# Helping Strategies for Child Sexual Abuse

A Whiting & Birch Ltd / National Children's Bureau Co-Publication

# Helping Strategies for Child Sexual Abuse

## Celia Doyle

Whiting and Birch Ltd

MCMXCV

Published by Whiting & Birch Ltd,
PO Box 872, , London SE23 3HL, England.
*USA:* Paul & Co, Publishers' Consortium Inc, PO Box 442, Concord, MA 01742.

*British Library Cataloguing in Publication Data.*
A CIP catalogue record is available from the British Library

ISBN 1 871177 22 7 (cased)
ISBN 1 871177 39 1 (limp)

Printed in England by Antony Rowe, Chippenham

# Contents

# Acknowledgements

As ever my thanks go to all my former colleagues who, in years gone by, encouraged and sustained me - Professor John Cooper, Margaret Oates, Peter Barbor, David N Jones, Maddy Collinge, Carl Blakey and Jean Moore from my days working in Nottinghamshire to name but a few. Then there are the more recent colleagues from Northamptonshire, Liz Brayne, Judy Fawcett, Jenny Still and Eddie Brocklesby.

I also owe a debt of gratitude to the children and adults, especially Lisa and her mother, who have had to cope with abuse and have been willing to share their experiences and insights with me and have given me permission to share their stories. I acknowledge, above all, the special contribution made by Jay through her poetry.

Special thanks must go to my mother, Joan Doyle who, as ever, undertook the sterling job of reading all the drafts of the book and providing wise guidance and comment. Moreover, it was through the help and counselling that she gave to Jay that Jay was prompted to share her poem and give me permission to use it.

I extend a warm and affectionate thank-you to my long suffering husband and children. Writing books would be impossible without your tolerance and patience, and authorship would be a tedious task master were it not for the fun we have when computer, printer and my attention to what is on screen are all firmly switched off.

Finally, I would like to acknowledge the contribution to our work on behalf of mistreated children made by people working in the entertainment and news media like Esther

Ranzen and Julia Stuart who have taken the time and trouble to inform themselves about child abuse and have then used their communication skills and information channels to reach the heads and hearts of the general public in a way that child protection professionals can only rarely achieve.

# Preface

I am waylaid in the college corridor by a student I teach who asks if I can spare a few moments to discuss a personal matter, a neighbour asks me if it is true that I work in the field of child care and could they have a quick word, the phone rings and a friend asks if I have time to talk. Whatever the scenario the question is often the same 'Please can you recommend something that I can read about child sexual abuse? The student, the neighbour, the telephone caller are all approaching me in their individual capacity as parent, foster carer, volunteer or professional. They do not normally deal with child protection issues, but have now come face to face with them through the disclosures of their own child, foster child, friend, patient or client.

I have found that, despite being acquainted with the massive literature on sex abuse, there has been no one book which I could recommend which would provide both a detailed overview and understanding of the problem as well as guidance on how to respond appropriately. Most books and articles are written for specialist child protection professionals. Other helpful material targets specific groups such as non-abusing parents, teachers or family doctors.

There appeared to be a need for an accessible book which could be read by a wide variety of concerned adults and which both enhanced understanding and provided practical guidance. It is hoped that this book will meet this perceived need and will prove useful for all lay, voluntary and professional people who have reason to be concerned about child abuse and, while not in the forefront of investigative work, may still feel the need to respond appropriately.

# Dedication

For my mother, Joan, and my husband, John,
and all the other special 'J's in my life.

# First thoughts:

# Is this book for you?

This guide is written for those who understand that sexual abuse causes pain and anguish to the victims and would like to be in a position to give effective help to sexually abused children. It will also be of interest to anyone trying to help adults troubled because they are survivors of childhood sexual exploitation or are closely related to a child victim.

### SHOULD YOU READ ON?

There are a number of people who may find the information and guidance contained in the following chapters beneficial.

### Professional and voluntary workers

For a number of professional people, such as child care social workers or paediatricians, who are dealing almost daily with child abuse cases the contents of this book may be all too familiar. Such professional workers probably receive specialist training and regularly read – as far as a busy work schedule will allow – the latest research articles. If you are in this category, you may find it useful to scan the remaining pages in order to check there is nothing that you have forgotten or overlooked. You could also determine whether or not this is a book worth recommending to other people who do not have your specialist knowledge but are eager to gain insight into child sexual abuse.

Professionals such as teachers, clergy and adult service social workers, though not regularly carrying full responsibility for cases of abuse, are aware that from time to time they may have some contact with an abused child. If this applies to you then you may find the guidance given in subsequent chapters helpful. You are probably not part of a target group for child protection training and yet may well be in the ideal position to give help to a particular child.

If you are a professional with a voluntary spirit or a volunteer with a professional out-look – a foster carer, playgroup leader, childminder or magistrate perhaps – this book is very much for you. Foster parents, in particular, are in a key position to assist abused children. Reading this will help you to understand the dynamics of child abuse, the needs of the victims and reasons for the various procedures which have to be followed and in which you might have a significant role.

Similarly, this guide will be useful if your interest in child protection work springs from your role as a volunteer from a voluntary agency – which nevertheless has professional standards – such as the Samaritans, Homestart, Relate, Citizens Advice Bureaux and church counselling services. You may well have freedom from statutory constraints which means that you can give the assistance that you feel is needed. It could help you to pick up signs of abuse and will also enhance your understanding of the impact of sexual abuse on victims and their families, both of which you may be in a unique position to assist.

### *Those personally involved*

You may have become involved as the friend, neighbour or relative of a child who has been abused. You could well be much the best person to support the victims and their families and this book should provide you with the insights which you will need to enable you to respond appropriately. If, however, you are the non-abusing parent or in a parental relationship with the victim you will probably need extra help. You might find it useful to turn to suggestions from the further reading section at the back especially *When Your Child Has Been Molested: A Parent's Guide to Healing and Recovery* by Kathryn B Hagans and Joyce Case.

You might be, or were in the past, the victim of child sexual abuse and are seeking assistance with the emotional legacy with which the abuser has burdened you. This book has been written with you in mind. You may find parts of it reassuring and helpful. Somewhat paradoxically, the section on understanding perpetrators will help you to appreciate why you were in no way to blame nor responsible for the abuse. But for you too, some of the publications in the further reading section will prove helpful.

WHY BE CONCERNED?

Why should sexual abuse of children concern us? The paedophile will argue that children benefit from sexual relationships with adults. When discussing physical chastisement of children many adults in support of its benefits declare 'I was beaten as a child and its done me no harm' – they stand there as living proof that it is acceptable to beat children. This line of argument is echoed by many a paedophile 'I had sex with adults as a child and its not done me any harm – in fact it did me good'.

There is now considerable doubt that childhood is a time of innocence and asexuality. Children have a lot to learn and many skills to master so sexual activities are usually low on a pre-adolescent's agenda. Nevertheless, most children are curious about matters which the adult regards as sexual. They are fascinated by how the body works, how babies are born and what it means to have a girl or boyfriend. The physical feelings aroused by sexual activities can be pleasurable. In view of this, is sex between adult and child or between child and child so undesirable?

Alexander Duncan, questioning his colleagues' concern, asked in a letter to a professional journal:

> *What is this 'sexual abuse' anyway? In families such behaviour is common and normal between siblings. It is so common in boarding schools that about 90 per cent would have to be closed down if it were ever taken seriously!... How much of recalled 'abuse' is like Freudian trauma, imaginary? Why is no weight ever given to the well established fact that, contrary to folk wisdom, many young people of both sexes from 12 upwards seek and even demand such experience from adults? (Letters,* Community Care *February 6 1986).*

### Causing harm

One argument against sexual activities between adults and children and, in some circumstances, between children

3

themselves is that it does harm. Professionals working with the victims of child sexual abuse have come across so many profoundly distressed children and adult survivors that they are left in little doubt of the truth of this argument.

There is, nevertheless, no evidence that all children who have engaged in sexual activities are harmed. So is the harm argument a sufficient one for intervention? The answer has to be, no. Many children suffer pain, are temporarily or permanently damaged or even killed riding horses but we do not ban horse-riding for people under 18 years old. The vast majority of young equestrians thoroughly enjoy the activity and they and their parents are willing to take some risks in the pursuit of their enjoyment.

There are a number of practical reasons for objecting to children engaging in sexual activities. Biologically children are unready for some activities. A small girl's vagina is too small for penetration by a grown man's penis. We need to protect children from the spread of venereal diseases and AIDS. The dangers of pregnancy in young pubertal girls is very real. Some start menstruating at the age of 10 or 11, and it is difficult enough for adults to practice reliable contraceptive methods never mind expecting children to do so. These practical objections however only really apply to penetrative sex.

### Informed consent

The main reason for taking action to stop certain sexual activities involving children is an ethical one. Children cannot give informed consent. The paedophile will often argue that the children that they molest welcome the activities and consented. But for true informed consent to occur 'two conditions must prevail. A person must know what it is that he or she is consenting to, and a person must be free to say yes or no' (Finkelhor 1979 p.694).

Until children and young people are about 16 to 18 years old they cannot fully appreciate the consequences of engaging in sexual activities. They cannot know how it will effect them physically and emotionally in their later years. Mark, when aged 8, agreed to have sex with a neighbour who was a type of grandfather figure to the local children. He liked the physical sensations and enjoyed the feeling of being special. However he was not to know at that age how these activities were to haunt his teenage years. It was not until adolescence that he became very confused about his sexual orientation because although attracted to young women he knew he had enjoyed sex with a man. He was also concerned about other people believing he was homosexual if they found out what he had done. He thought that if a man could find him attractive then women could not do so. He also thought that he might have been physically damaged.

It is worth clarifying that the example of Mark is not a condemnation of homosexuality. Instead it is an illustration of how inappropriate it is for children – who have enough to cope with in coming to terms with their sexual development – to be additionally burdened by worries which arise from having been exploited at an early age by an adult.

Children and young people are often in the power of adults or older children. They are not in a position to refuse to engage in sexual activities. Tobias was at a boarding school when an older boy who was a prefect found him attractive. Tobias had learnt very quickly in his first few months at school that teachers and prefects demanded absolute obedience. Even though the prefect did not use threats, Tobias felt he had to do exactly as the older boy demanded.

Basically people, whether adults or children, have a right not to be involved in sexual activities unless they give informed consent. It is unlikely, because of their lack of knowledge of the issues and their comparative powerlessness, that children and young adolescents are ever in a position to give such consent.

The reality is that many of the children and young people who are abused have no opportunity to give or withhold consent, informed or otherwise. Obvious examples are babies and toddlers as well as older children who cannot easily communicate their objections due to physical or severe learning difficulties. Finally, in many cases children are assaulted or exploited without being given the opportunity to agree or disagree. Some are tricked so that they find that they are being used sexually before they realise what is happening. Others are suddenly attacked without any chance to object.

## THE EXPERIENCE OF SEXUAL ABUSE

To continue reading may for some, whether professional, volunteer, relative or survivor, be the start of a painful journey into the world of sexually abused children. This may not be something that you want to experience. To find this out perhaps you could start by taking a few steps with a child who has been molested by reading a poem by Jay and then seeing how you feel at the end of it.

Jay, does not regard herself as a professional poet and has had no literary training. Poetry is the means by which she expresses some of her feelings about what has happened to her. The poem has been reproduced here in exactly the same way that Jay wrote it down.

### Violate

*To go out with a group of friends*
*but, be alone with a man in the end,*
*to realise you have been manoeuvred there*
*and that you are young and immature.*

*An unknown feeling creeps up your spine,*
*instinct tells you, leave at this time*
*in a house alone in an area you don't know*
*the door is locked, no key, you cannot go.*

*Talk and behave quite naturally,*
*it will be alright, you'll see,*
*you tell yourself with good cheer,*
*then understand the feeling, it is fear.*

*Find yourself being mauled about,*
*your throat's closed up you cannot shout,*
*No! No! No! you beg and plead,*
*No ears listen, no mind heeds.*

*Hands on your throat threaten your life*
*you kick, you struggle with all your might*
*but in the end its to no avail*
*the outcome's certain, you know you've failed*

*Hands, with dirty black fingernails*
*abuse your body like a thousand flays*
*nails cutting flesh never touched before*
*know you're being treated like a whore*

*Tearing pain of intrusion*
*The mental confusion*
*Emotion does abhor*
*you're a virgin no more.*

*To be laughed at*
*and ridiculed, poked fun at,*
*and told green as grass, a virgin as well,*
*never had one before, now go to hell!*

*Now wait, sit down, you look ill, drink this tea*
*Sit quietly there while to my dinner I see,*
*wriggly eggs sliding round on a plate,*
*stabbed with a fork the yolk to break*

*That's how I felt,*
*like the eggs on the plate,*
*wounded, bleeding and sore,*
*broken, cut and – so much more.*

*How I found my way home I do not know*
*But, there was nobody in – and so*
*to my bedroom I made a hasty retreat,*
*blood-stained clothes to hide under the sheet*

*Cried myself to sleep that night in bed,*
*I slept, but it went round in my head*
*the morning arrived as is its way*
*to begin another dreadful day.*

## Feelings about abuse

How do you feel after reading the poem?

Some people feel numb, shocked and do not want to believe such incidents really happen. This is a natural and very common reaction to something which potentially causes distress. Denial that upsetting events have occurred means that we can retreat from them, regaining a more comfortable state. However, it is important that we accept that children and young people are sexually abused and that something can be done to help.

Perhaps you feel angry. Are you angry with Jay? Are you thinking 'She deserved all she got. She was stupid to go back to a man's house on her own. She probably egged him on until he couldn't control himself? If you feel that, I hope that you will be willing to continue with the rest of the book; maybe you are right but maybe by the end of it you will feel a little differently.

Perhaps instead you feel angry with the man who raped Jay. If you do then it is possible that by reading the following chapters you will find ways of harnessing your anger in a constructive way.

Perhaps you feel distress and confusion as you realise that the sort of thing that happened to Jay also happened to you when you were young. Maybe it was a single event of sexual assault or maybe you were abused over a long period of time. If you have never given yourself time to come to terms with this you might well need assistance. Reading this book should lead you to appreciate both why you might need help and also why you are worth helping.

Perhaps you already know that you were abused as a child. You know that you share Jay's feelings but you have been helped or have healed yourself so that the pain is no longer as raw nor as real. You are in an excellent position to help other victims of abuse. Here you can learn how you can best assist fellow sufferers.

Perhaps you are worried that what happened to Jay might happen to someone you know and love. The following pages will help you understand how children become vulnerable, how they can be protected and how, if protection fails despite your best efforts, the ones you love can be enabled to cope with their experiences.

### *Responding to abuse*

How did Jay's carers respond? Did they support her in a constructive way. Jay tells us in the continuation of her poem:

> *I looked in the mirror, the shock the disgust to see,*
> *the state of me,*
> *love bites and bruises the difference to tell*
> *you'd have had a job, I did as well.*
>
> *Out with the make-up to cover it all*
> *would have taken the stock of an entire store,*
> *now downstairs to face the day,*
> *put a brave face on and nothing to say.*

*There could never be another day like that,*
*my father disowned me, that was that,*
*words rained down on me, I had no hat,*
*my mother called me names, there I sat.*

*I tried to explain what had happened to me.*
*Nobody listened, nobody believed me.*
*The shouting went on, nobody believed me.*
*The silence hung there, nobody believed me.*

*The day went on with looks of disgust.*
*Silent looks, saying tut, tut, tut,*
*brooding eyes, that just stare.*
*They see you, but you're not there.*

*The pain I suffered, both outside and in,*
*No more to say, the words locked in,*
*out of the window, go love and trust,*
*and in its place, shame and disgust.*

*How I felt at the end of that day?*
*Torn asunder in another way,*
*there was no one there, to care,*
*to help me live through 'my nightmare'.*

*The days went by but I don't recall.*
*Then the phone rang in the hall.*
*The abuse and the threats did start,*
*the police arrived to take their part.*

*The questions, the answers, to say it out loud,*
*they listened this time, they were not 'proud'*
*by then I didn't care what anyone thought*
*now they knew the truth, and so they ought.*

*They never said, 'I'm sorry' for doubting you*
*never asked if I was alright, they knew it wasn't true*
*they tried to help me then, but, too late in the day,*
*the damage was done, from both of them I turned away.*

*Eventually it blew over and no more was said*
*and gradually I learned to hold up my head,*
*those traumatic days changed my world for me,*
*lessons learned, a different way to see.*

**J.L.B. 1990**

## Feelings about the response

How are you feeling now that you know how the adults in Jay's life responded to her. It is possible to feel that her parents were quite right to act as they did. She was lucky not to have had a good hiding and be thrown out into the street there and then. She had behaved little better than a promiscuous hussy and deserved all the recriminations. If you agree, it is important to try to understand why you feel this so strongly.

Maybe you feel nothing very much, you do not know how you would respond if a child told you that they had been molested. This book may help you to realise how very much the child needs your assistance and how you can give it in a positive way.

Your response could be one of anger against Jay's parents. You would like to think that you would never be so uncaring and unsympathetic. Yet Jay's parents were not unloving or callous. They simply did not understand what the experience meant for Jay nor did they appreciate how vulnerable children and young people are in the hands of a determined sexual abuser. Many adults have responded inappropriately through ignorance rather than malevolence; even some of the most caring responses are not the most helpful.

One common reaction is to say as little as possible about the assault in the hope that 'least said soonest mended'. It is a widely held belief that if you talk to children about bad experiences, old wounds will be opened and they will become distressed. This is to an extent true but sometimes distress and the opening of wounds is part of the healing process, lancing a boil is perhaps an apt analogy. By the end of this book you should be able to make an informed decision about the best way to respond to a sexually abused child.

You might be wishing that you could sweep Jay into your arms and comfort her and tell her that everything will be alright. Unfortunately life is not so simple. Some children can no longer tolerate being touched, let alone cuddled, by an adult. Often after disclosure everything is far from alright. The child may have to leave home or give evidence in court against the perpetrator. He or she may have to have at least one medical examination and suffer the medical consequences of assault such as pregnancy, internal and external injury and disease including AIDS. There is the emotional aftermath with the almost inevitable feelings of guilt, shame and fear.

A caring, sympathetic response will be immensely more helpful than a punitive one but children often need more than just sympathy. Through these pages you can learn to build on your initial caring response so that you can continue to give, or help others to give, the care and assistance required.

Another possibility is that long-forgotten feelings were awakened in you as you remember the unsympathetic response that greeted you when, as a child, you tried to tell someone you had been sexually abused. You know what you needed at that time and you know what a victim needs now. However you may not have experienced some of the situations encountered by other children who have been sexually abused. Reading this book should enhance your ability to respond in a positive way even when the situation differs from your own .

### CAN YOU REALLY HELP THE VICTIMS OF ABUSE?

You may be asking yourself 'Can I really help – shouldn't I leave it to the experts'. You may worry that you are not specially trained. You may be even more worried that you could do more harm than good.

Some activities have to be left to the experts – activities such as medically examining a child, investigating incidents and collecting evidence for legal proceedings or providing a deeply disturbed child with intensive therapy. But there is much that the informed and committed 'non-expert' can do to help.

It is also probably true that in some respects you are an expert yourself:

- you might have skills and possibly training in counselling and other forms of giving help;
- people close to the victims are probably, after the victims themselves, the experts on how the children are likely to react and cope;
- finally, many adult survivors have a level of knowledge and understanding that could well be defined as expertise.

An abused child's first need is for the abuse to stop – you can help stop it. Details of how are given later. In addition, children who manage to tell someone about the abuse need to feel that they are believed and are not condemned for telling . Jay, in her poem, twice repeated 'Nobody believed me'. You can believe and praise the child for having had the courage to disclose. Even when the child seems not to be telling the absolute truth is it possible to believe they have experienced something distressing and to say 'I am taking what you say seriously'.

Above all, victims need to know that they are not to blame for the abuse, have the right to be angry and are worthy of help. You can avoid casting the blame onto the victim, you can allow expressions of anger and, by giving assistance in very many other ways, you can show abused children that they are worth helping.

It is sometimes possible to do more harm than good. But if you have a clear understanding of the issues involved then you are unlikely to respond in an inappropriate way. A useful analogy can be drawn with what happens in an accident. If you have an understanding of how the body responds and the dangers of shock then you can administer appropriate first aid and give proper, possibly life-saving support, even if you are not a doctor, nurse or paramedic.

The first part of this book is designed to give you as clear an understanding as possible of child sexual abuse. Without this you might not respond appropriately.

The second part provides guidelines. It draws largely on what we have learnt from the victims of abuse. Children, and adult survivors, have identified for those of us working in this field responses that have helped them and made them feel better.

# One

# Understanding what is meant by child sexual abuse

WHAT IS CHILD SEXUAL ABUSE?

Some of the shortest and most straightforward questions are the most difficult ones to answer. The question 'What is child sexual abuse?' is no exception. It poses many other questions, for example 'What is a child?' We may immediately see the need to protect a 4-year-old from sexual assault but many a 15-year-old is equally in need of protection. Other queries which spring to mind include 'When is touching a child a sexual act and when is it demonstrative loving?' 'Can sexual activities between children be defined as abusive?'

Over the years the term 'child sexual abuse' has expanded to mean not only incestuous relationships between fathers and their young daughters but any sexual activity involving a child or young person which is experienced as abusive. One of the reasons for this is that much of the distress experienced by incest victims is shared by people sexually abused by non-family members. Furthermore, it has now been realised (Salter 1988) that people who offend sexually against their relatives are also quite likely to do so against neighbours or other more distant acquaintances.

## What is a child?

The word 'child' includes any person who is 'under age', that is younger than 18 years. Teenagers pose some dilemmas for adults who have to decide whether or not they have been sexually abused because it is lawful in Britain for a young person on reaching the age of 16 to have certain sexual relationships and to marry. In other countries the ages of consent and of marriage are as low as 12 years. Another matter

13

of debate is how far an adult with learning difficulties and the comprehension capacity of 5-year-old should be protected from sexual abuse in the way that a primary school child might be.

## What is sexual activity?

Sexual activity can refer to a wide range behaviours. There is non-touching behaviour such as exhibitionism (that is the displaying of genitals, often referred to as 'flashing'), watching children undress through a spy-hole and other forms of voyeurism, making obscene telephone calls, forcing children to look at sexual activities or pornography or making them pose for pornographic photographs and videos.

Behaviour involving touching can include stroking the breasts, vagina, penis and bottom, masturbation of the child or of the perpetrator by the child, rubbing the penis between the victim's legs in simulated intercourse, penetration of the vagina, anus or mouth by the penis and pushing objects or fingers into the vagina or anus. In some cases the children are tied up, gagged, dressed in strange clothes, spanked or whipped in a sexualised way and in a few cases subjected to torture, suffocation or killed in a sadistic manner.

The activity is sexual when at least one participant gains sexual gratification from the activity and when it involves the genital or erotic parts of the body

## When is behaviour sexually abusive?

Not all activities involving the genitals are abusive. Intimate medical examinations and cleaning a baby's nappy area are obvious examples of non-sexual touching although they can become abusive if performed not for the benefit of the child but for the sexual gratification of the person undertaking the examination or cleaning.

Children will explore each other's bodies, often through games such as 'doctors and nurses'. One colleague described to me how as a very small boy with a couple of equally small friends, during a hot summer, he played a delightful game of 'milking cows' with the part of his anatomy which, when he was on all-fours dangled down like the udders of the cows that they saw in the nearby field.

In a study by Sharon Lamb and Mary Coakley (1993) sexual games were played mostly with the same age friends and if they were 'discovered' by adults, unlike most instances of sexual abuse, the children did not feel unduly ashamed or guilty or that any harm had been done, nor did the game feel abnormal. In the majority of cases there was no coercion although when girls played with boys, even same age ones, this increased.

## Power and coercion

One of the important features distinguishing acceptable from abusive activities is that all parties to the activity join in willingly without coercion. There is a balance of power between the partners or group members and all are more or less aware of any consequences. This reflects the discussion of 'informed consent' discussed in First Thoughts. It is worth repeating that because children have limited knowledge and experience they cannot give informed consent to sexual activities with adults. We should recall that youngsters may like the feeling of being caressed and sexually aroused but they may not realise that they run risks of disease, pregnancy or future guilt and distress.

Maya Angelou, a black American writer describes how, when as an 8-year-old she was fondled by her mother's boyfriend, she felt comforted, 'He held me so softly that I wished he wouldn't ever let me go.' She was not to know that this would lead to her rape by this man, his death and her becoming literally struck dumb for much of her remaining childhood. (Angelou 1984 p.71).

Sometimes a child is tricked into giving apparent consent. There have been cases of children duped by strangers who pretend to be a family friend. They may ascertain the child's name by spotting it emblazoned on the youngster's bag, T-shirt or bracelet. Children often assume that people cannot be 'strangers' if they know their name.

Another important feature mentioned in First Thoughts is that there is a power imbalance between perpetrator and victim. It is not uncommon for parents to use parental authority to coerce a child into sexual activities. Some abusers use superior physical strength or weapons. Others use threats of physical violence to the victims themselves, to their pet animals or to the people they love. Threats can also have an emotional focus, 'Do this, or you will not be my special princess any more', 'Do it or you will not get that bike for Christmas' 'Get your clothes off if you don't want me to tell your teacher you cheated in that exam.'

More subtle forms of power can include the use of status and influence such as when a teenage gang leader tells a younger boy he must agree to sex if he wants to stay in the gang or a music teacher promises to promote a child's musical career in return for sexual favours.

A popular definition which enshrines many of these concepts is:

> *The involvement of dependent, developmentally immature children and adolescents in sexual activities that they do not truly comprehend, are unable to give informed consent, and that violate the social taboos of family roles. (Schechter and Roberge 1976 p. 129).*

The great merit of this definition is that it includes as victims both children and adolescents. It ensures that abuse of children by other children is not excluded. We are not just thinking of sexual activities between child and adult we are also including those between children when one of them is unwillingly or unwittingly being used for the sexual gratification of the other.

Although the definition includes the concept of violating the social taboos of family roles it does not just limit sexual abuse to instances of inappropriate sexual activity between family members. There are a great many abusive activities which take place in non-family settings. The next section will examine this.

### THE FORMS AND CONTEXT OF SEXUAL ABUSE.

Sexual abuse can take many forms and occurs in a wide variety of contexts. The perpetrators can be male or female. They can work alone, in pairs or in groups. They can be family members, more distant acquaintances or strangers. This section will consider the different types of abuse in different settings. It is however important to remember that the various forms are not mutually exclusive. A boy abused by his parents could then be involved by them in an organised vice-ring, or a girl molested by her step-father might also be attacked by a stranger. Sylvia Fraser (1989) in her autobiography describes how she was sexually exploited for many years by her father but also suffered an incident of vicious sexual assault by a lodger.

The perpetrators of abuse may engage in a variety of activities. A boarding school headmaster was sent to prison for abusing the boys in his care. Shortly after his imprisonment, his daughter felt safe enough to reveal that he had been having an incestuous relationship with her for a number of years.

Until recently there was a popular belief that broadly speaking only two forms of sexual abuse existed. One was incest and the other, attack by a stranger. Both were thought to be rare.

Many of us as children were taught to be wary of strangers particularly ugly ones in dirty macs offering us sweets. We would not, we were assured, come to any harm if we avoided such people. If we were unlucky a stranger might be lurking in the shrubbery and take us unawares, so girls in particular were warned not to take short cuts through parks on their own and under no circumstances were they to linger in front of suspicious looking bushes.

The other form of acknowledged sexual abuse, incest, was, it was fondly believed, confined to rural areas where there were no other diversions on cold winter evenings. There might also be some incest 'going on' in very poor families in overcrowded conditions in city areas who could ill afford any other entertainments and whose members, adults and children alike, all had to share one bed. Eccentric aristocrats were also believed to indulge in a little incest but such families were in the minority.

It was only subsequent to the sexual revolution of the 1960s that society was forced to recognise that incest is not uncommon and can occur in any type of family including 'respectable' middle- or working-class ones. It is as much a problem for affluent suburbia as it is for inner city or rural communities.

### Incest and family-member abuse

Under English law incest is narrowly defined as sexual intercourse between a man and a woman within the prohibited relationships of a man with his daughter, sister or half-sister, mother or granddaughter or a woman over 16 with her father, brother or half-brother son or grandfather. It does not mention a woman with her grandson and yet such cases are known. It does not embrace foster, adoptive or step relationships nor does it include activities which fall short of intercourse. This is mostly because the legislation was drawn up more to protect inheritance and property rights than to protect children.

---

### EXERCISE

Try drawing a family tree of a family where the father has had intercourse with his daughter and subsequently has a son by his daughter. Is the baby the father's son or grandson, is he the girl's son or her brother? Is the father's sister the child's aunt or great-aunt?

---

As victims of child sexual abuse started to talk openly about their experiences we began to realise that the experience of the victim in an abusing family was often equally distressing whether the abuser was a natural parent or step-parent, a sibling or an adopted sibling, a natural grandparent or a foster-grandparent. All abuse within a family could give rise to feelings of helplessness, betrayal by the very people that you rely on to care for you, and of being trapped in a situation of divided loyalties. The term 'incest' is often used particularly in American literature to refer generally to any form of sexual abuse within families.

Until recently abuse by brothers and sisters was thought not to require any attention unless it was a case of an adult causing serious physical damage to a much younger sibling such as an adult brother inserting knives into his little sister's vagina. Only a few years ago when my colleagues tried to protect a very unhappy 12-year-old girl from being abused by her 16-year-old brother they were met with outraged protests from the school and family doctor who maintained that the police and social workers were upsetting respectable parents and intruding into a happy family.

We now know that abuse by another child can lead to considerable distress. It is worth bearing in mind the feelings expressed by Helen who from the age of six was used as an experimental sexual object by her brother, Frank, who was only five years older:

*I was terrified for both myself and Frank in case our secret was discovered. I would not let anyone get close to me in case they saw through me and found out what I was really like - a dirty, rude little girl. My father still wanted to cuddle me when he was at home but I held him at arm's length, in case he came so close that he saw how dirty I was. Once, as I backed off from him, I caught the hurt look in his eyes, I felt unworthy of his affection...even after the sexual abuse stopped I still carried a weighty secret and felt unclean and guilty (Doyle 1990 p.24-5).*

Children can be abused by family members who are not living with them. One of the most difficult areas for investigating agencies to deal with are those involving divorce or separation where a parent is accused of molesting a child while on an access visit. This becomes particularly difficult if the child is unable or unwilling to give an account. Even if there is medical evidence it is often difficult to determine who caused the damage. Parents on access visits can and do molest their children but equally parents who resent their former partner having access have been known to falsely accuse them of abuse. Sometimes a parent will accuse an estranged partner in order to protect a new one who is really the perpetrator. What is certain is that children do not readily falsely accuse anyone close to them of sexually abusing them.

Both boys and girls might start refusing to visit their grandfather, uncles, aunts or other relatives for no apparent reason. It may be that they are being molested in their relative's household or even in a park or car when their relatives take them out for a 'treat'.

### Non-family members of the household and baby-sitters

Children can be abused by people living in a household although they are not family members. Perpetrators sometimes seek out homes containing children and young people when they are looking for lodgings. On occasions a lodger gains the parents' confidence and offers to babysit.

Children have been exploited by casual, non-resident babysitters. One male babysitter was sent to prison for a year after simulating intercourse on a 6-year-old girl and forcing anal penetration on her 7-year-old brother. When asked to chose animals to represent the abuser the girl chose an elephant because she had been so frightened that he would squash her with his weight. The boy chose a tiger because he had felt ravaged and torn by the babysitter. Both children had shown behavioural changes in school. The boy had become withdrawn, quiet and unable to concentrate. The girl had become very talkative and constantly demanding attention from the teachers. Eventually the little girl was able to ask her mother if the babysitter was really allowed to do the things he was doing. The children had thought that their parents had given the man permission to indulge in sexual activities just as they had given him permission to smack them if they were naughty.

A child should always be listened to carefully if he/she is reluctant to stay with a babysitter. It may be that they are not simply 'spoilt brats' who want to stop their parents going out and having a good time.

### Substitute carers

As we noted with lodgers, people who molest children tend to put themselves in positions where they have contact with children. If they are given sole charge and care of children so much, in their eyes, the better. For this reason some substitute carers are in fact perpetrators of abuse. Childminders, nannies, foster parents, nursery nurses, boarding school teachers and staff of children's residential homes have all been implicated in cases of child sexual abuse.

In an informative study David Finkelhor and his colleagues found that abuse occurred in a wide variety of nursery settings. Pre-school children are as vulnerable as older ones. One of the most important factors particularly for parents to take into account is how 'open' the nursery or playgroup is. 'Programmes with few limits on parental access and in which there are strong, sustained levels of parent participation should be at reduced risk' (1988 p.150) Unfortunately a good reputation, registration and inspection and a qualified officer-in-charge were no guarantees against abuse.

In recent years the dangers to children in residential establishments have been exposed. In Northern Ireland there were allegations of abuse in the Kincora home in 1980s. In 1991 the iniquitous career of Frank Beck and his associates in Leicester was exposed. He was officer-in-charge in a number of children's homes in Leicestershire from 1973. On 29 November 1991 he was 'found guilty on 17 counts involving sexual and physical assault. Those convictions included four for offences of buggery and one for an offence of rape. Mr Beck was sentenced to life imprisonment for each offence of buggery and for the offence of rape' (Kirkwood 1993 p.1). Two of his colleagues were also found guilty of lesser offences and a third committed suicide, while visiting Holland, before he could be brought to trial.

For nearly twenty years Frank Beck had had the care of vulnerable children. He was found guilty of sexually and physically abusing some and there were allegations that he had abused many others. As the trial judge said 'You exploited your authority and the undoubted power of your personality to satisfy your lust'.

Beck also applied to be a foster parent and was approved as one in 1984. In the course of his application one of his referees stated 'He is without doubt responsible sexually and would not under any circumstances take advantage of a minor within his care' (Kirkwood 1993 p.225). When the father of PQ, a boy Beck wanted to foster, accused Beck of abusing his son, the boy's worker dismissed the allegations as 'an attempt by PQ's father to jeopardise the placement with Mr Beck, which PQ's father had not wanted to go ahead.' (Kirkwood 1993 p. 223).

This illustrates how some potential abusers seek to be day or residential care staff or foster carers in order to exploit children placed in their care. That having been said, foster carers are in a particularly difficult position in relation to sexually abused children. Some children coming into care have been brought up to think that they can only gain the affection of their carers or at least male ones if they attract them sexually and give them sexual favours. Some small children automatically associate a male figure with sexual activity. They may attempt to touch their foster father's penis or kiss members of their foster families in sexualised way. They can generally behave in a manner often termed 'provocative'.

This behaviour is difficult for foster carers who want to cuddle and comfort a child physically but fear that such intimate contact will be misinterpreted as a sexual advance. What is certain, however, is that a foster child will not turn a foster parent into a sexual abuser. As will be seen in the next chapter, if foster carers are not sexually attracted to children in the first place, they will not molest them, however overtly sexual and 'seductive' the child's or young person's behaviour is.

Residential workers encounter similar problems of having to give physical care and comfort to children who may see this as sexual activity. But again children or young people will not manage to 'seduce' a worker into molesting them unless the worker has a sexual orientation towards children in the first place. If you care for children and find that you are sexually attracted towards any of them then I would recommend that you change your occupation and ensure that you only work with adults.

## Organised networks

There is increasing concern about sex rings involving children. In England a number of these have been uncovered such as the one in 1984 in Leeds involving 11 child sex rings in one working class community:

> *The rings contained 14 adult male perpetrators and 175 children aged 6-15 years. Most perpetrators used child ringleaders to recruit victims; others became a 'family friend' or obtained a position of authority over children. Secrecy was encouraged and bribery, threats, and peer pressure used to induce participation in sexual activities, Offences reported included fondling, masturbation, pornography, and oral, vaginal, and anal intercourse. Eleven perpetrators were successfully prosecuted; all but one received a sentence of three years or less. Behavioural problems were common among those children who had participated for a long time (Wild and Wynne 1986 p.184).*

Although in the case quoted above it was a working class area and the victims were predominantly female, other rings in America and England have thrived in middle class communities and the victims have sometimes been boys.

In some instances children are targeted and enticed to join in organised rings because they have a disadvantage which would make them unreliable witnesses. Youngsters with learning difficulties are vulnerable in this respect.

Similarly, children labelled 'psychiatrically disturbed' or 'delinquent' may also be targeted because they are seen as not to be trusted. In the early 1990s an 11-year-old boy involved in a vice ring eventually confided in his social worker. The boy had been in and out of care and had been in trouble several times for petty criminal offences. The reaction of the police officer to whom the matter was referred was 'Don't believe anything that lad says, he's nothing but trouble. He's always leading us a dance.' The social worker, who believed the boy, insisted that the matter was fully investigated and a substantial neighbourhood ring was uncovered.

Despite the example just given of friction between a social worker and a police officer, there have been several very effective joint police and social services investigations. Operation Hedgerow in the London Borough of Brent succeeded in breaking a ring which involved some 150 or more boys. 653 allegations were collected and 14 men were subsequently sent to prison for sexual offences against the youngsters. One of the leaders befriended neighbourhood children by selling toys on a Sunday market. 'He also had his living room kitted out with three computers, an oval of train sets, sweets laid out on the mantelpiece' (Redding 1989 p.15).

The Detective Chief Inspector in this case was quoted as saying:

> *The trouble with paedophiles is that they work underneath the community... They work themselves into key jobs which bring them into contact with children. I don't believe that Kilburn is particularly unique in this. It must be fairly typical, certainly of any deprived London borough. If that's the case, the scale of this activity across London is colossal, and I'm sure it's replicated in other major cities (Redding 1989 p.15).*

Not only is it likely to be replicated in deprived city areas but also in the more affluent ones as well as in rural communities.

### Ritual abuse

There is little doubt that child sex rings exist. However the claims of some children and adults that they have been abused as part of satanic worship has been met with a degree of scepticism. We have enough difficulty believing an abused teenager when she accuses a charming, respectable-looking man of attempting to rape her. The difficulty becomes almost an impossibility when she accuses that same man of taking her and other youngsters to a strange place where there are adults who tie her up, inject her with drugs, force her to eat faeces, kill animals as sacrifices, worship Satan and generally terrorise her. The more bizarre a child's story the more unlikely most people are to believe her.

Another problem with ritual abuse is that apart from the

accounts of victims there has been little supporting evidence. There have been claims that babies have been sacrificed and yet no bones have been found. The various law enforcement agencies have never managed to discover an overtly abusive ritual ceremony in progress.

A definition of ritual abuse was formulated by the Leeds Ritualistic Abuse Study Group in 1993:

> *Ritual abuse is the involvement of children in physical, psychological or sexual abuse associated with repeated activities ('ritual') which purport to relate the abuse to contexts of a religious, magical or supernatural kind (McFadyen, Hanks and James 1993 p.37).*

In many cases this type of abuse takes place within an extended family with perhaps neighbours also taking part. In America grave concern has arisen because of allegations of pre-school day nurseries being used as cover for organised ritualistic abuse (Finkelhor 1988). In America, members of a family called McMartin were accused of extensive ritual abuse of the children attending their day nursery in an affluent, middle-class area of Manhattan Beach in California. The case was largely inconclusive and has simply added to the controversy.

In England, in Nottingham and on Orkney, there have been accusations of ritual abuse. These were dismissed as the fantasies of children or the delusions of social workers. It may have been right to dismiss them. But the problem is that in such cases the only evidence is provided by the victims, but the more fantastic a child's story the less likely it is to be believed; the more unpalatable the truth the more certain it is to be ignored.

### *Danger stranger*

What society in general, and parents in particular, have worried about more than any other form of sexual abuse is molestation by a stranger. Repeated studies have shown that children are often abused by someone they know. Baker and Duncan (1985) in a study of over 2,000 people in England found that 51 per cent were abused by strangers while nearly as many (49 per cent) were abused by someone they knew.

It is easier for a perpetrator to seduce a child quietly into engaging in sexual activity rather than leaping out from the bushes thereby risking the victim's screams. Molesters will usually try to befriend their intended target. As already mentioned they often obtain a position where they are naturally in contact with children. Some regularly encounter children and young people in a professional or occupational context such as a teacher, doctor, priest, school groundsman or park keeper. Others engage in voluntary activity which brings them into contact with children maybe as a scout leader or a youth club official. Sometimes they are those really good neighbours who help the parents and never object to children hanging around their garden.

But some children are abused by complete strangers. Exposing the genitals (flashing) accounts for many of the statistics of people abused by strangers. However there are a small number of cases each year of people, predominantly men, who assault children unknown to them. They sometimes abduct their chosen victim and occasionally kill the child either in a panic or in a few rare instances in order to gain sadistic satisfaction. Working with a group of male sex offenders Mezey and colleagues noted:

> *Certain men enjoyed the passivity and submissiveness of the child. Others described an increasing sense of sexual excitement with the child's fear and resistance. For one man the climax would have come with the child's murder ... Although initially shocked by one offender's preoccupation with killing a victim, most men reluctantly recognised their own potential to act in a similar way for sadistic reasons or out of sheer panic (1991 p.19).*

Although such cases are few and far between they are so distressing that parents are wise to advise children to be wary of strangers - that is as long as children are also told that people they know and like can sometimes behave inappropriately towards them.

## HOW MANY CHILDREN ARE AFFECTED?

This is another very difficult question to answer. To arrive at an exact figure researchers would have to overcome a number of major obstacles not least because of the problems of definition and of secrecy. We tend to have to be content with the best estimation of the numbers.

## Problems of secrecy

One of the key features of child sexual abuse is its secrecy. Most forms of sexual activity take part in private and when children are involved and the activity is unacceptable to society it is hidden away as far as possible from public scrutiny. The perpetrators fear at best that what they are doing will be curtailed, at worst that they will be punished. The victims are frightened that either they or the abuser will face recriminations. They may also be terrified that threats that the abuser used to ensure their silence will be carried out.

Many victims, even as adults, do not want to disclose their childhood abuse because they are still protecting the perpetrator or other family members. Furthermore they feel deeply ashamed of having been molested even though it was not their fault. This means that we may never know for certain how many children are sexually abused.

## Problems of definition

There are also problems, as noted in First Thoughts, over deciding what is, and is not, abuse. Some studies trying to determine the incidence of abuse have included non-touching sexual activity such as being distressed by a 'flasher'. Other studies only include sexual activity involving direct physical contact. Again, while some researchers define child sexual abuse as happening to people under 16 years, others include young people up to 18 years. Some surveys have only looked at girl victims. Others include both sexes. Some have excluded abusive experiences perpetrated by children. Others include any form of sexual experience perceived to be abusive even when it involves child-to-child activity.

## Prevalence and incidence

When looking at the research, a distinction has to be made between prevalence and incidence. Prevalence refers to the proportion of the population subjected to child sexual abuse. Incidence describes the numbers of children victimised during a given period of time, usually a year. Therefore one study such as the American National Incidence Study 1981 will talk about an incidence rate of 0.7 per 1.000 children or 44,700 children in one year. Other studies will talk of abuse as a percentage for example Baker and Duncan quote 10% of a sample population (Baker and Duncan 1985).

### Collecting statistics

There are a number of different ways in which statistics can be gathered. Each way has both merits and drawbacks.

- From child victims: there are a number of obstacles to collecting statistics from the victims. How do you discover if children are being abused? Babies and toddlers cannot say what has been happening. Older children and young people are unlikely to trust a researcher with such an important secret and some may not realise yet that they are being abused or may have blanked out the experiences from their consciousness.

- From adult survivors: some researchers have asked adults if they remember being abused as children. Survivors may have pieced together their experiences and can give a reliable and lucid account. But many may well have forgotten that they were abused. We know that people sometimes cope with difficult events by blotting them out of their memories. As in the case of children, a number of adults may not wish to tell a researcher an intimate secret which they have kept for years; they may still feel too ashamed of what happened to talk to anyone about being victimised.

- From perpetrators: some research projects have asked the perpetrators of abuse about the children they abused. However this leads to an under-reporting of abuse because most perpetrators, even convicted ones, fear reprisals if they admit to abusing more children than the 'authorities' know about. Other offenders will have forgotten some instances of abuse particularly if they have been regularly exploiting children. Others only give half the story, for example they may be willing to admit to abusing girls but will not tell researchers that they abused boys because of the stigma that still clings to homosexuality. Similarly others will admit to abusing teenage girls excusing themselves on the grounds that they were 'seduced' but will not speak about the much younger children whom they also abused. So while studies of offenders give some valuable information they may not reflect the true rate and nature of sexual abuse.

- From official records: other studies look at the number of cases of reported sexual abuse. However many instances are only discovered by chance. We are aware from adults abused as children that at the time they never told anyone. We know from telephone help lines such as ChildLine that there are children and young people being abused at this moment who wish to remain anonymous and who may never disclose their abuse to anyone who can identify them. This leads workers to believe that the number of reported cases are the tip of the ice-berg.

We know that most perpetrators given the opportunity will abuse more than one child. Gone are the days when we thought that a man 'fell in love' with his teenage daughter and because his wife was 'failing' to satisfy his sexual desires gave his physical affection to his daughter. We have learnt through research and practical experience that people who molest children are sexually attracted to them and will abuse any available child if the circumstances are right.

### Paul's story

Some perpetrators molest a considerable number of children in their life. Paul, a colleague, described how he was molested by a teacher, Mr T, who used to touch all the 8-year-olds in his class between the legs putting his hands up the boys shorts - this was in the 1950s when small boys used to wear shorts all year round. He would also put his hand up the girls' skirts and sometimes down their knickers.

He used to make the children come out to his large desk to have their work marked. The desk hid his surreptitious activity in the event of another adult or older pupil walking in.

This was also the days when corporal punishment was permitted in state schools and he used spankings as an excuse for removing pants and feeling the children's private parts. When the children tried to tell adults, their parents assumed that they were complaining about being chastised and simply told them that they had probably deserved the punishment.

Often Mr T ensured he was able to get what Paul describes as 'his daily fix' by putting his pupils in a 'no win' situation such as spanking the last child out of the changing room after the PE class; however quickly the children dressed themselves there had to be someone who was last. Some pupils tried coming out last together - he simply smacked them all. Paul and his friends knew that Mr T was 'being rude'. They knew that his spankings had nothing to do with bad behaviour and even at the age of eight recognised that he enjoyed punishing them.

It left Paul feeling ashamed and guilty about the way he allowed himself to be used. He also became fearful of, and confused about any sort of punishment. Some of his classmates became extremely disturbed about what was happening and a significant number had very real sexual difficulties in their early adolescence; the roots of these difficulties could well have been traced back to the activities of their teacher.

The point about Paul's story is that Mr T molested all the children in his class - about 35-40 pupils a year. He had a fresh group of 8-year-olds annually. He also molested a handful of other pupils who were not in his class but whom he caught perhaps committing some minor misdemeanour when he was on playground duty. He was a teacher for over forty years. This means that one man molested at least 2,000 children.

The other moral of Paul's story is that parents should closely question the motivation and sexual orientation of those teachers, still employed in private schools, who cling tenaciously to their right to use corporal punishment.

It can be seen that it is impossible to answer the question 'How many children are abused?' with any firm and reliable figures. Studies have ranged from 6 per cent to 62 per cent for females and 3 per cent to 31 per cent for males. It is felt that 10 per cent is a conservative estimate. But if, for the sake of simplicity, we use the figure of 10 per cent, it still means that if you are a teacher with a class of thirty pupils, three of these have been, are being or will be sexually abused before they reach late adolescence. If you are a governor of a comprehensive school with 2,000 pupils aged 11 to 18 it is likely that about 200 of these have already been abused or will be abused during their time in your school. Child sexual abuse is therefore not to be dismissed as a rare and insignificant problem.

## WHAT SORT OF CHILD IS ABUSED?

The short answer to the question 'What sort of child is abused?' is 'Any sort'.

### *Gender*

Time and again studies which look at the proportion of sexually abused males to females report that more girls than boys are molested. There are however indications that a significant number of boys are sexually abused but they feature less prominently in the official statistics. This may be due to the fact that boys and men molested as children may be less willing to talk about their experiences.

There are a number of reasons for this. Firstly, men are not expected to be victims and they may be reluctant to admit to having been unable to protect themselves. Jean La Fontaine (1990) cites a friend who was an Old Etonian and who informed her that small boys would find it impossible to resist the overtures of a prefect or 'head of house'. In the school system and other all male institutions it is the 'weak' who are abused. So for a boy to admit to abuse is to admit to being weak.

As long as there is a stigma attached to homosexuality, boys abused by fellow males may be reluctant to speak out in case they are thought to be homosexual. We now know that, although some perpetrators prefer one gender, many such as Paul's teacher will abuse any available child regardless of gender.

Boys abused by women have equal difficulty. To be abused by an older boy or man is to be considered weak but to 'allow yourself' be exploited by a women is even weaker. This is not of course true, small boys are as much at the mercy of their mother, female teachers, school matrons and other women in authority as they are in the power of male figures. Older boys are expected to enjoy being introduced to sex by a skilled and knowledgeable woman and they are not expected to complain or feel exploited, although again if they cannot give fully informed consent then they are being exploited.

La Fontaine (1990) noted in one study that only 11 per cent of cases were boys where there was a single victim. But in cases where there were several victims such a sibling group the proportion of boys doubled to 22 per cent. This was because the offences were revealed by another member of the family, rather than the boy victims themselves.

According to Baker and Duncan's (1985) research more girls are subject to abuse from immediate relatives such as parents, grandparents or siblings. Boys are more likely to be abused outside the family by someone whom they already know. Girls are only slightly more likely than boys to be abused by strangers.

## Age

Children of all ages from a few days old to 18 years can be abused. The youngest child on my own caseload was a 16-day-old baby with damage to the anus thought to be caused by her natural father. It is difficult to detect abuse in very young children unless there are clear medical signs because pre-verbal children cannot talk about their experiences. Some toddlers simulating sexual activities with toys and other children give rise to the suspicion that they have been abused but it is difficult to confirm precisely what has happened. When older children or adults are asked when their abuse first started they may be unable to remember earliest experiences. This means that the sexual abuse of pre-school children is probably under-reported.

The age at which children are most vulnerable differs from study to study. Most find that the statistics peak between six and 12 years old. The age at which children disclose abuse is rather older. There is usually a significant gap between the time of onset and time of disclosure. This is largely due to the skill of the perpetrators in ensuring that children find it difficult to tell anyone about the abuse.

## Class and family income

It was once thought that sexual abuse was class related. As earlier mentioned it was assumed that incest only occurred in the families of isolated agricultural workers, the poor of rundown inner cities or amongst eccentric aristocrats. Professional and business middle-classes and the 'respectable' working-classes were thought to be immune from incest and sexual abuse. Children who were attacked by strangers or used for prostitution were thought more likely to be from the 'lower' orders of society.

It is true that children from lower income groups may figure more frequently in abuse statistics for a number of reasons.

Studies of all forms of abuse tend to identify mistreatment among poorer families. This is because poor families, especially if they are receiving state financial assistance, are likely to be under greater scrutiny than wealthy families. Furthermore poor parents cannot buy their way out of trouble. In addition, some poorer children could be more tempted than wealthy ones by material bribes and might have to play on the streets or use public transport unaccompanied, all of which can render them more vulnerable to a potential molester.

However, numerous accounts from the survivors of sexual abuse show that children from all classes are abused. One of my earliest cases was of a wealthy business man who was simulating intercourse with his daughter. The family's long sweeping drive behind the high hedge led to a huge house extensively carpeted, exquisitely decorated and expensively furnished. Perpetrators come from all walks of life and so do their victims.

### *Ethnicity, culture and religion*

'Across the board, studies have consistently failed to find any black-white differences in rates of sexual abuse' (Finkelhor 1986 p.69). As we will see later black and minority ethnic children have an added burden when trying to disclose in a predominantly white society. However perpetrators can be black or white and similarly victims can be black or white. We have accounts of black victims of sexual abuse such as Maya Angelou (1984) and of white victims such as Sylvia Fraser (1989).

Some ethnic groups figure more prominently in some studies and some much less. This could be due to the social systems within a particular group which may afford greater or less protection for the group's children. It could on the other hand be due to a failure to recognise and disclose abuse within some groups. Bandana Ahmad cites an example of some of the problems of recognition of abuse relating to cultural factors:

> *Some years back I was approached by a school in relation to a Punjabi girl who was sexually abused by her father and his friends regularly. Although the school was aware of this abuse for some time, no action was taken as the 'culturally sensitive' school was anxious to check whether 'incest' was accepted in Punjabi culture!...The school which had a responsibility to take*

*action in protecting the Punjabi girl against sexual abuse not only fell into the trap of a liberal and safe approach, but also reinforced the pathological stereotype of 'ethnic minority culture' (Ahmad 1989).*

Victims also come from a wide range of religious traditions as well as those who are atheist or agnostic.

It must also be remembered that we are talking of all forms of sexual abuse including molestation by non-family acquaintances or strangers. This means that a child could be molested, even if he or she came from a family with a culture and creed - which according to statistics - has a low abuse rate, because the perpetrator could be an acquaintance or stranger from a different cultural tradition.

## *Personality and physical factors*

We have already noted that neither age nor skin colour is a barrier to being abused. Nor are any other physical features. Children can be fat or thin, tall or short, good-looking or not so attractive. Maya Angelou (1984) who was raped as a child described herself as a too-big Negro girl, with nappy black hair, broad feet and a space between her teeth that would hold a number-two pencil. Comparing herself to her brother she said 'Where I was big, elbowy and grating, he was small, graceful and smooth. When I was described by our playmates as being shit color, he was lauded for his velvet-black skin. His hair fell down in black curls, and my head was covered with black steel wool.' (p.21). Sylvia Fraser (1989) on the other hand remembers being admired as a 'fairy tale princess'.

Children with a physically disability can be vulnerable because perpetrators realise that some will have difficulty escaping from the abuse. One victim explained:

*Because of my disability I can't get off my back without help, so all he had to do was force me to the ground and I was fair game for him and his friends (Corcoran 1987 p.106).*

Some victims are very intelligent, both Maya Angelou and Sylvia Fraser were achievers academically. Most are probably of average intelligence. Children with learning difficulties, sometimes referred to as people with mental handicaps, are vulnerable. They may be more easily tricked as they can be more trusting and less street-wise than their peers.

Perpetrators may think that they are less likely to be believed and will make less reliable witnesses if they do attempt to disclose.

No formal research studies to date have demonstrated beyond doubt that particular physical or personality features make children more or less vulnerable. I have certainly met every type of personality from the out-going talkative child to the quiet, nervous one. I have encountered abused children who can test an adult's patience to the limit as well as well-behaved, compliant ones. Some victims are aggressive, some passive. However the quiet, obedient, passive child may be easier to abuse than the more assertive child. For this reason helping children to be challenging and assertive may protect them from exploitation.

Children who have a special interest or talent may be more vulnerable. A child who, for example, is musically gifted could be offered additional tuition by a teacher who uses these special sessions as an opportunity to molest the child. Children who are very good at sport have been befriended by coaches who have built up a bond of trust and reliance then abused them. Perpetrators are adept at tuning in to the enthusiasms of young people in order to gain the confidence of both victims and parents; caring and careful parents who - had they realised what was happening - would have protected their offspring.

One feature that is common to most victims is that of isolation. It is, however, difficult to disentangle cause from effect. Children who are on their own and apparently unprotected by family or friends are easy targets. Lonely children may be readily befriended by an adult or older child who offers them bribes and affection in exchange for sexual favours. On the other hand being abused may set children apart from their family and friends. Marie, whose father was physically and sexually abusive recalls:

> *It was difficult to have friends because they couldn't understand why I was friendly one moment and suddenly distant the next. It was easier not to have friends, so I became isolated (Doyle 1990 p.21).*

### In conclusion

Any type of child can be abused. We cannot look at a group of children and identify those that are likely to be abused and those who are safe from abuse, although some perpetrators of abuse can spot the child who is likely to be the safest target. This of course means that no parent can be sure that their child will not be abused. Nevertheless, as will be shown in later chapters there are ways of attempting to protect children and ways of helping those who have been abused to recover from their experiences.

In order to help abused children or to prevent abuse from happening it is important to acquire a thorough understanding of how the victim perceives the abuse, how the perpetrator's mind works, how the family is likely to react and how you and others trying to help will think and feel about events. The next section should help you move towards that understanding.

# Two

# Understanding ourselves

Without an understanding of our own emotions and limitations, any help given to victims of sexual abuse may be ineffective or even damaging. It is true that there are some people who naturally say and do the right thing at the right time. An example is given by Sarah who was sexually and physically abused by her father and who recalled how as a young adult living in digs:

> She met a woman who accepted her and hearing of her experiences commented, 'It isn't fair, why should it have happened to you'. This helped Sarah realise that she was not to blame for what had occurred and there was nothing bad about her, she did not deserve such treatment. She learnt about friendship from that woman and was able through her to make other friends (Doyle 1990 p.117).

Even people with this type of natural sensitivity will still find that their abilities are reinforced if they acquire a greater understanding of child sexual abuse.

There are a number of reasons why child sexual abuse is a particularly difficult and poignant subject. The issues and emotions that this form of abuse provoke are worth examining.

### Attitudes to human sexuality
The very many excellent animal studies, nowadays conveyed to a wider audience through television programmes about nature and wildlife, have shown us that even among animals there are rituals and rules about sexual relationships. Among many of

the higher mammals, the young males are not allowed to mate with any female of their choosing. They are sometimes chased out of their original group and have to find a female in a new group.

It comes as no surprise therefore that human beings have various taboos and controls about sexual behaviour. In the animal kingdom these rules are designed to avoid the genetic problems arising from in-breeding and to ensure the survival of the species. However because humans are intensely social beings who manage to achieve so much by working in co-operative teams, relationships have to be further refined in order to avoid conflict and the destruction of potentially beneficial groupings.

These rules and taboos have to be powerful ones because the drive to procreate is strong, ensuring as it must human survival, just as thirst and hunger have to drive us to find food and drink. This means that there is constant conflict between the basic human desire for sexual activity and the need to control, channel and constrain that desire.

Children have to be taught society's taboos and rules long before they can understand the reasons for them. Small children may enjoy touching and rubbing their genitals but, because in most cultures sexual activity is confined to the private setting, children may be punished for masturbating without really understanding why they are being chastised. This leads to a degree of guilt, shame and confusion about sexual matters which most of us carry into adulthood.

As a consequence when we are having to deal with sexual abuse we have to cope not only with the distress that all cases of child mistreatment cause but also with the feelings of embarrassment and guilt engendered by the subject of sex.

Because the exact rules and taboos on sexual behaviour vary from culture to culture, from family to family and from person to person there is the potential for distress and conflict when society attempts to define and impose appropriate limits. This serves to add to the difficulty of trying to respond positively to cases of child sexual abuse.

Many adults also have strong feelings about sexual abuse cases because they have had an unpleasant sexual encounter at sometime during their life. Even as adults, people may have felt powerless in the encounter. For example a young man, Sean, proudly joined up as a regular soldier only to find himself totally humiliated when he was molested by his Sergeant Major. Similarly Zeta, a female secretary, to her great distress and embarrassment soon found out why her colleagues called her boss, whose official title was Group Manager, the 'Grope Manager'!

We all grow up with a certain degree of familiarity with physical abuse, neglect and emotional abuse. From the cradle onwards most cultures incorporate fairy tales, nursery rhymes, children's chants and games that contain the mistreatment of children. In Europe, we only have to think of Cinderella.

In English folk songs there are variations on the theme of the cruel mother:

> *Oh, she was walking on her father's lawn*
> *Where her fine sons they were born.*
> *She took out her penknife*
> *And there she took away their three lives.*

In another version she had two 'pretty babes' and 'stabbed them right through the heart'.

In the Orkney's the children skip to the ancient Norse rhyme 'Bang willa gas glay, bang willa gas glay, takken leggen sloggen, vekken, bang likka slay' which means 'and the baby won't be quiet, the baby won't be quiet, take it by the leg, hit it against the wall.'

---

### EXERCISE

Try to think of other children's stories and rhymes familiar to your own culture. How many of them include instances of cruelty or abandonment of children?

---

As children grow older they read books and see plays or television shows which again familiarise them with physical and emotional cruelty towards children. Emanating from Britain and translated into many other languages are the stories from Charles Dickens – his story of Oliver Twist is read world wide. The popular Australian soaps *Neighbours* and

*Home and Away* to which children of the 1980s and 1990s sit glued each evening occasionally touch on physical or emotional cruelty. Again think of the books, plays or poems that you read as a schoolchild or teenager. How many of them contained instances of cruelty to children?

Psychologists have shown that we can become less shocked and upset by objects, situations and events if we become familiar with them. We steadily become 'desensitised' to them. From earliest childhood we are introduced to the fact that young people are physically and emotionally mistreated and abandoned. This means that when we come across a case of cruelty to children we may feel shock and distress but our feelings are probably manageable because of the process of desensitisation.

---

### EXERCISE

Now look again at all those fairy stories, rhymes, popular children's television programmes and stories. How many of them explicitly described a child being sexually abused? Any at all?

---

If you are Roman Catholic you may recall St Dyphne who chose death rather than be subjected to an incestuous relationship with her father. However such examples are few and far between. Nursery stories and rhymes, it is true, sometimes have sexual innuendos and symbols but very rarely do they describe in graphic detail the suffering of a sexually abused child in the explicit way that the physical and emotional distress of Cinderella or Oliver Twist are described.

This means that we are not 'desensitised' to child sexual abuse. Therefore unless we have been the victims of sexual abuse the discovery of our first case, a graphic newspaper report or explicit television programme comes as a profound shock. The impact is all the greater if we have been led to believe as many people have, that childhood is a time of relative sexual innocence and that sexual abuse is a very rare event.

### *Emotional responses*

---

### EXERCISE

This might be painful so do not try it until you are feeling fairly calm and resilient.

Try to think of a recent shock that you have had – a burglary, a car stolen, bad news about a friend.

Can you remember your very first feelings on hearing the news or seeing that items were missing? Try to write them down.

---

The natural human reaction to any shock is a state of numbness followed by denial and disbelief. Can you remember feeling 'Oh no, it can't really have happened' or something similar when you tried the last exercise? Elizabeth Kubler-Ross observed:

> *Among the over two hundred dying patients we have interviewed, most reacted to the awareness of a terminal illness at first with the statement, 'No, not me, it cannot be true'. This initial denial was as true for those patients who were told out-right at the beginning of their illness as it was true for those who were not told explicitly and who came to this conclusion on their own a bit later on (Kubler-Ross 1970 p.34).*

We now know that on being faced with the shocking fact of child sexual abuse, many people deny that it occurs, or if it happens at all then it does so in remote and far-removed areas or among some helpless, hopeless underclass that knows no better. They will not accept that it could take place in their own community, neighbourhood or family.

Others can accept that sexual abuse exists and is relatively widespread but still find it hard to believe that it could occur close to home. Like a serious road accident or natural disaster, it happens to other people.

Those of you who are the parents or close relative of an abused child can be reassured that if your first reaction was one of numbness followed by disbelief then you shared a common response with the rest of humanity. Denial is not arrogance or stupidity but a normal defensive reaction. When it is a temporary state it gives the body, or even a whole community, time to muster its energy and resources before the pain of what has really happened is felt in full.

Those of you who were the victims of abuse may recall, perhaps with some bitterness, that those around you found it difficult to believe you. It could be that as ordinary mortals they had to defend themselves through denial and disbelief against the unacceptable truth and emotional pain.

Society in general supports this denial and disbelief. The news media and politicians berate those like Drs Higgs and Wyatt in Cleveland who tried to tell them that a significant number of children are being anally abused, or the social workers in Nottinghamshire who exposed the sexual exploitation of children during ritual ceremonies.

But as long as we, as individuals or as representatives of society, are trapped in a state of numbness, denial and disbelief we shall never be in a position to help the victims of child sexual abuse. When dealing with this topic you have, as the staff at the Faithfull Foundation in Birmingham put it, to:

> *Think the unthinkable*
> *Believe the unbelievable*
> *Imagine the unimaginable*

Some former victim's first response will be denial – 'It wasn't really abuse, we were just kids playing'. 'Dad didn't really do that to me, it was just some kind of fantasy'. 'It didn't do me any harm'. Some adults manage to push the memories back into a safe place but in doing so may collude with the more general denial found in society. One wonders how far some professionals who have the evidence before them but have found ways of denying the realities of child sexual abuse, have personal reasons for doing so.

A substantial number of adults have pushed their abuse to the back of their minds or have forgotten about it completely. Being faced with the issue of child sexual abuse they might suddenly recall the abuse. They could well share the feelings described by a professional worker who had just taken part in a training session during which a colleague described an incident of child sexual abuse:

*The session did not end for our subject. There was no forgetting the incident described by the distressed group member. She pictured it increasingly clearly but then recognised that the victimised child in her images was her own self. Night after night the reason became apparent as she recalled long forgotten sexual exploitation. Between the ages of 5 and 12 years she had been used as an experimental object by an older male relative.*

*She relived the experiences; the discomfort, terror, pain, the struggle to breath under the weight of his body, the smell of his sweat, the damp patch on the sheets and the screaming in her head – not out loud for fear of being heard and discovered.*

*She now had to face the fact that she had been a victim. As she described 'Its like having had a disfiguring accident, then years later someone holds up a mirror and forces you to look at every scar, every blemish, every abnormality.'*

*She wanted to end the nightmare, she wanted to die. Never before had she contemplated suicide but now she saw herself as irretrievably damaged goods; she saw little purpose in carrying on living (Doyle 1986 p.8).*

Adults sexually abused as children who suddenly find themselves recalling long forgotten events might experience an even greater shock than those who encounter child sexual abuse for the first time as adults.

Other survivors will find that they can no longer deny their experiences as day after day they experience 'flash backs'. During these flashbacks abusive events are recalled in all their detail to the extent of being able to feel the pressure of anal penetration or the pain of vaginal intercourse. Former victims can smell the sweaty excitement of the perpetrator. They can hear the abuser's threats, see his distorted features and taste semen or their own tears. This recall is so vivid that victims relive the events along with all the feelings of shame, guilt, powerlessness and humiliation that they originally felt. They cannot control these flashbacks which creep up unawares and may continue long after the adult feels the problem should have been dealt with.

Once denial cannot protect us from facing what has happened we often begin to feel angry.

People who were not abused as children may still feel a sense of outrage at what has happened. We do not have to be a dog, cat, whale or badger to find ourselves seething about cruelty perpetrated against animals.

If you are a former sexual abuse victim you are likely to experience anger. You might be angry with society for not having protected you, angry with your family for having exposed you to danger, angry with the perpetrator for having inflicted so much pain on you, angry with parents or teachers for not having believed you, angry with your present friends and partners for not being able to take away your pain, angry with yourself for not having stopped the abuse and for not having told someone sooner, angry with yourself for your inability to control the flashbacks and for spending hours in an incoherent heap crying helplessly. Unfortunately the anger turned in on yourself can lead to self-hatred, despair and thoughts of suicide.

If, at the same time, you are being expected to cope with a case of child sexual abuse you may find your anger in relation to the case directed inappropriately, such as turning it against victimised children because you cannot bear to carry their pain as well as your own. You might be furious with the perpetrator or with the child's family. You could well become overwhelmingly exasperated by the investigating workers, procedures and legal requirements as you can see how limited they are in their ability to heal the pain of the victim – professional workers and systems are fairly safe targets for your anger.

We might also speculate about just how many social workers, police officers and doctors have become the target of journalists, politicians, other professionals or members of the general public who have a personal reason for projecting their anger against those in the front-line trying to cope with the issue of child sexual abuse.

Often the stage of anger is followed by depression. Former victims might become very unhappy and despairing. Depression can cause a lack of appetite, sleep impairment, inability to work or to complete tasks, forgetfulness, irritability, isolation and loneliness. This further compounds the problem. You are meant to be helping someone who has been sexually abused yet you feel tired, lethargic, ill, unhappy and maybe even suicidal. The fact that you are unable to cope makes you feel even more helpless, useless and depressed.

People can and do recover from the profoundest of shocks. Elizabeth Kubler-Ross (1970) in her work with the terminally ill found that given time and help patients can reach a stage of peace and acceptance. Similarly the former victims of child sexual abuse can reach a stage in which the pain goes and they can lay down their burden of secrecy and guilt. There may be occasional flashbacks but these are no longer so vivid nor prolonged. They cannot be controlled but can be tolerated.

This stage however is not reached without time, effort and help. If you have started remembering earlier abuse it may take two or three years before you feel strong enough to recall it without distress. However in those years the distress will not always be so profound. You will fluctuate from stage to stage; sometimes denying the significance of your experiences, sometimes feeling numb, sometimes angry, sometimes sad and sometimes getting on with your life as if nothing had happened. The pain will come and go but over time it will probably diminish.

The most important thought to hang on to is that you were not to blame. Later in the next chapter when we look at perpetrators I will try to show you why this is so. You are not the only person this happened to and there is nothing particularly odd or aberrant about you, it can happen to the nicest of children.

Finally, you are worth helping and you have the right to ask for and receive assistance. Many survivors are eventually able to use their experiences in a positive and constructive way to help other victimised children. They understand why they were abused, know it was not their fault and know that they do not need to carry a burden of secrecy, guilt and shame. They feel emotionally strong.

If this applies to you then you may be in a very good position to help abused children because you know what the journey to recovery and healing is like and you can lead abused children and young people along that same road. However, do remember that you may have forgotten how rough some of the way was, or perhaps you did not find the journey a hard one whereas the children and young people you are trying to help may have much more difficulty coping with it.

Even if you were not the victim of any sexual abuse you may have experienced the various stages associated with coping with unpalatable truths. Returning to the first part of this stage you could well at first have denied that child sexual abuse exists or denied that it is the very real problem that some of the 'experts' say it is. You may then have felt angry with the victim, his or her family, the perpetrator, society or the system for allowing such things to happen. You might subsequently have felt confused and unable to respond constructively. You could still be feeling this which is why you have reached out and started reading this book hoping that it can wrest you from the despair and depression which is creeping over you.

Hopefully it will help but you may also need to accept that these feelings are a normal consequence of the shock of learning about the reality of child sexual abuse. Be gentle on yourself, give yourself time and do not be ashamed of admitting you are having difficulty coping and need assistance. You are on the way to acceptance of the issue of child sexual abuse and its attendant problems. Once acceptance is achieved you will be in a far better position to help the victims than other people who are stuck in denial or anger.

### A MESSAGE TO THOSE WITH SPECIAL SECRETS

There may be those of you reading this book who know deep down that you have sexually abused a child or have had fantasies about having sex with a child or young person. I guess that you would welcome some guidance.

You may have engaged in sexual activities as a child or young adolescent and now realise that you were in a powerful position in relation to the other child or children so were basically an abuser.

Were you also sexually abused as a child? If so, your activities with other children might have been a way of coping with what happened to you. You may have found the way out of your feelings of helplessness was to have other children in your power. Do you never now – and here be honest with yourself – have fantasies about sex with children, are not sexually aroused by children or young adults who have childlike characteristics and are in no way attracted to child pornography? If this is the case you can allow yourself to accept that you are not likely to be a child molester.

You have to realise that what you did as a child or young

person was more in the nature of bullying which was expressed in a sexual form. What you need to do is to examine whether or not you still bully people now. Are you attracted to helping in child sexual abuse cases because of the power you have over other people involved in these cases who may be vulnerable? If so it is better to avoid such work. If however you know that you have grown out of your childish bullying you may be able to help in a constructive way despite your earlier activities.

*If* – whether or not you have ever actively abused a youngster – *you have any fantasies about sex involving children, find the idea of sex with children sexually arousing or are attracted to child pornography then you must leave working with sexually abused children to others.* We would not advise an alcoholic to work in a pub, nor someone addicted to drugs to work in a pharmacy. Similarly I am advising you not to put yourself in a position where your fantasies may be reinforced and where you might find it impossible to resist temptation.

### UNDERSTANDING ABUSED CHILDREN

Children caught up in abuse whatever its form, physical, emotional or sexual find it difficult to ask for help. At first sight this might seem strange. Surely if people are being ill-treated they will seek assistance? If you are attacked in a busy street, assuming the assailant is unarmed, you would probably cry out for help, struggle and attempt to escape as quickly as possible. You will also be extremely grateful to anyone who intervenes and saves you from further attack.

However, if you are mugged you have some hope of escape, there is the chance that someone will hear your cries and attempt a rescue. You would react very differently if you had no such hope. We know this from studies of adult hostages and people who have felt trapped and unable to escape their assailants.

### Frozen fright

When people realise that they are facing a hijacker, a hostage-taker or a kidnapper with no chance of escape the first thing they do is to freeze. This is rather like the numbness experienced in any situation of shock.

In the same way, children who realise that they are being

sexually abused often stay very still and do not resist. Moira age 16 describes being abused by her older brother, 'He also pushed [his penis] into my vagina but – this might seem silly – I'm not sure if he was inside me or not. I was really scared of him by then and half the time I didn't know what was happening. I just seemed to cut myself off from it' (Bain and Sanders 1990 p.40).

Children who become aware that their brothers or sisters are being sexually abused can become similarly frozen by fear. Marie whose father sexually abused her sister describes how at night when her father came home she would:

*Clamber back to bed and pretend I was asleep. My father would creep into our room, ostensibly to tuck us in but he seemed to be trying to see who was in the deepest sleep. Sometimes he would stay by our bedside for two minutes, sometimes for fifteen. At that stage he didn't touch me but there was always the fear, the dread, wondering if it was going to be my turn (Doyle 1990 p.20).*

Some children are slowly and gradually seduced into sexually abusive activities. Sonia describes how her aunt, who used to baby-sit 'Would sleep beside me in my bed. At first, I thought this was good fun.' When her aunt started pushing her fingers in Sonia's vagina she asked her to stop but the aunt said 'She would tell my parents I was doing bad things, and that I would get the blame' (Bain and Sanders 1990 p.39). Such children dare not tell anyone what has been happening because they feel they might be punished for having sometimes willingly participated at first or for having allowed the abuse to continue.

### Denial

Having read the earlier section it will come as no surprise to you to learn that children, like adults, trapped in a frightening situation protect themselves from the pain of their fear by denying that their abusers intend them any harm. We have already seen how important denial is when people receive a shock. Being kidnapped or finding yourself in the power of a sexual abuser is a profound shock.

One passenger who was the victim of the hijack of TWA flight 355 in 1976 declared 'They didn't have anything [the bombs were fakes], but they were really great guys. This was despite the fact that a bomb disposal officer was blown up trying to diffuse one of the bombs (Strenz 1980 p.144). Similarly for a shorter or longer time the victims of sexual abuse may deny that their molester was harming them in any way.

### Anger and fear

Anger, we have seen, follows hard on the heels of denial. However sometimes the trapped victims are too frightened to turn their anger against their abuser yet they have to do something with it. Adults in hostage situations sometimes turn it against the people trying to rescue them. There is a feeling of 'its us against the world'; a bond is forged between abuser and abused. Hostages have been known to protect their captors against the police. Similarly abused children will sometimes try to protect the people who have been abusing them.

Anger, if not turned on the perpetrators nor the outside world, might be turned by the victim against him or herself. This gives rise to the feelings of depression and unworthiness felt by some hostages and abused children alike.

Adult hostages and abused children may of course behave in a compliant manner and not seek escape because of a real fear of the abuser's threats. The kidnapper may say 'Attempt to escape and I will kill you'; the victim very sensibly does not try to escape. The father of Sylvia Fraser threatened that if she told her mother she would be sent to 'The place where all bad children go. An orphanage where they lock up bad children whose parents don't want them any more' (Fraser 1989 p.11).

Hostages may fear for others. One hostage taker said 'See, once you have a man and wife – especially if they're young – you can control one through the other .... Whatever I want you to do, I can threaten your husband and you'll do it' (Knutson 1980 p.124). Similarly the abused child might be told 'If you tell anyone our secret your mother will be so upset she will end up in hospital'. Maya Angelou (1984) was told by her mother's boyfriend who raped her that if she told anyone he would kill her much loved brother.

### Shame

From a very early age children learn that they must not be rude nor talk about rude things; adults have inconsistent and often angry reactions when children do so. Anything involving the private parts seems to be considered 'rude' by adults. Children will therefore be reluctant to admit they have been involved in activities in which private parts played a significant role. Only very young children will be free of embarrassment and shame.

Children often do not have the vocabulary to tell adults about what has been happening to them. Once children learn that you simply do not talk to grown-ups about 'willies' and 'fannies' how can they tell adults that someone has touched those most private of parts? Many little girls do not have a word for the vagina apart from 'bottom' and who is going to take notice of a small child who says 'Mummy touched my bottom.'? Similarly will adults understand a youngster who declares 'My brother put his 'thing' in my mouth'?

Sexually abused children often feel sullied and ashamed because such abuse involves the parts of the body often referred to as rude and associated with toiletting. They are naturally reluctant to let others know how 'dirty' they are (which of course they are not).

### Guilt

Perpetrators are adept at making their victims feel guilty – 'You dirty minx, you seduced me'. They will call the children devils and temptresses.

Children may also feel guilty because they have accepted bribes or they have broken some rule or other. I can recall being approached by a man in a quiet street. Being a polite child I thought it would be discourteous just to run off until I realised he was asking me to look at what was in his trousers between his legs. I never told an adult because I had broken the rule of not talking to strangers. My behaviour was the result of two conflicting injunctions – 'Be polite to grown-ups' and 'Do not talk to strangers'. How many of us put our own children in similar Catch 22 situations?

### Doubt

Abused children are made to feel that they are merely objects who are really worth very little. Many victims doubt that they are worth helping. They may also have found that the people whom they thought they could trust are the very people who are abusing them. This means that they may doubt the intentions

**Figure 1: Forces which can bind a child to an abuser**

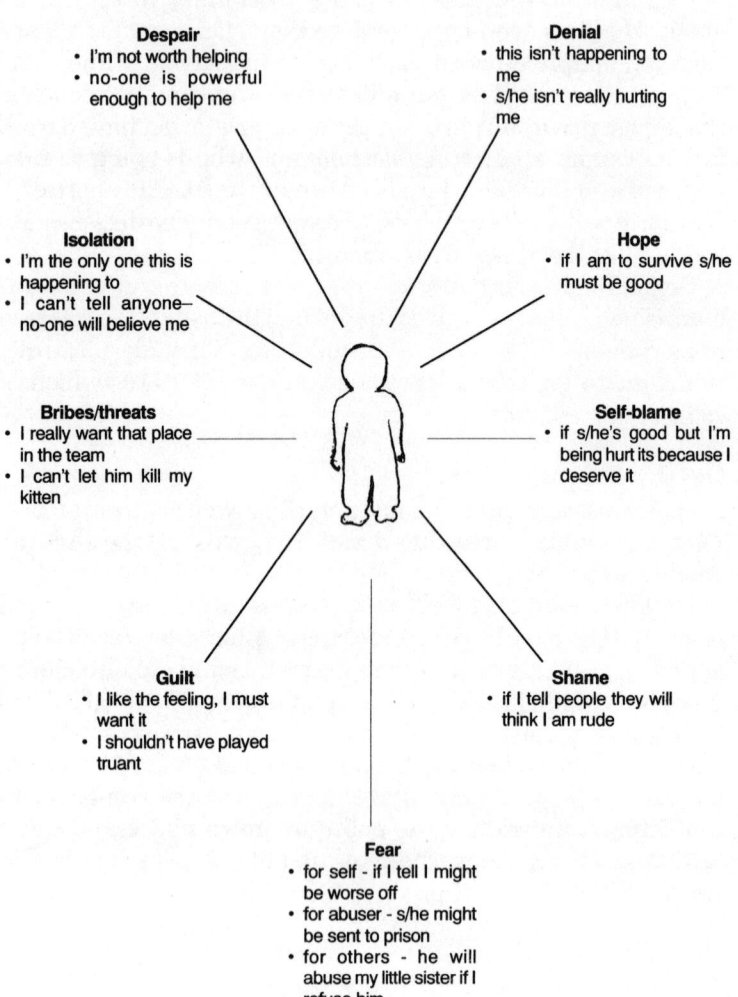

**Despair**
- I'm not worth helping
- no-one is powerful enough to help me

**Denial**
- this isn't happening to me
- s/he isn't really hurting me

**Isolation**
- I'm the only one this is happening to
- I can't tell anyone— no-one will believe me

**Hope**
- if I am to survive s/he must be good

**Bribes/threats**
- I really want that place in the team
- I can't let him kill my kitten

**Self-blame**
- if s/he's good but I'm being hurt its because I deserve it

**Guilt**
- I like the feeling, I must want it
- I shouldn't have played truant

**Shame**
- if I tell people they will think I am rude

**Fear**
- for self - if I tell I might be worse off
- for abuser - s/he might be sent to prison
- for others - he will abuse my little sister if I refuse him

of other adults who could be in a position to help them. The result is that they are fearful of disclosing and entrusting their secret to any adult.

## Do children lie?

We have learnt from the previous section how difficult it is for sexually abused children to seek help and tell someone about their experiences and yet for years people have refused to believe those children who have tried to confide in an adult.

Among the patients of the famous psychoanalyst, Freud, were a number of distressed, disturbed young women. As he listened to them pour out their life stories, time and again he heard them talk about having been sexually molested by their fathers or other male relatives. He had no reason to disbelieve them, they could gain no advantage by telling lies. Although at first he was inclined to accept his patients' accounts, ultimately he could not face the truth. He also knew that his colleagues and society as a whole would not believe the accusations being made against respectable, middle-class men of the time.

He therefore convinced himself (for a while) and others that small girls fell in love with their fathers and had fantasies about having sexual relationships with them, the Electra Complex. Similarly small boys fell in love with their mothers and felt a rivalry with their father. This is popularly known as the Oedipus Complex.

Freud was very influential and even today people will assume that stories told by children against adults are the normal fantasies which children have from time to time. Now that we have learnt to listen to children and piece together all the facts logically, we know that most youngsters simply do not have such fantasies. If they can talk about sexual activities it is because they have been exposed to them in some way. If they talk about being abused the usual reason is the obvious one – they have been abused. We do not have to look for elaborate and convoluted explanations emanating from deep within a child's subconscious.

There are some occasions when children do not tell the truth or the whole truth. This usually happens when they are unwilling to disclose everything that happened either because they are frightened of being punished for not having stopped the abuse or are trying to protect someone they care for, possibly the abuser him or herself.

It is sometimes argued that children make false accusations motivated by revenge or a wish to get rid of the accused. This becomes all the more plausible when a child does not like someone such as a baby-sitter or a new step-parent. *But*, the reason why the child does not like the baby-sitter or step-parent may be because he or she is being abused by them.

We need to realise that from a child's perspective it is far safer, if you are seeking revenge, to accuse someone of being cruel in a way other than sexual. If you complain of being sexually abused you run the risk of being thought rude and dirty yourself and you may be punished for engaging in forbidden sexual activity.

Occasionally the wrong person is accused. An example is that of Rose who maintained that she was being abused by her step-father when in fact the perpetrator was her grand-father. The step-father had in fact made some sexual comments, or as he viewed them 'jokes', relating to Rose which were at best insensitive. Rose's grandfather who for many years had been her only father figure and whom she loved very much had been forcing her to have intercourse. Rose desperately wanted help and was worried about getting pregnant. She felt degraded by her step-father's 'jokes' and feared that they were a prelude to something more sexually abusive. By accusing her step-father, Rose thought that she would prevent him from molesting her, get help for herself and protect her grandfather.

Again some children are thought to be attention seeking by maintaining that they have been sexually abused. A colleague admits that, as a child, following a Danger-Stranger campaign she made up a story about being approached by a stranger as an excuse for being late for school. However, as she acknowledges, she would never have made up a story about someone she knew well. Furthermore, she would not have had the knowledge to make up any explicit sexual details.

Many young children simply do not have the sexual knowledge to make up a story of molestation. They may have watched explicit videos but then how do they get information about how semen feels and tastes from a video?

Children often retract their story and some people argue that this proves that they must have been lying in the first place. However, children often disclose because they want the abuse to stop. They do not want to get the abuser into trouble nor cause distress to their family. Yet having disclosed they find that they are under enormous pressure, often from their family, to retract. They find that their parents are upset, the perpetrator arrested and they are subjected to medical examinations, police questioning and threats of legal proceedings. Their world falls apart and they are made to feel uncomfortable. Cindy describes her experiences:

*I asked for protection...[I was sent] to live with strangers in another place, with a different school. I lost my part in the school play and the science fair while he and the others all got to stay at home... I asked you to put an end to the abuse – you put an end to my whole family...You've exchanged my private nightmare for a very public one (MacFarlane 1990 pp.148-9).*

It comes as no surprise that many abuse victims retract, it is more of a wonder that many of them do not do so.

Children's stories are sometimes vague, inconsistent or garbled. This does not mean that they are lying. In order to protect themselves they may have tried not to remember distressing events – they may have attempted to 'blank them out'. Sometimes children do not have the words to describe what has been happening to them. Other children are frightened of using their own words for private parts or interviewers fail to understand the terms that the children are using.

Sometimes they do not understand what the abuser was doing. They are often having to infer by feel what is happening because they cannot see. In cases of anal penetration the abuser may be behind them. Many perpetrators cover the victim's face so the victim can only guess what is happening. Many children especially younger ones do not have a clear image of their own body or that of an adult. They are confused by such things as male ejaculation. Maya Angelou wrote of her experience after being sexually assaulted when only 8-years-old:

*He pulled off his shorts that had fallen to his ankles and went into the bathroom. It was true the bed was wet, but I knew I hadn't had an accident. Maybe Mr Freeman had one while he was holding me. He came back with a glass of water and told me in a sour voice, 'Get up. You peed in the bed.'...I knew when to keep quiet*

*around adults, but I did want to ask him why he said I peed when
I was sure he didn't believe that (Angelou 1984 p.71).*

Although as an adult Maya can make sense of this event, we
can imagine that were she to have been asked, a few months
after these events, to describe how she had been molested she
would have been very confused about who had wet the bed.
Ejaculations and semen were until this point outside her
knowledge and experience. She might well have omitted this
important (to an adult investigator) piece of information for
fear of being punished either for wetting the bed or for accusing
Mr Freeman of doing so.

So, if a child tells you they have been sexually assaulted they
should be believed in much the same way that the police will
believe an adult who reports that his or her car is stolen. The
police will start with the assumption that the adult is telling
the truth and that the car has indeed been stolen. An
investigation on that basis will be started. The police may
eventually find that the driver simply made a mistake about
where the car was parked or was involved in an insurance fraud
or a hit and run accident and was reporting the theft as a cover
story. But the police do not start from a point of assuming an
ulterior motive.

Adults can deliberately lie or be mistaken but we do not
initially assume that they are doing so. Yet in the past many
adults started with the belief that sexually abused children
were lying and either ignored or punished them. This is rather
like the police responding to the report of a stolen car by either
sending the driver away with the proverbial 'flea in the ear' or
charging him or her with an insurance fraud without even
investigating.

To reiterate, as with adults, children may occasionally lie or
be mistaken. But it takes a very reckless, disturbed or
distressed child to do so when it comes to an allegation of sexual
abuse especially against someone they know and possibly love
deeply. Whatever the truth of the matter, a child telling an
adult about being molested needs to be taken seriously, listened
to and helped.

## WHO IS TO BLAME?

The child victim is never to blame.

The child victim is often blamed for the abuse and its consequences. And yet because children and young people cannot give informed consent and do not fully appreciate the consequences of their actions they cannot be to blame. It is the perpetrator and the perpetrator alone who holds the power and it is he or she who abuses the child's trust, helplessness, vulnerability or naivety.

Perpetrators will of course blame their victims and will often do this so convincingly that they will draw other people into condemning the child. They will also make the victims believe that they, not the perpetrator, were to blame. They will say that the child seduced them 'She used to lift up her skirt and show her knickers', 'He would come to my house and expect to be paid', 'She would wander round the house half-naked', 'He started it, asking to see how big my penis is'.

Perpetrators will blame the child for not having stopped the abuse. 'She seemed to like it, she didn't tell me to stop.' Most children do not object either because they are too frightened to do so or because they are confused about what is happening. Younger children may think it is what all adults do. Some children genuinely like the feeling of being caressed and enjoy physical contact so at first they do not want it to stop. Maya Angelou remembered before she was raped 'then came the nice part. He held me so softly that I wished he wouldn't ever let me go. I felt at home' (1984 p.71). *But* it is the perpetrator who is the person in the more powerful position. He or she alone has the strength, knowledge and/or authority to make the ultimate decision over whether or not to exploit the child's willingness or vulnerability.

Children and young people may possess characteristics that make them more vulnerable but that is not the same as saying they are to blame. They may behave in ways that make them more susceptible but they are still not to blame. Maya Angelou again describes how 'I began to feel lonely for Mr Freeman again and the encasement in his big arms...One evening when I couldn't concentrate on anything I went over to him and sat quickly on his lap' (1984 p.73). Yes, it looks as though Maya initiated contact this time but it was Mr Freeman who was to blame for taking advantage of her need for physical comfort.

Sometimes blame is cast on other children in the family. The eldest daughter is blamed because she refused to have sex with her father, 'If you had let me do it to you I wouldn't have had to have sex with your little sister'. Siblings who were aware of the abuse may be blamed because they did not tell someone or try to help. Yet we know that brothers and sisters are just as fearful of disclosure as the victims themselves. They are made to feel powerless by the perpetrator who will then turn round and blame them for not exerting a power they never really had.

Occasionally when one small child abuses another or a child is abused by an adult with the mental age and understanding of a young child the concept of 'blame' is unhelpful. In this case the abuser may have as little understanding of the consequences as the victim. A five-year-old who has been sexualised through having been abused by her grandfather cannot be blamed when she repeats what has happened to her with her three-year-old brother.

### ISSUES FOR BLACK CHILDREN

Most children are abused by someone whom they either love or who at the very least has befriended them. When youngsters disclose they often feel that they are betraying their loved relative or friend. If the abuse occurred within their family they will feel guilty for betraying their family. Abused children from minority cultures may feel they are betraying not only their family or friend but their community as well. This is a particular concern for many abused Black youngsters because at quite an early age they may become aware that a part at least, if not the whole, of the white population will seize on any opportunity to denigrate Black people.

Black children who have already had a taste of racism in a predominantly white culture may fear that their disclosure will expose them and their community to yet more racist attacks. Charmaine, a Black 11-year-old, born and living in England whose parents originated from the West Indies wrote, 'I couldn't tell about my dad because I loved him and I didn't want to get him into trouble and I thought white people would make racist comments' (Rouf 1991a).

Black children may already have a negative self-concept because of the very many negative black images in white

Western cultures. Being sexually abused may compound that image. Let Celestine explain in her own words:

*I was of mixed race – my mother black, my father white. Consequently I was dark brown. I remember at school I was always made to feel my skin was dirty. I remember when I was about eight years old a class mate said 'Isn't your skin dirty'. I used to sit in the bath trying to scrub myself clean but I could not get rid of the brown. My skin would just start to bleed. I used to rinse my hair in lemon juice as I had heard that this made it lighter but it did not change colour, the juice just made it sticky. I used to pray to wake up with blue eyes but each morning they were the same dark colour.*

*At school I was never chosen to be an angel or a fairy or a princess or a May Queen. I was a shepherd, a witch or just one of the crowd. I did not have lovely peaches and cream skin or clean blond hair. There was one other black pupil, a West Indian girl, who had shiny ebony skin. I envied her because her skin was clearly black and her white eyes and teeth shone. I, with my brown skin, just looked dirty.*

*When my uncle came to live with us he started to abuse me sexually, taking my clothes off and rubbing his penis between my legs. He would sometimes 'wee' on me. This confirmed my feelings of being dirty and defiled. I knew people thought I was dirty but I never wanted them to know quite how dirty and sullied I really was.*

It is to be noted that although Celestine referred to herself as 'mixed race' a preferred and more accurate term is 'dual heritage'. Similarly here the word 'Black' is used in a positive sense to denote all those people who challenge the racism to which they are subject on the grounds of their colour.

Black children living in a white society have the burden of racism and discrimination to carry. Sexually abused black children in a white society have a double burden – a heavy load indeed.

### ISSUES FOR CHILDREN WITH DISABILITIES

The terms physical or learning disabilities or difficulties have superseded the now discredited terms physical and mental handicap. However, even the term 'disability' had its drawbacks as many so labelled have considerable abilities, the artists who paint with feet or mouths spring immediately to mind. Nevertheless, in the context of abuse the additional physical or learning limitations of some children render them vulnerable both to abuse itself and to an adverse emotional aftermath.

It was once thought that children with disabilities were protected from sexual abuse partly because they tend to be closely supervised and partly because it was believed nobody could be so heartless as to abuse children with disabilities. All these beliefs have been open to question in the past few years.

A number of points relating to the vulnerability of children with disabilities have already been made. Some youngsters cannot easily escape 'I have to use crutches all the time. I couldn't really get away could I' (Concoran 1987 p.106). Some children with communication problems cannot tell a perpetrator to go away or stop.

Children and young people who need a considerable amount of intimate physical care may be confused about the distinction between touching of the private parts which is necessary in order to clean or dress them and that which is sexually exploitative.

There has been a coyness about accepting that people with disabilities have sexual needs. Some children and young people are not given education about sexual matters or even a basic understanding of their anatomy and therefore again they are very confused about what is happening.

When they do realise that their treatment is unacceptable they may have difficulties seeking help. There are the physical constraints, particularly if a youngster has limited speech. Some children have adequate linguistic skills but the denial of their sexuality has meant that they have not been provided with a vocabulary with which to describe what has happened.

There are also the emotional constraints particularly if they are very dependant on an abusive carer. Even in cases where they are not dependant on, and attached to, the perpetrator they may feel that they have caused their parents and other carers enough trouble already and do not tell for fear of giving them yet more problems. They may believe that they would seem 'ungrateful' if they complained of being abused. This is on top of the concerns about causing problems and not being believed that they share with all victims. Some children have been made to feel 'second-class' or less worthy because of their disabilities and believe that they deserve to be abused.

Perpetrators can recognise these limitations and vulnerabilities and so target children with disabilities by becoming a voluntary helper or by finding work in residential establishments and special schools. It is important however not to cast the shadow of suspicion on the majority of people who work voluntarily or professionally in disability services without abusing their position of trust.

Even if a child with a disability manages to disclose, there are sometimes problems in relation to the help that can be given. Margaret Kennedy illustrates this with reference to deaf children:

> *The four year old prelingual profoundly deaf child whose communication consists only of pointing, shouting and much pulling and pushing may achieve her objective in obtaining a drink of lemonade. It will not however be enough to determine whether she has been sexually abused, and if so, how she is feeling about it. Nor would it be enough to establish in her mind the subtleties of a safety / prevention programme (1989 p.3).*

Often the negative feelings that children experience because of their disabilities are mirrored and compounded by the emotions evoked by the abuse and so they, like black children, suffer a double burden. These feelings include:

- self-blame 'I cause my family problems by being deaf/blind/ in a wheel-chair/abused';
- shame, guilt, lack of confidence 'I'm faulty, I'm bad, I'm dirty';
- anger 'why did God make me like this? What right had that person to do that to me?';
- isolation 'I'm not like other children because I am deaf/ disabled/abused.

Children with disabilities have the same rights as any other children to protection from sexual exploitation and help with emotional distress. This requires careful selection of volunteers and care staff, a willingness to listen to and believe the children, a commitment to provide them with education and information about their bodies, sexual matters and self-protection, and finally a development of therapeutic skills geared to the their emotional needs.

# Three

# Understanding the perpetrators

## Who is to blame?

It is worth examining this question again in the context of a discussion to sex offenders.

Sometimes blame is cast not on the victim but on non-abusing parents or other family members. There are many fathers and step-fathers that have claimed that they only had sexual relations with their daughters because their wives did not meet their sexual needs – therefore of course they were not to blame, it was all the fault of the child's mother. A judge in England not so long ago excused a man's sexual assault on his step-daughter on the grounds that his wife was pregnant so could not satisfy his sexual desires!

Non-abusing parents are blamed when their children are molested by acquaintances outside the family or strangers: 'They shouldn't have let her walk to school on her own'; 'They ought to have kept a check on where he was getting the extra money from'; 'They should have been more careful about choosing a piano teacher'; 'What can you expect if you let her go to that youth club'.

As parents we can reassure ourselves by believing that the victim's parents were negligent and to blame in some way. We can convince ourselves that sexual attacks only happen to children with deficient parents – then, because we are such careful parents ourselves, we can rest assured that our children will not be attacked in the same way. Unfortunately that is simply not true. A child may merely be in the wrong place at the wrong time, however careful the parents are. So if you are the parent of an abused child and if you were not the actual perpetrator then you are not to blame.

Occasionally parents have taken risks or not taken proper precautions. They have left their children to their own devices while they go out to the local pub. They have not bothered to send their son to school, allowing him to hang around with a gang of older youths. But although parents may fail to fulfil all their parental responsibilities they are still not to blame for the abuse.

Is society to blame for the abuse? Societal attitudes do play a part. The majority of known abusers are male and data gathered from people who were abused as children seems to confirm that sexual abuse is mainly perpetrated by men.

Various myths that abound help male sexual abusers justify their actions to themselves and others; beliefs such as 'might is right' which seems to be a prevalent attitude in many societies. In sophisticated modern societies it may not be so obvious as the power of brute force but authority tends to be vested in the fittest and strongest in society. How many politicians in Britain are female or have a marked disability? How many captains of industry or heads of public services are women or registered disabled?

Men, predominantly fit, middle-aged, white men totally dominate all the positions of power. The least powerful sections of the population are children, the severely disabled and the frail elderly, that is the people with the least physical strength. This means that what an able-bodied male says carries more weight and authority than a child's account of events. This is despite the fact that the child may have no obvious motive for lying while the male, accused of sexual abuse, has a very strong motive indeed for avoiding the truth.

There is a widely held belief that men have strong sexual urges that they cannot control. They are driven beyond reason by sexual desire and have to find an outlet for their pent up libido. This myth serves as a way of excusing men who abuse others to fulfil their sexual needs. A man who breaks into a house and steals valuables is branded a thief or burglar and is held totally accountable for his actions. A man who rapes a woman or child is believed to be at the mercy of wild and uncontrollable drives and passions and not really responsible for his behaviour.

Little boys are brought up to believe that as men they should dominate situations. From the earliest stories for children it is the male figure that takes the initiative and commands events – Postman Pat, Fireman Sam, Thomas the Tank Engine, Paddington Bear, Sooty, Muffin the Mule, Bart Simpson, Captain Planet, Dan Dare, Spot Dog, the Turtles, Peter Rabbit, Noddy, Big Ears, Winnie-the-Pooh – they are all male.

Where are the assertive females? The coaches, not the engines, are female in Thomas the Tank Engine. Female figures are passive having things done to them. Alternatively, they are the sensible voice of reason – like Sue in Sooty films – given responsibility for rescuing the male from his occasional indiscretions.

It is hardly surprising that male sex abusers need to feel powerful, dominant and in control of the situation, expecting women and children to be passive recipients of their attentions. If they recognise the inappropriateness of their behaviour they blame females for not having done something to stop them. They hold the child or the child's mother responsible for what has happened.

Ultimately the only person to blame is the person who commits sexual acts against children. It is, nevertheless, worth acknowledging that sometimes the concept of blame is not useful when, for example, a small child sexually abuses another child or, very rarely, when the molester has severe learning disabilities.

Before moving on it is worth commenting on people with learning difficulties, sometimes referred to as people with a mental handicap. Parents can feel that their children may be more at risk from such a person. There is however no evidence to show that this is the case. As will be seen in later sections, the highly intelligent man or woman with a wide range of social skills is far more dangerous and can continue abusive activities for far longer than people whose intellectual limitations render them less able to plan strategies and conceal what they have done.

### Definitions

The word 'perpetrator' is defined as 'One who perpetrates, performs, executes or commits a crime or evil deed' (*Oxford English Dictionary*). The term is now commonly applied to adults who sexually abuse children and its use makes clear that child sexual abuse is, in most circumstances, a crime. The person responsible for a crime ultimately is the person who commits it, unless the person cannot be held criminally responsible by virtue of their youth or mental condition. Anyone who has worked for years with the child victims or adult survivors of this type of mistreatment would possibly agree that it can be described as an 'evil deed'.

Some professionals prefer to use the term 'offender' to describe those people who sexually abuse children. In America the term molester is frequently used and the word 'molest' is used as a noun, as for example in the question 'Where did the molest occur?'

Understanding the perpetrator especially in the case of adult males is the key to understanding many other aspects of child sexual abuse such as why victims find it difficult to resist and how caring, responsible non-abusing parents may nevertheless find that their child has been molested.

It is important to recognise that for an adult, abusing children sexually is a compulsive behaviour which cannot be cured but can only be controlled.

### *Adult male perpetrators – features*

All present indicators point to the fact that the overwhelming number of perpetrators are adult males. Nevertheless, individual male abusers cannot be readily identified. They can come from any and every cultural and social background. Some are in work and nearly all occupations are represented; others are not in work being students, retired people or those in some other way unemployed. They may be rich or poor, young or old, clean and tidy or scruffy and ill-kempt, black or white, handsome or ugly, tall or short and fat or thin.

Many perpetrators are attractive, plausible and socially skilled. They use their charm to gain the trust of the children they abuse and of any parents or other adults who could protect the child. They are often very good with children and know the sort of activities and presents that will delight the children they will eventually abuse. They are also in tune with children's fears and worries and they use this knowledge to intimidate children and ensure that their victims do not tell anyone else about the abuse. Often they do not need to use explicit threats, saying instead something like 'You are special and you will keep our special secret, won't you?'. Even in this there is the implied threat – 'If you tell you will no longer be special, you will no longer be important to me'.

Others however are less subtle. Mr Freeman who raped Maya Angelou knew how much she loved her brother Bailey. He guaranteed her silence for a while with – 'If you tell, I'm gonna kill Bailey'. Sylvia Fraser's father threatened to kill her kitten:

> *My father needs a permanent seal for my lips, one that will murder all defiance. 'If you say once more that you're going to tell, I'm sending that cat of yours to the pound for gassing'...The air swooshes out of me as if I have been punched. My resistance is broken. Smoky's life is in my hands. This is no longer a game, however desperate. Our bargain is sealed in blood (1989 p.12).*

There are a couple of myths which have to be dispelled at this point:

- One is that men who abuse little boys will not abuse little girls and vice versa – men abusing girls will not abuse boys. This has been a very dangerous myth and I have worked with families where, in our ignorance, we have removed the girls from home and left the brothers unprotected only to find several years later the boys in the family having themselves been molested are seeking help. Some abusers seem to prefer one particular gender but there is no guarantee that they will not abuse members of the other sex.
- Another myth is that if a man abuses children of a particular age then he will not abuse children outside his preferred age range. Child protection workers have left babies in a household in which a teenage daughter was abused only to find a few years later the small child left at home has also been abused.
- A third myth is that a man who abuses his step-children will not abuse his natural children. Experience and research has shown that abusers can be a step-parent to some victims and the natural parent of other victims (Doyle 1987).

There are some features that perpetrators have in common.

The first is that they have a very low self-esteem. They feel worthless. Very often this has arisen because they were themselves abused as children – not always sexually but perhaps emotionally or physically – and were made to feel guilty and ashamed.

Sometimes this lack of self-esteem is cleverly masked. Perpetrators collect positive labels in an attempt to convince themselves and others that they are really wonderful people and so they become respected members of society – 'pillar of the community', 'school governor', 'regular church-goer'. Some engage in occupations that give them a high status or a lot of power especially over children. I hasten to add that many people who serve schools, their church and the community or have high status occupations are motivated by a genuine desire to use their abilities and capacities constructively and are not child molesters.

Another feature is that perpetrators' low self-esteem leads them to believe that nobody can really love them, they are simply not lovable. They are isolated and have no close relationships. Sometimes this is evident and neighbours will comment that a particular abuser was 'quiet, kept himself-to-himself, no bother to anyone.'

On the other hand a number of perpetrators seem to be surrounded by family and friends. But usually these apparently close relationships are built on a facade or are maintained because the perpetrator has power over the people who seem close to him. They may appear to be attractive personalities with a lot of charm. Sarah who was sexually, physically and emotionally abused by her father described how 'My father was handsome and charming and when he came to school the pupils would all try to catch a glimpse of him and say how lucky I was' (Doyle 1990 p.28).

The other very important feature is that, for whatever reason, perpetrators are sexually attracted to children. Some also have sexual relationships with adults whether male or female but if a man does not find children sexually appealing then he will not have sex with them, apart from the rare example of someone being forced to do so by a third person who is sexually stimulated by watching adult-child sex. This is illustrated by Figure 2.

**Figure 2: Sexual Preferences of Abusers and Non-Abusers**

Some adults only enjoy sex with another adult:

non-abuser

   sexually attracted only to

adult
male or female

adult
male or female

Some adults whether male or female enjoy sex with other adults but could also enjoy sex with children:

child abuser

   sexually attracted only to

adult
male or female

adult and child
male and/or female

Some adults can only enjoy sex if it is with children:

child abuser

   sexually attracted only to

adult
male or female

child
male and/or female

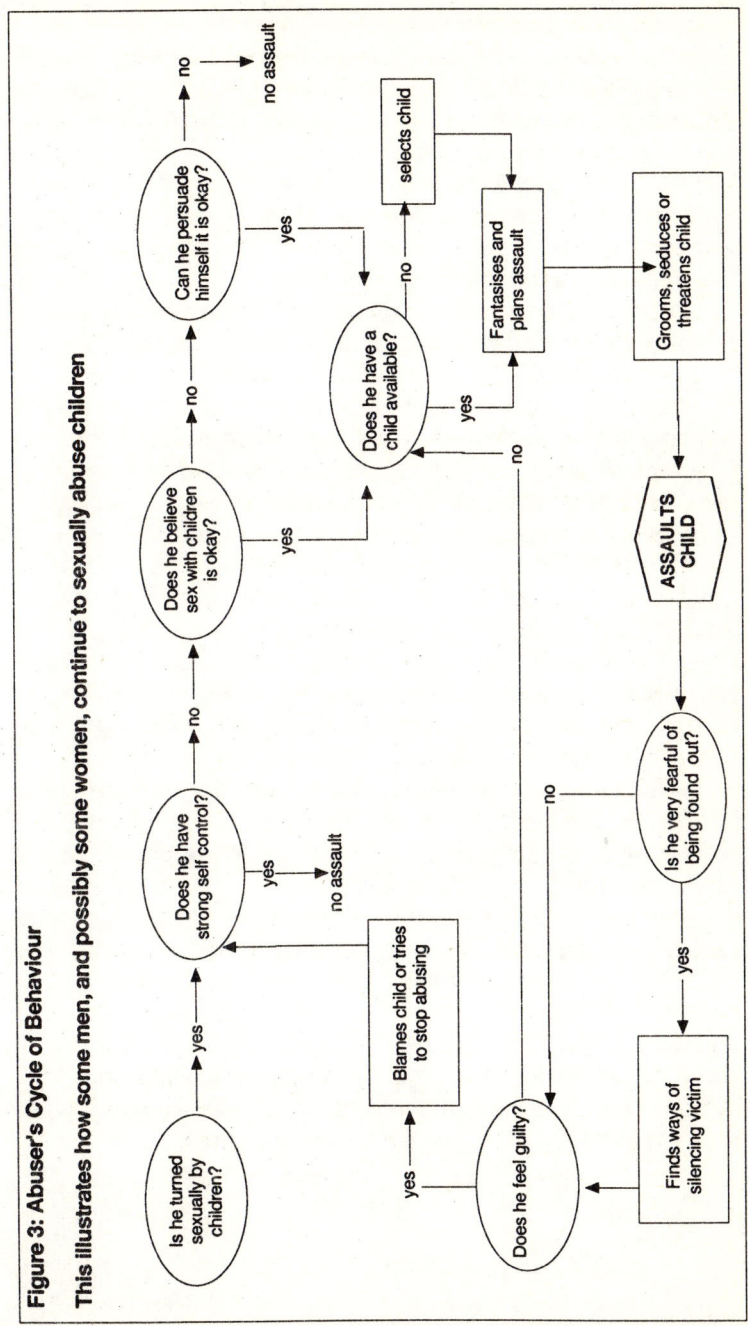

**Figure 3: Abuser's Cycle of Behaviour**

**This illustrates how some men, and possibly some women, continue to sexually abuse children**

### Adult male perpetrators – behaviour

As already noted, sexually abusive behaviour is compulsive. It is impossible for a perpetrator to completely stop abusing children without enormous determination and he will probably need a considerable amount of assistance. It is worth repeating that there is no cure only control. Ultimately, unless an offender is permanently incarcerated away from all children the only person who can control the behaviour and stop youngsters being abused is the man himself.

Over recent years our knowledge of the compulsive nature of sexually abusive behaviour in adult males has increased. Some of this knowledge has been gained through formal research programmes, some through the insights gained by people working with child abusers and their victims, some through information given directly by abusers and some through a general understanding of compulsive behaviour.

By piecing together all these sources of information it is possible to draw up a 'cycle of abusive behaviour'. This is illustrated in Figure 3. We know that the perpetrator is sexually attracted to children and has a feeling of being worth little. Some event or memory or simply lots of small pressures conspire to bring his feelings of worthlessness to the fore. He then retreats from these painful feelings into a fantasy world, the most pleasurable fantasy being a sexual one. Inevitably he will think about sex with children. He is likely to masturbate at the same time which generates even more pleasurable sensations. He may feed his fantasy with pornography especially when it involves children.

Some argue that pornography is a healthy outlet for the sexual feelings and desires. However, we have to think of what the children in pornographic photos and videos have been through in order to be filmed. Tim Tate (1990) in his definitive book on child pornography makes this point graphically as does Judith Ennew (1986) in her book on the sexual exploitation of children.

Secondly does looking at pictures of the desired but forbidden object really help people control their appetites?

## EXERCISE

Try to think of an occasion when you tried to give up something you did habitually – maybe giving up sweets or chocolate.

Did looking at pictures of luxury ice cream, boxes of chocolates and Black Forest Gateau really strengthen your resolve?

If you cannot think of an appropriate example, then try to give up something you enjoy doing – if you are a smoker or enjoy a tipple try to abstain by watching advertisements of people having a long, slow, satisfying drag or a clear, refreshing pint. If your weakness is going on a spending spree then try reading all the shopping catalogues you can find. My guess is that you will soon be gasping for the real thing.

So it is with sex offenders, day dreaming and looking at pictures can only satisfy them for so long. Sooner or later they need the 'real thing' – if only to give them material for a new set of fantasies.

This leads the sex offender to prepare to change fantasy into reality. He does not want to be caught so he has to plan how to immobilise anyone who could protect his chosen victim and ensure that the child will not tell.

Most parents fear the stranger who leaps out on a child from behind a bush. We teach children not to talk to 'strangers' and we picture these strangers as ugly caricatures with distorted features so children only become wary of threatening looking strangers. But as I have mentioned earlier, most sex abusers do not want to draw attention to their activities by frightening a child who may scream and attempt to resist. They prefer instead to have a quiet, compliant victim whom they can use and abuse several times.

They therefore seek out or target a child who meets their needs and who is likely to be an easy prey. This may be the neglected, lonely child who is truanting from school. Such a child may be desperate for an adult who treats them as special and who is kind to them. If after the abuse the child threatens to tell, the abuser can threaten to tell the child's parents or the education authorities about the truancy.

Sometimes the abuser manages to achieve a position in society such that parents will almost automatically trust him, such as a headmaster, a choir master, an athletics coach. He may then target a child with a particular talent and suggest he gives them extra coaching or tuition. Abusers may target well-behaved, compliant children or friendly, happy children. They may get a perverse thrill from gaining the trust of very caring parents and managing to molest that child despite the vigilance of the parents. *So if your child has been molested it might be because you or your child has a special quality*. It is not just lonely abandoned children who are molested, it can be popular, well-cared for ones as well.

Abusers occasionally adopt quite a long-term strategy, moving into a family over time. Della had three children and her husband had left her. She was not coping on her own. She was a poor cook, not good at keeping the house clean and tidy and could not manage the family finances. She was then befriended by Gareth. He moved in, cooked delicious meals, did all the housework, earned a good income and organised the household budget. He was a sex offender who was now an essential part of a household containing three young children and a mother who had a struggle coping with the demands of life. It had taken over a year to get himself into that position but he now had three children readily available to him at any time of day (apart from school time) or night, in the privacy of what was now his own home.

Having chosen a particular victim the perpetrator has to prepare the situation. He has to ensure that anyone who could protect the child or witness the offence is prevented from doing so, preferably by being removed from the scene.

Sometimes fathers will persuade their partners to take an evening job offering to babysit. Gareth encouraged Della to go to Bingo. Other fathers may wait until the child's mother goes shopping or visits her own mother. Older brothers, grandfathers, uncles, neighbours may agree to babysit while parents go out. Perpetrators may follow and observe a child for weeks in order to determine when the youngster is left alone.

Bart, an athletics coach targeted Winston aged 12 who had considerable potential as an athlete. Bart persuaded the boy's parents that he would go further with individual coaching which, thanks to a sponsorship scheme, would be free. Winston's father initially came to watch him in training but Bart indicated that his son would concentrate more if his father was not present at the individual sessions. This meant that Bart could freely molest Winston during coaching sessions.

The perpetrator also has to gain power and control over the child. Very occasionally this takes the form of pouncing on a youngster in a lonely lane and using physical force to subdue the victim. However more often there is a more gradual process termed 'grooming'.

Bart used to touch Winston's legs and body during coaching showing him how to do exercises 'properly'. Slowly this touching became more intimate. At the same time Bart made the boy feel that he could only be a successful athlete if Bart was his coach. Winston came to believe that if he rejected Bart he would be turning his back on his career, fame and fortune. Meanwhile Bart was ingratiating himself with Winston's parents who kept telling their son how lucky he was to have such a magnificent coach.

Sometimes grooming involves alienating the child from his or her protectors. Todd moved in with Pam and her two teenage daughters. He told Pam that he had been to prison for molesting his own daughters. However, he assured her, they had falsely accused him and he had only pleaded guilty because he felt sorry for his daughters and he wanted to spare them the stress of appearing in court. He said that often teenage girls had a 'crush' on him and fantasise about him. He also warned Pam that he would leave her if her daughters tried accusing him of sexual abuse. He then set up several situations in which the girls were seen to be liars such as arranging for Pam's missing make-up and jewellery to be found in the girls' bedroom. Gradually Pam began to believe that her daughters were untrustworthy. When one daughter tried to tell her mother Todd had molested her, he feigned anger saying he would not tolerate such lies against him again. Pam by now had been convinced that her daughters were manipulative liars and did all in her power to defend and placate Todd.

Other abusing fathers buy one favourite child lots of presents. This results in the other children and their mother feeling resentment towards the favoured child who in turn feels isolated and dependant on the perpetrator's love. The targeted victim is fearful of losing the abuser's affection and attention.

In one such case the perpetrator said, of his daughter 'She begged me to have sex with her'. The victim, alienated from her brothers, sisters and mother, found herself being bullied by them and sought protection from her father. When she refused to have sex with him, he withdrew his protection. She then agreed to have intercourse. He in turn refused but still failed to protect her. As the bullying became worse she went to her father and, desperate for his protection, pleaded with him to have a sexual relationship with her in the hope that he would protect her again.

Grooming can take the form of a slow seduction in which abusers befriend their victims and gain their trust, gradually abusing them starting with a 'harmless' touch during horse-play perhaps opening the way to more intimate touching. The child hardly realises what is happening until he or she is completely trapped in a web of secrecy and guilt.

Grooming can also be a matter of imposing authority on a child by using threats or physical strength. Some fathers accuse their child of a minor misdemeanour then use anal abuse as a form of punishment. The child feels too guilty to resist. These sexually abusive punishments may then increase in frequency and severity.

During the assault itself the child is objectified. The abuser no longer sees the victim as a person but simply a means of satisfying his or her sexual needs. For a while I could not understand why so many children that I interviewed described having their face covered by clothing or a towel during the abuse. It is now apparent that by covering the face perpetrators can deny the personality and human nature of the child they are victimising. This is of course one of the reasons why sexual abuse is so dangerous. The perpetrator is oblivious to the pain and distress the child is suffering so may inflict physical damage or kill the victim without fully realising what he is doing.

After the offence has been committed the perpetrator feels some satisfaction and has new material with which to feed his sexual fantasies. However he may also feel some guilt. He may push the guilt onto the victim, 'It was her fault for seducing me, she is a slag in any case', 'He was really asking for sex coming to see me in my own house'. He might dump his guilt onto the child's parents 'They don't really care for him', or his wife 'If she was more exciting and not so frigid I wouldn't have had to do it', or society 'If they legalised brothels I would have been alright'.

The perpetrator will probably have to ensure the child's silence by persuasion 'You are special and this is our special little secret'. He may have to restore the 'Good guy' image in both his own eyes and that of the victim by buying the child more presents, by saying 'Sorry, it will not happen again' or by being especially kind and charming. Alternatively he may have to use threats.

Ultimately the offence will make the perpetrator feel even more worthless and isolated from society and incapable of 'normal' relationships. To escape once more from the feelings of isolation he will retreat into his world of sexual fantasies and these will include sexual relationships with children, and *so the cycle starts all over again.*

Another offence may be committed later the same day or the perpetrator may not have the opportunity to offend again for a number of years. But what is certain is that he will eventually offend again unless he is prevented from doing so or is helped to make a determined effort not to molest a child again.

## Adult female perpetrators

There seem to be far fewer adult female child sex abusers than there are male ones. Only about 3 per cent of the people convicted of sex offences against children in England and Wales each year are women and this figure is echoed in many other countries. Research among adults recalling childhood abuse overwhelmingly implicates men rather than women (Finkelhor 1984, Fromuth 1986). Children disclosing abuse repeatedly indicate a male abuser.

Nevertheless there are some adult women who sexually abuse children, the estimated figure has been rising steadily. The fact that the figure is still a low percentage of all sex offenders may be due to a number of factors. One theory is that the way men are brought up or socialised makes them more likely than women to meet their needs through child molestation. A related theory is that while men gain status in their own or other people's eyes through sexual conquest, women gain status through maintaining sexual 'purity' and through the role of carer. The ideal woman is a type of 'Madonna'. Molesting a child can be seen as a conquest, however puny, for a man, molesting a child is a complete betrayal in the case of a woman.

Some theorists maintain that there are a much higher number of female perpetrators than we think but they go undetected because sexual activity in a woman is masked by care-giving activity. Generally women are permitted by society to handle the more intimate parts of a child's body.

It is also argued that children and adult survivors may find it harder to talk about abuse by a female because girls may fear the label 'lesbian' if they reveal that they were molested by a woman, whereas boys may fear being seen as weak and unmanly if unable to resist a woman's domination and control.

There is no evidence that vast numbers of women are sexually abusing children undetected – however as stated, some do.

Some women who feel threatened by adult males or who, for some other reason, have no adult males with whom to relate sexually use young boys in order to meet their sexual needs. In a similar way some women with a lesbian orientation who are unable to relate to adult women may form sexual relationships with girls.

Some women start sexually abusing their own infants in the neo-natal period (Chasnoff et al. 1986). Usually the victims are boy babies but some mothers have abused all their infants regardless of gender.

In a number of instances the perpetrators were themselves sexually exploited and we have examples of girls who, having been abused, then molest younger children. The reason for this may be associated with an awakened sexual curiosity which they can fulfil by exploring the bodies of other children and the bodily sensations that intimate contact can create. There are also issues of premature sexualisation and regaining power that are applicable to adolescents of both genders and will be explored further in the next section.

So far research has not shown for certain that women are bound up in the same cycle of abusive behaviour which we saw related to adult male perpetrators. However there is no evidence that women abusers are not subject to the same compulsive processes.

What we do know is that even if statistically there are few

women child sex abusers, they do exist and numerically form a fairly large group. This means that there is a significant number of victims abused by female perpetrators and they may have special problems. This is because most of the literature and therapeutic approaches are geared to people who have been molested by men. Furthermore most of the members of self-help groups are the victims of male perpetrators.

There are some myths about female perpetrators which it is worth dispelling. These include: women cause less harm than men; boys always enjoy sex with older women; and women are always coerced by men.

- Female sex abusers can do as much physical and emotional damage as their male counterparts. They have been recorded as inserting twigs, knives, bottles, sticks, hoses and all manner of objects in to children's vaginas and bottoms. As far as emotional damage is concerned, the accounts in Michelle Elliot's book (1993) of male and female survivors abused by women makes truly harrowing reading.
- Adolescent boys enticed to have sex with older women do not always think themselves lucky and enjoy the experience. Andrew started to have sex with his aunt, Ruth when he was 12 years old, 'I've been through the bravado bit in the pub with mates. I was fucking my Aunt when I was only 12... but I now feel different. It's as if my growing awareness has made me feel more guilty, more dirty. I looked at her and she is now 60, she looks like my gran. I felt sick when I thought that' (Elliot 1993 p.192).
- Female abusers are not always coerced by dominant or threatening males. In his study of sexual abuse in day care and nurseries Finkelhor and colleagues (1988) found that several of the female perpetrators were the directors of the nursery and themselves coerced their staff into taking part in the activities. Other women acted alone. In an account of the youngsters using ChildLine it was recorded that an absent father was a feature of many reports by the child callers who were concerned about female abuse (Harrison 1993).

Female abusers like males ones can come from any social group, class, culture or creed. Some appear to be competent and socially skilled, others less so. They vary in educational background and occupation. Many seem to be happily married.

Their relationship to their victims can be as diverse as male abusers. They can be mothers, grandmothers, sisters, aunts, neighbours or other non-relatives in professional or voluntary roles. Some are strangers although it is probably true that few victims have reported being assaulted by unknown women lurking in the bushes. Nevertheless there have been abductions and assaults by women strangers very occasionally working alone but more frequently accompanied by a male.

If you or someone close to you has been abused by a woman it may be helpful to read *When You're Ready* by Kathy Evert and Inie Bijkerk (1987). Kathy was physically and sexually abused by her mother.

UNDERSTANDING THE CONSEQUENCES

The consequences of child sexual abuse are widespread. It impacts upon the victim in various ways. It affects the non-abusing parents, the victim's brothers, sisters, extended family and anyone else who is fond of the victim such as a best friend or a close neighbour. It has repercussions for the professional workers in contact with the child: teachers, doctors, health visitors and others. It affects the person to whom the child discloses. It affects foster carers and residential staff. It has consequences for the perpetrators themselves and their families. Its reverberations are felt within society as a whole.

We cannot look at all the consequences in this section, there are too many and some are covered in other chapters. This part will highlight some of the most significant consequences not discussed elsewhere.

### Adolescent abusers

One aftermath of abuse is that victimised children may be made more vulnerable to becoming abusers themselves. We all learn by example therefore it is hardly surprising that some children who are abused learn to copy their abusers. On the other hand children can also learn by example what not to do – some successful road safety campaigns show the dire consequences of what happens if safety is disregarded. A high proportion of sexually abused children grow up determined not to abuse children and to protect other children from mistreatment. Most will not abuse.

But a number of sexually abused children who do not want to victimise other children, do so and continue to do so in adulthood despite their good intentions. They manage to convince themselves that their activities are not really harmful. Henry was 'gently seduced' by his father. He was also violently gang raped by a group of men. As an adult he was convinced that he was doing no harm by indulging in mutual masturbation with young boys as long as he used no violence.

A third group give very little thought to their victims or sincerely believe that engaging young children in sex benefits the children.

The latter two groups may well progress from victim to victimiser almost imperceptibly and start abusing children younger than themselves when children or adolescents.

Work with sexually abusive young people has indicated that there are couple of possible processes at work here:

Firstly, abused children cannot immediately forget abusive incidents. They will remember, whether or not parents and other adults allowed them to talk about their experiences. Part of the pain of remembering is the humiliation of being out of control and in someone else's power. This is particularly difficult for boys who are socialised to be strong and powerful. One way of escaping from the pain is to become the abuser in fantasy. By this means the children recall the events but change the circumstances so that they are in control. Metaphorically and sometimes literally they imagine 'being on top'. This becomes a powerful fantasy and because it is related to sexual activities may well lead to masturbation. This especially if it results in an orgasm is itself pleasurable so reinforces the fantasy. Eventually fantasy may not be enough, victimised children now have to have sex in a situation where they are in control. They are unlikely to be in control if having sex with an adult so they target a weaker child instead.

Another similar process occurs when children are subjected to sexual activities which give pleasure. The child likes to remember and masturbate to the memory of the pleasurable activities. But again the way to avoid the pain of having been dominated and humiliated is to imagine being in control of the situation – being the person with the power in the relationship.

At the same time such children are 'sexualised'. Their sexual interest and drives have been stimulated at an age when they cannot find a legitimate outlet for these. Sometimes they may seek sexual satisfaction from adults and are deemed 'promiscuous', possibly becoming child prostitutes and rent boys. Other children do not want to risk being dominated and abused by adults so seek sexual satisfaction from children younger or weaker than themselves.

The heady mixture of needing sexual satisfaction from other children and a fantasy life around adult/child sexual relations leads the original abused child to become an abuser in childhood and adopt powerful behaviour patterns which are continued into adulthood.

---

### EXERCISE

Try to think of an occasion which gave you great pleasure especially one when you were paid attention by someone you really liked and admired.

After the event did you simply forget about it only to recall it now or is it so vivid in your memory because afterwards you liked to daydream and think about it, savouring the 'best bits'? My guess is you did the latter.

Now imagine that the occasion had been marred by something which embarrassed or humiliated you. You had a big boil on your face, you said something entirely foolish or inappropriate, your knicker elastic broke and they fell down or your 'flies' were undone.

You could then only remember the occasion with pleasure if you could blot out the embarrassing incident. Alternatively, you could picture that you met the person a second time when you were more in control of the situation – when your face had cleared, when you said exactly the right thing at the right time, when your clothes were perfect.

This exercise is designed to help you to understand the victims of abuse especially where the abuser is someone who has gained the affection and admiration of the child and who gives the child pleasure, despite causing humiliation and shame.

---

### Consequences for non-abusing parents and other family members

The first reaction of a non-abusing parent can be to try to deny what has happened. The parent hopes that the child is mistaken or is just making up a story to seek attention. It is much more comfortable to believe that your child's imagination has run riot than to believe he or she has been interfered with by an older child or adult. The need to deny is all the stronger if the perpetrator is a relative of the non-abusing parent – a spouse, parent, son or daughter. Some parents are never able to move through this initial stage of denial. Others, when the whole truth becomes too painful, retreat back into it. This results in a permanent rift between parent and victimised child

In a similar way other relatives including the siblings may also be stuck in a stage of denial. Grandma cannot believe that her son could possibly be a child molester and so blames her granddaughter for causing all the trouble. Brothers and sisters may similarly blame and reject the child who discloses especially when the perpetrator is a family member. Sometimes this happens even when the siblings know what is happening and are co-victims themselves.

Parents, if unable to deny what has happened have to cope with overwhelming feelings of guilt – 'I should have protected him/her better' – and feelings of bitter anger. If for any reason this cannot be expressed against the perpetrator, perhaps because he or she is also a much loved spouse or a child, then the anger may be projected against the victim, neighbours, society or the self. The non-abusing parent has a churning anger which damages relationships with the victim or other people or leads to self-recrimination and depression.

Depending on the circumstances the non-abusing parent has a lot to lose. If it was stranger abuse there may be a loss of trust in the outside world, loss of 'face' with the neighbours, loss of privacy especially if the media becomes involved. The losses are almost overwhelming if the abuser was the father or mother-figure in the family. There is the loss of the companionship of an adult partner, of a sexual relationship and of self-esteem – 'what sort of person am I to have loved and admired a child molester?' There are often huge financial implications if their partner leaves the household. Child molesters are particularly adept at creating financial and material dependency in their partner.

Other children in the family will be affected by the loss of a parent whom they do not view as abusive or may want despite abuse. They can also suffer from a deterioration in family finances, less money means fewer toys, presents, clothes and activities. They may be subjected to discrimination and ridicule by other children if the abuse becomes known outside the immediate family and professional circles.

In this way the abuser causes damage and distress not only to the victim but to the rest of the victim's family who can, especially if the abuser is also a member of the family, be thought of as co-victims.

### LONG TERM CONSEQUENCES FOR THE VICTIMS

We have just seen that for a minority of victims one long term consequence is that they become abusers themselves. But by no means all do.

Sexually abused children can grow up with a low self-esteem and do not know how to prevent themselves from becoming victims in other situations. They may have long term sexual problems including avoidance of sexual activity altogether. Difficulty in trusting other people results in anxiety and isolation. Depression, self-destructive behaviour and substance abuse are all possible long-term effects.

If a person seems to have difficulties in relationships and in liking and looking after themselves and there is no apparent reason then sexual abuse in childhood may be the root cause.

It is however very difficult to determine the exact cause of problems in adulthood because some children are targeted by abusers due to other problems relating to the child's care. For example the child maybe emotionally neglected by his or her parents and so hungrily accepts the friendship of a neighbour who is a child molester. Is it the sexual abuse which causes the long term problems or the parental neglect?

Some children appear to be resilient and seem to suffer no long term adverse effects. It could be that they have a natural resilience or maybe they have had profoundly positive nurturing and have grown up with a deep sense of being lovable and valued despite the abuse. Other youngsters have received constructive help that has enabled them to overcome potential problems.

The consequences of sexual abuse for the victim will depend on the type of abuse and the circumstances, such as the relationship of perpetrator to child. There is some evidence to suggest that the type of incident that most parents fear – an attack by a stranger – is less damaging (assuming the child is not killed) in the long run than repeated abuse by a close relative (Baker and Duncan 1985). Other factors which will effect the outcome are the child's general family situation and childhood nurture, the child's nature, the response if and when he or she disclosed and above all the help given to the child. Which is what the rest of this book is about.

# Four

# Recognising the signs

'No professional diagnosed abuse in childhood, let alone sexual abuse from a woman. No one attempted to ask the right questions or gave me time to talk'. So observed Jane, a former victim of abuse (Elliot 1993 p.144). Statements similar to this have been echoed innumerable times throughout the accounts of survivors.

These next few sections are designed to help you to pick up possible signs of abuse so that you, whether you are professional or lay, can be the person to 'ask the right questions' and give the victim time to talk or express distress, thereby helping to release the child from a living nightmare.

It can be difficult to recognise a child who has been sexually abused. Hopefully I will have convinced you that there is no particular 'type' of child you can look out for. So many adults abused as children recall how 'normal' they must have seemed to the outside world. A significant number, like Sylvia Fraser and Maya Angelou, perform exceptionally well at school and shine academically. As in Sylvia's case, children can sometimes 'compartmentalise' their experiences so that they blank off abusive events and show no obvious behavioural difficulties.

Other children on the other hand may show their distress by being disruptive, aggressive or mutilating themselves but for many children their behaviour can be attributed to another cause. The case of Lisa serves as an example.

## LISA'S STORY

Lisa was a 15-year-old, who had what her parents regarded as a 'crush' on her English teacher. She was keen on drama and she had a part in the school play although usually only sixth formers took part. Her parents who cared for her deeply were glad that she was enjoying the production and proud that she had been chosen to play a significant role. They were pleased that the English teacher who was attractive, 'happily married' and well respected in the community was interested in her talent. They believed, because Lisa was basically a sensible girl, that the crush would eventually pass.

Lisa's father obtained promotion which meant that the family had to move to another part of the country. The parents thought about the effect of the change on Lisa but decided that she would accept it as long as they waited until after the school production before moving. Lisa however became very upset and angry with her parents because she did not want to leave her friends, her English teacher and the school she was enjoying so much.

Just before the first performance of the play Lisa suddenly became unusually tearful and spent all her spare time in her room. Her parents assumed she was still upset about the proposed move. But her withdrawal from her parents continued during and after the family had moved. Her parents felt that they simply had to give her time and space to accept that the family had had to agree to the relocation.

It was not until three years later that Lisa told her parents that the English master had raped her. They knew that he had always given her a lift to the bus stop. She explained that he had started kissing her in the car. At first she had felt flattered and delighted and thought it harmless. He then began to touch her between the legs. She was uncomfortable about this but when she tried to resist he would hint that he might get someone else to play her part.

Shortly before the performance he had raped her. He ensured her silence by telling her that if she said anything she would not be believed. If by any chance her parents did believe her then they would, he assured her, think her promiscuous. If anyone else believed her he would be arrested and the performance would not go ahead. Everyone would blame her. Lisa could not risk all that.

Lisa's parents were very fond of their daughter and there was a close relationship between all family members. Had the family not been moving the parents would probably have been more concerned about the change in Lisa for which, without the move, they could not have accounted. They would then have gently encouraged her to tell them what was wrong and we can be fairly certain that, although she was anxious not to hurt or worry them, her trust would have enabled her to confide earlier in them. But because Lisa was so upset about the house move her parents assumed that all her distress was due to this particular change.

The outcome of Lisa's story is that when she did eventually tell her mother, the parents gave her their full support. Although some three years had passed the matter was referred to the police. Several other girls had made allegations against the teacher and these were looked at again. One girl had been expelled for 'making up lies' against him when she had tried to disclose. The teacher was found guilty on several counts including rape and sent to prison for a substantial period.

Some children are already suffering from other forms of abuse such as living in a violent household or being neglected. Others are coping with obvious stresses like a significant bereavement, school bullying or their parents' divorce. In all such cases, as it was with Lisa, it is difficult to determine whether all the change in behaviour and distress shown by children is due to sexual abuse or some other more obvious trauma in their life. As we have seen from the previous chapter perpetrators are skilled at choosing children who are distressed or in turmoil and therefore vulnerable to pressure or befriending.

In many instances non-abusing adults should feel able to forgive themselves for not picking up the signs or cries for help of a victim. Lack of knowledge, children's capacity to adapt to abusive conditions and the skill of sex offenders all conspire to blind even the most devoted of parents or the most concerned of professional helpers from the reality of what is happening. However there are some signs which should alert you to possible problems and which deserve closer scrutiny.

## SIGNS – PHYSICAL

There are some physical signs which can be strong indicators of sexual abuse. Many of these will require the specialist interpretation of a paediatrician or gynaecologist and most will only be indicators, other aspects of the victim's history will need to be investigated before any confident conclusion can be drawn. There are some physical signs that are conclusive evidence that sexual abuse has occurred but only in rare cases will they point with certainty to a particular perpetrator.

### General injuries

There may be injuries to various parts of the body which help to corroborate the victim's account and which can be seen without an intimate medical examination. These could be picked up by non-medical acquaintances of the child although they would need to be examined more closely by a medical specialist.

Children may say their hands were tied during the assault or the abuser attempted to strangle them. Rope marks on the wrist or bruising to the throat would be significant in such cases. There may be soreness round the mouth where the victim has been gagged with tape. Some children have marks where they have been injected to ensure their compliance or as part of ritual abuse. One 'child was repeatedly treated for infected 'mosquito bites' later identified as injection marks' (Snow and Sorensen 1990 p.483). Another victim, Karen, recalled:

> *I was sexually abused by my mother from the age of one until I was ten years old. When I was 13, she forcibly broke my hymen so that my father and brother could rape me. When I was 19, my parents injected me with a tranquilliser so that my father could rape me again' (Elliot 1993 p.145).*

Generally, any unusual marks on a child's body for which there is no adequate explanation should lead to further inquiries. A young or a very fearful child might not be able to explain how the injury was caused. However, a skilled investigation may supply other pieces of the jigsaw puzzle to give a clearer picture.

There will sometimes be bruising where the child has been physically abused. Youngsters may be beaten into submission or to stop them telling. Sometimes parents and other carers use and abuse their children to satisfy all their emotional needs whether hitting, pushing, burning, shaking and throwing the youngster when they are angry or sexually exploiting them when they want sexual satisfaction.

Bruising and weals to the bottom and back should not be too readily dismissed as 'over-chastisement'. Adult survivors accounts repeatedly show how flagellation or sexualised spanking formed a part of the abuse.

## Genital abnormalities

The lay person may also be able to pick up signs of genital injury not through an intrusive inspection but because there are semen stains or blood on the child's clothing. Maya Angelou's mother realised that her daughter had been raped after finding her 'red-and-yellow stained drawers under the mattress' (1984 p.77).

Children may also pass blood when going to the toilet and be in considerable pain 'It must have been obvious that I was torn down there; I remember bleeding a lot and both weeing and pooing hurting terribly; not just stinging, but really hurting me inside' (Elliot 1993 p.161).

Damage to and abnormality of the genitals obviously needs to be investigated. Sometimes accidental injury, congenital abnormalities, self-inflicted injury and infection may be the cause. Nevertheless sexual abuse has to be considered in some cases. Although it was thought that young teenagers whose periods have started could tear the hymen by the insertion of a tampon, research findings have confirmed that this is a myth (Bays and Chadwick 1993). Similarly masturbation cannot cause a torn hymen. There may be bruising and scratches to the genital area which again could be accidental or self-inflicted but are also indicative of a sexual assault.

In Cleveland in 1987 much of the controversy centred around a physical finding called 'reflex anal dilatation'. In this the anus which appears to be closed initially opens up or alternatively one which appears open first closes then opens again. There is the strong possibility that this is caused by something large and hard passing through the anus but of course this 'something' may not only have passed from the outside upwards but from the inside downwards. A history of severe constipation is a possible explanation, but so too is anal abuse.

At the time of the Cleveland crisis there was a lack of knowledge about the extent of anal abnormalities in non-abused children. Researchers have subsequently addressed this issue (McCann and colleagues 1989) and it is now felt that anal dilation of more that 15 to 20 mm without a stool (faeces) in the rectal ampulla is a very strong indicator of sexual abuse and repeated episodes of dilation under 15 mm is a possible indicator. The test for anal dilation should only be undertaken by a trained doctor. There are also some other differences in and around the anus that provide substantial evidence of sexual interference of which a specially trained doctor should be aware but which would not be evident to the lay person.

Some redness and soreness can be caused by a child scratching because of itching to the bottom. But this should in any case be brought to the attention of a nurse or doctor because it may be a symptom of a medical condition requiring treatment.

### Forensic signs

Other rare but conclusive physical signs are semen and blood of a different group from the child's, in the vagina or rectum. Hairs not belonging to the child especially around the genitalia are important as are lubricants. The blood, hairs and semen may not only be strong indicators that the child has been abused but they may also point to the identity of the abuser.

If a child reports an intrusive assault immediately, then he or she should be seen by a police surgeon straight away so that vital evidence is not lost. The child's clothing should not be removed nor should he or she be washed. This may cause additional distress but is necessary if the perpetrator is to be apprehended and other children kept safe and secure.

### Disease

The symptoms of a sexually transmitted disease are possible physical signs of sexual abuse. Infections of the genitals need to be treated and the source of the infection traced if possible.

Sexually abused children nowadays not only run the risk of the traditional diseases such as gonorrhoea and syphilis but may well be infected by HIV. A number of sexual abusers have very poor sexual boundaries and will have intercourse with a large number of adult partners and child victims. This activity increases the risk of catching and transmitting the virus which can lead to the development of AIDS.

A nightmare worry for every parent whose child is raped whether vaginally or anally is the possibility of AIDS, particularly if the assailant is stranger or distant acquaintance. There are two crumbs of comfort that can be offered. Firstly a diagnosis of HIV is not an automatic death sentence. A substantial number of infected people may not develop AIDS, that is the virus may not attack and deplete the person's immune system. Secondly research in America has shown that only a small proportion of sexually abused children contract AIDS from the abuse (Bennetts et al. 1992).

The fear of AIDS should not be used as an excuse for discrimination against homosexual people. Any penetrative sex, oral, anal or vaginal, can lead to the transmission of the HIV virus and therefore a heterosexual man who has several relationships with adult women and also targets young girls and who has unprotected penetrative sex with them poses a greater risk than a man who only has relationships with young boys.

Not all children with sexually transmitted diseases have been abused. Some babies are born with these diseases through their mother's infection. A small number of children have developed AIDS after being infected by contaminated blood transfusions, although careful screening has now largely eliminated that risk in Britain. Children who come into contact with intravenous drug users could be infected by dirty needles. Sadly some drug users discard needles in parks and playgrounds which are then picked up by small children.

### Pregnancy

Another obvious yet much overlooked physical sign in a girl whose periods have started is pregnancy. How many girls in the past, and indeed the present, have refused to name the father of the baby because they know only too well that he is their own father, grandfather, brother or other close relative.

### Absence of physical signs

Sometimes, paradoxically, the absence of physical signs can be indicative of sexual abuse. Some abused children complain of stomach pains when investigations reveal no physical cause.

Forced to have oral sex, a child may constantly complain of a lump in the throat when no lump can be seen. Children may indicate they hurt between the legs despite the fact that there is no obvious soreness or damage.

Children may also feign illness in order to avoid an abusive situation, for example a boy once keen on soccer may suddenly have a bad leg every time a session with a particular football coach is due.

Any pattern of illness should be observed and the causes fully investigated. Children do not feign illness just for fun. Children, unburdened by undue emotional problems, would generally prefer to be out and about playing, mastering skills and enjoying life.

SIGNS – SEXUAL BEHAVIOUR

Behavioural signs can give important clues but rarely provide conclusive evidence of sexual abuse, although it is true that sexual behaviour, especially in younger children, can be a sign that a child has been exposed to sexual activity. On the other hand it is worth remembering that some behaviour which through adult eyes appears to be sexual may not be indicative of abuse.

Children, from babyhood to adolescence, will explore their own bodies. They will find that rubbing certain parts gives pleasure. Most children will start to masturbate. At first they will have no inhibitions about this but as the adults in their life show a measure of disapproval they will learn to do so only in private. A child beyond about four or five years old who continues to masturbate frequently and openly despite adult disapproval may have needs which have been aroused by being sexually assaulted. On the other hand, children distressed by other events such as the loss of a beloved grandmother, may find much needed comfort in masturbation.

### *Advanced sexual knowledge*

A relatively small number of young children demonstrate that they have detailed knowledge of sexual activities such as intercourse which are usually confined to consenting adults. 'Accidentally' seeing pornographic films is an explanation sometimes offered for this and one which is growing in popularity. However how is a 5-year-old able to describe the sticky texture or taste of semen from watching a film? How can a 10-year-old girl know what an erect penis feels like without having experienced one?

Even seeing activities such as anal or vaginal intercourse on film is unlikely to teach young children how to engage in these activities. They will only get a broad impression initially because many of the pornographic films are of poor quality. Secondly, they do not show what actually happens inside the various body orifices. Thirdly, young children's knowledge of human anatomy is so limited that, even given close-up shots, they will simply not understand the activity they are seeing.

Children from protective homes may catch sight of a pornographic video film perhaps at a friend's house. However if children are to copy any sexual activities they will have to be exposed to very explicit material more than once. A child who is allowed or forced to watch pornography on a regular basis is without a shadow of doubt a sexually abused child. Being a child he or she by definition cannot give informed consent and will be witnessing activities which lead to confusion, fear and possibly a sexual arousal for which there is no legitimate outlet. The abuse may be indirect but nevertheless it is abuse.

The question 'How did that child gain that piece of knowledge?' always has to be asked. We know now in physical abuse cases we have to ask 'How did that child obtain that injury?' If the explanation given goes beyond the bounds of credibility we have to look for a simpler cause; an obvious one being that the child has been abused.

## Sexual abuse of other children

Children who sexually abuse other children are very likely to have been abused themselves – as was discussed in the last chapter. A child attempting or pretending to have vaginal or anal intercourse with other children, toys or animals, one who tries to lick or suck other children's private parts or who kisses in a sexual way using the tongue may well have been abused, although whether directly or indirectly is something that has to be investigated.

On the other hand, it is important not to jump to conclusions whenever children are seen to be exploring their own and other children's bodies. 'Doctors and nurses' can give children an excuse to undress each other and there is a natural curiosity about the opposite sex. Young children may copy their teenage brothers and sisters whom they have caught sight of indulging in some sexual play with their girl or boy friends. If we suspect that a child has been sexually abused it is possible to read into the child's natural sexual curiosity and exploration abnormalities which are not really present.

Some parents, foster parents, childminders, playgroup leaders, nursery nurses, teachers and health visitors are very familiar with children and their activities. Because they see so many average children they will know when the behaviour of one particular child is far from ordinary. If one child's behaviour seems remarkably more sexualised than the others it is worth investigating.

## *Promiscuity and naivety*

In older children and younger adolescents promiscuous behaviour, especially in girls can be a sign of a young person who has been sexually aroused when she is too young to control that arousal and is also too young to have satisfactory outlets for her prematurely aroused sexual needs. However not all promiscuous children have been sexually abused and by no means all sexually abused children become promiscuous.

Some teenagers who show no interest at all in sexual activities can have been abused. Helen who was abused by her elder brother from the age of five explains:

> *My fellow pupils used to jeer at me because I was regarded as so naive about sexual matters. The others would gather in little groups to read the 'juicy bits' of various salacious novels. I did not join in because I was frightened that I might 'let something slip' and show that I knew too much. I also didn't have boy friends because I could not abide the feeling of being experimented upon by an inexperienced youth (Doyle 1990 p.25).*

### SIGNS – OTHER BEHAVIOUR

There are a number of other non-sexual behaviours which could indicate that a child has been sexually abused, especially if there is no other apparent reason for the behaviour. However if there are other upsets in a child's life it is – as we saw in the case of Lisa – all too easy to attribute the distressed behaviour to those more obvious upsets, thereby failing to recognise the signs of sexual abuse.

## Changes and extremes

A sudden and very obvious change in behaviour should not be dismissed lightly. A child who is normally fairly quiet and compliant might suddenly become noisy and demanding or very talkative and rather volatile. A boisterous youngster might become quiet and thoughtful. A gregarious one might want to be left alone. But we must not overlook the normally quiet child who becomes withdrawn and depressed or the usually noisy child who becomes overwhelmingly boisterous and uncontrolled.

Extremes of good or bad behaviour may be significant. Some sexually abused children feel so guilty and so 'bad' that they behave in a way which confirms the image they have of themselves. They may almost welcome the punishment their bad behaviour attracts because they feel that they need to be punished for their sexual activities. Their behaviour will continue to be atrocious until someone discovers the underlying cause and convinces them that they were not to blame for the sexual abuse and they are not guilty of wrong doing in relation to the sexual activity.

Fire raising seems to be a feature of some boys who have been sexually assaulted although it appears to be less common in girl victims. It may be associated with issues of power and control because a fire once started is difficult even for groups of strong adults to control. In a sense the helpless victimised child has achieved power in which he has placed the adult world in a relatively uncontrolled and powerless position. Fire is also associated with anger and destruction but also with cleansing and starting afresh.

Some abused children's behaviour, in contrast, may be extremely good. They may be exceptionally helpful at home and work very hard at school in an attempt to win praise in order counter-act their feelings of guilt. Helen who, we remember, was abused by her elder brother explains:

> *I had done something so wicked that I deserved a dreadful punishment. I tried to be good and work hard in order to avoid any punishment. I could not bear being given a bad conduct*

*mark at school as it only served to confirm how dreadful I was (Doyle 1990 p.25).*

## Fears and refusals

Sexually abused children may become very fearful of certain places or situations. They may refuse to stay with a particular babysitter or grandparent. They might become bad tempered or withdrawn after having a class with a particular teacher. They might insist on walking a different, maybe longer, way to school. If a child shows distress which has a clear pattern or relates to a particular situation then the cause for this should be sought and the possibility of sexual molestation should be borne in mind.

Many abused children experience night terrors or recurrent nightmares. There may be an alternative explanation for these but they may form one piece of the jigsaw and also sometimes their content can be revealing such as the small boy who clings to the end of his bed screaming 'no, not again, please not again.'

Truancy and school refusal is not uncommon. Sexually abused youngsters feel different from their school mates. In their shame and isolation they want to hide away. They may fear they will be 'found out' if they mix with other children in school. They often feel that other children know their 'guilty secret' and are making fun of them behind their backs. Marie whose father sexually abused her sisters recalled:

*I couldn't mix in school; I used to sit alone. From thirteen years onwards I played truant continually. We were cut off from the other children for fear of letting anything slip... You can't concentrate at school while wondering what will happen when you get home. I was very wary of all the male teachers. I couldn't learn from them because of the need to put up all the defences. I assumed that underneath they were all like my father and I was hostile to them (Doyle 1990 p.21).*

## Self-mutilation and eating disorders

Self-mutilation especially amongst teenagers is not an uncommon sign of sexual abuse. The emotional pain of guilt, shame, degradation and self-hate is so great that some youngsters gain temporary relief by inflicting physical pain on themselves, a pain which will eventually diminish and stop and so by focusing all their painful feelings on the purely physical, youngsters will feel some emotional relief. For some children it may be a way of attacking a despised object, namely their body, which they feel is defiled and no longer their own. Some victims are also punishing themselves for their perceived guilt through self-mutilation.

Becoming grossly obese or painfully thin is a form of self-mutilation. There is an element particularly in young people suffering from anorexia nervosa of needing to feel in control of their own body at last. Extremes of fatness and thinness can also be a way of making themselves sexually unattractive and therefore safe from any further sexual advances. Diets, calorie-laden or calorie-controlled, will not be of lasting benefit unless the root cause which is the fear, mistrust, shame, guilt and powerlessness arising from sexual abuse is recognised and dealt with.

It is important to remember that not all obese or anorexic children and young people have been sexually abused nor conversely, do all sexual abuse victims develop eating disorders.

### Escape and suicide

Children may flee from the realities of persistent abuse by becoming over-absorbed in films, books, computer games or by escaping into a world of their own, appearing to be absent-minded day-dreamers. Other children blank out some of their pain through drugs and drink. Yet others run away. A colleague who is the warden of a hostel for homeless young boys told me that a high proportion of the residents disclose to him that their real reason for leaving home is to evade further sexual abuse.

A number of children and young people chose the ultimate means of escape. Until recently sexual abuse was rarely recognised as a possible reason for suicide and attempted suicide especially among adolescent girls. The publicity about sexual abuse and the greater freedom that children have to discuss sexual matters with adults has meant that some victims have been able to disclose if gently questioned after an 'unsuccessful' suicide attempt.

Marie, remembered the suicide attempts of her sister, Pauline:

*At around this time Pauline told me that our father had sexually abused her. He had done nearly everything except penetrate her,*

*She wanted it to stop. He kept saying 'Have you come yet?' to her but she didn't know what he meant. Not long after this conversation Pauline ate a hundred aspirins in front of me. I didn't realise what was happening, I thought she was eating crumbly white cheese. She tried to commit suicide six times after this (Doyle 1990 p.19).*

For many abused children the feelings of being violated, defiled, of having had innocence stolen from them, and of guilt leads to despair – a loss of hope for the long future that they see stretching before them. In this state they may see death as the only relief from their emotional pain. Some others simply want the abuse to stop and oblivion seems to be one way of ensuring it does stop.

Again not all children and young people who attempt or commit suicide have been sexually abused nor do all sexual abuse victims have suicidal thoughts.

We have also become aware that suicide or attempted suicide can be a feature of some adult survivors who are able to recall incidents of sexual abuse in their own childhood. For them there comes a point where they can no longer stand the pain of the reality of the 'flashbacks' they recall. A few survivors look back at a damaging and unhappy childhood, a painful and distressing present and a bleak future. They feel unloved and unlovely and suicide becomes the obvious answer.

### Signs – children trying to tell

Sometimes children will talk about their abuse or ask for help and yet these communications go unrecognised as a sign of sexual abuse.

### *Communication problems*

Small children, under about 5 or 6 years old may not speak very clearly and what they are saying can be misinterpreted or ignored because the adults are unable to cope with the thought that children of such tender years could be talking about sexual experiences.

More commonly small children do not have the words to describe a particular activity or a part of their body. One little boy described his uncle 'gooing' on him. When asked what he meant he said his uncle had 'wee'd on me, but it was sticky'.

Because the boy was encouraged to explain what had happened the possibility that the uncle had ejaculated on him became clear.

For many years we failed to recognise the extent of anal abuse. When little girls complained of men putting their penis in their bottoms we tended to assume that 'bottom' was the word used for vagina; an understandable assumption because many girls do not have a special word for their vagina. Only by using anatomical dolls or drawings of parts of the body have we been able to ascertain whether when children use the word 'bottom' they really mean the anus or the vagina.

If young children do have an elaborate but uncommon, non-medical vocabulary then they may have been abused and/or forced to watch pornographic videos. Usually families have one word for each part of the body and children may pick up additional words from friends. However a pre-school child who stays at home most of the time and yet has several words for the vagina could be being abused, especially if those words are derogatory ones like 'cunt'.

Some cultures do not refer openly to sexual matters and some languages do not have acceptable words for the genitals. Children from such backgrounds will have added difficulties disclosing. However, European and American cultures do not make it easy for children to talk about sexual experiences either.

### Attempts to tell

By the time children start school they will have learnt that certain words should not be used openly. They may therefore find it difficult to tell anyone about the abuse. How do you tell someone that your dad has tried to have intercourse with you if 'intercourse' is not part of your vocabulary and you do not like to use the words for your private parts. Children may therefore try telling in an obscure way:

*Daddy hurts me.*
*How does he hurt you?*
*I don't really know.*
*But you must know.*
*I can't say.*
*Why not?*
*I don't know.*

By this time many an adult would be getting impatient and no doubt the impatience would be showing. This makes the child even more hesitant and fearful and so he or she will decide to let the matter drop.

A perceptive adult who remembers that it is very difficult for children to talk about certain experiences will approach the initial 'Daddy hurts me' in a different way which will be discussed in the next chapter.

Older children may have the clarity and vocabulary to disclose what has been happening to them but will be more aware of the possible upsetting consequences of disclosure. They may be torn between wanting the abuse to stop and not wanting to cause a lot of trouble. They might also be worried about upsetting and giving offence to the person they would like to tell.

This means that they may start off with a tentative question or statement. A 10-year-old asked her favourite teacher 'What is intercourse?' Had the teacher brushed the youngster away with 'What sort of question is that for a girl like you to ask?' we may never have known that her father was sexually abusing her and her younger brothers.

Children may talk about 'a friend something happened to' when they are really talking about themselves. They want to check the adult's reaction before taking the risks involved in disclosure. Young people may also talk hypothetically. 'What would you do if a child told you he was sexually abused?' or 'Do you really think that children can be sexually abused?' This enables them to test whether or not you would blame them for what has happened, get angry, become distressed – or, as no doubt they hope, remain calm and supportive.

### Non-verbal ways of trying to tell

Many children cannot speak for themselves because they have a physical disability which prevents them from doing so. Physical disability can range from a severe stutter which will usually worsen when a child tries to disclose abuse to having no speech at all. An adolescent who had severe cerebral palsy could not speak. He was molested several times by a man who thought that the boy would not be able to tell anyone. The lad was however able to communicate effectively to his main carers through a word board and so was able to explain what had happened by pointing to the appropriate words and letters on his board. It is essential that children who cannot use spoken words are taught to use other ways of communicating distressing events. It is also essential that children with disabilities are taught how their bodies work and are given education about sexual matters. The young man above was only able to disclose because of the explicit education in bodily and sexual matters that carers and teachers had given to him.

Some children choose to use drawings and writing to let people know what is happening to them. They might draw pictures of genitalia and obvious sexual acts between various people and sometimes animals. This can lead to a horrified response by adults and an even greater entrapment for the victim. Richard was fostered by his aunt who systematically sexually and physically abused him. He explained:

> When I was around 10, I stayed after school had finished and drew rude pictures of myself and my aunt on the pages of the class register. They soon found out it was me and I was expelled for three months. Nobody asked how I knew about such things, they just called my aunt to the school, told her what had happened, and she took me home. Of course she wasn't very pleased and left me in no doubt what my fate would be when she got me home. It was the first time she used a cane on me, telling me as she hit me that, for the next three months, I would always get the cane as she didn't have to worry about leaving marks on me (Elliot 1993 p.172).

Other children write poems or essays. One teenager found her experiences of being abused by her uncle flooded out into an essay she was writing for English. The teacher who marked the essay wrote in red ink 'I do not expect such disgusting rubbish from a girl like you'. That teacher in her ignorance and narrow perspective, like those in Richard's case, compounded the abuse the child had already suffered.

### Indirect attempts to tell

Finally, the abused child may confide in a friend who in turn decides to seek the advice of an adult. This can be an enormous responsibility and burden for the child who informs the adult. This second child needs to be listened to carefully and helped to unburden him or herself. We will return to the issue of one child disclosing on behalf on another in the next chapter.

# Five

# When children seek help

Apart from professionals whose task it is to investigate allegations of sexual abuse, many other people may be able to help sexually abused children unburden themselves, whether through speech, play, demonstration, drawing or writing. This chapter offers guidance on how to gain sufficient information to decide whether or not the matter should be passed on to an investigating agency. It should enable you to respond to the abused child in the most helpful way possible.

It must be emphasised that if any child under the age of consent describes sexual activity with an adult it should be reported to an investigative agency, as should any sexual activity which appears to have a distinctly coercive element or an unequal power relationship even when the activity is between children.

There are a number of reasons why suspected abuse should be reported to investigating agencies. One important reason is that adults and young people who sexually abuse children are dangerous. They may kill or damage their victims and they could be carriers of disease. The child you know will almost certainly not be their only victim. The perpetrator needs to be stopped and helped to control his or her activities.

Do not deceive yourself into believing that the child comes from such a 'nice' family that no real harm could be done or that the suspected perpetrator is such a charming person that no one could imagine him or her abusing children. Sexual abuse has occurred in the most 'respectable' and respected of families. Time and again survivors have told us how their abuse went undetected because no one would believe that any mistreatment could be taking place in their apparently happy families. Remember also that perpetrators have a vested interest in appearing to be above suspicion.

Another reason for informing investigative agencies of suspected sexual abuse is that the victim may need more help than you can give and the abuser's other victims – and there are likely to be other victims – need to be identified and offered help.

INITIAL RESPONSES

You would probably like to feel that your reaction to a disclosure or to the suspicion that a child is being sexually abused will be less damaging than the response of Jay's carers or Richard's school or the teacher with the red pen. It is likely that anyone who is sensitive to children and has a good understanding of the victims' perspectives will be able to respond appropriately.

## *Observing and recording*

You may come across a child whose behaviour gives you cause for concern. You might find that you are unable to ask the child directly what is causing upset or that the child is unforthcoming when asked. In these circumstances it may be useful to write down a careful description of the behaviour you believe to be significant. If you do not have enough information to pass on to an investigating agency then continue to keep a detailed record.

When keeping notes try to record facts rather than opinions or judgements. For example instead of 'Six-year-old Zoe was dressed sexily' you should write 'Six-year-old Zoe was dressed in a skimpy low cut top, a tight skirt, short enough to reveal lacy stockings held up by a suspender belt and high heeled shoes'. How appropriate this attire was would very much depend on all the circumstances which the investigating professionals would take into account before making their judgements or forming an opinion.

You should make sure the notes are 'contemporaneous', which means that you make a record at the time of the events or as soon as possible after they have occurred. It may be necessary to record events a considerable time later and a delayed record is better than none but the validity of any notes made more than 24 hours later will be considerably diminished.

It is important to ensure that your record is kept in such a way that it remains confidential until shared with the appropriate authorities. Make sure that, to the casual observer, there are no significant identifying details unless you can be certain that the records will be kept securely.

As you make the record try to note if there is a pattern. Try to find out if there are a number of alternative explanations for the behaviour. Retain any questionable drawings or poems as long as the child does not mind you doing so.

If drawings, writing or activities seem to be sexual try not to get angry and condemning but remain calm. You may have to restrain or divert youngsters if they are distressing other people. A child in nursery who is trying to simulate intercourse with another child will have to be stopped. Kind firmness rather than punitive anger will cause less damage in the long run. Evident revulsion and telling the children they are rude will only damage their already vulnerable self-esteem.

### Talking and listening

You could also spend time talking and listening to any child whose behaviour and comments worry you in order to find out if he or she is ready to confide in someone. You must find somewhere where you will not be disturbed nor overheard. Do so at a time when you will be able to stay for a while with the child; a time when you can afford to be patient.

What you say will depend on the age of the child and the circumstances. However it is useful to pick up on the children's demeanour or something they have done. Maybe,

> 'That looks an interesting drawing, can you tell me about it?' or
> 'You are very quiet nowadays, is something worrying you ?
> 'No'
> 'Are you sure, you look quite sad sometimes?'
> Silence
> 'You know, I will listen if you want to tell me something.'
> Silence.

The silence could well mean that the child is struggling to find the right words or is trying desperately to work out whether this is the right time to tell, whether you are to be trusted, whether you will cope with what he or she has to tell you.

Give the child time. If necessary say 'It's alright, take your time'. If the child looks very worried it might be worth saying 'Don't worry, I won't be angry with you'. It hardly needs saying that you must of course not get angry if the child eventually plucks up the courage to tell you. You must not even show anger towards the perpetrator or about the injustice of the situation. Children in distress will sense an adult's anger and will automatically assume it is directed towards them.

If you are in a position of authority over the child such as a parent, foster-parent or teacher and the child seems afraid it might be worth giving the reassurance that you will not punish him or her – only if you can guarantee that you will not. It is worth emphasising that no victim should ever be punished for the sexual activity. However, a child who is sexually abusing another or who is behaving in an inappropriate manner will have to be restrained.

Some children may not be ready to tell you what is happening to them. Occasionally they are not sure that they really want the abuse to stop because there can be positive associations such as the feeling of being wanted, needed or special. Helen whose brother Frank had abused her, recalled feeling 'sad and rejected' when he stopped coming to her room at nights. Some children may be too frightened of getting themselves or the perpetrator into trouble. Again Helen would not tell anyone because she did not want to cause problems for her brother. This fear *for* the abuser rather than fear *of* the abuser is especially true where the offender is loved by the child.

Children can be aware that they are distressed but do not know the cause. They erase abusive experiences from their memory. Sylvia Fraser (1989) recalls 'I did not remember my daddy ever having touched me sexually' (p.15). Such children may feel upset but simply cannot tell you what is wrong because they do not know themselves.

Other children may not be able to tell their parent or other people they love for fear of upsetting them. They do not want to have to witness the anguish of their adored mother, grandparent, foster carer or teacher. Nor do they want to tell people they admire for fear of losing the good opinion of these important people. They may eventually choose to tell someone more distant and less important to them.

Tony's history is an example of this. He is an adult male survivor who was sexually abused for several years by his grandfather who had been invited by his parents to live with them after his wife, Tony's grandmother, died. Tony could not tell his parents for fear of upsetting them.

He was a keen Boy Scout and wanted to confide in his Scout leader, Angus, whom he admired and respected. But he could not bring himself to do so, despite the fact that Angus was a very perceptive adult who sensed that something was wrong and tried to encourage Tony to talk to him.

Tony, on several occasions, nearly disclosed but each time his (undeserved) sense of shame and guilt held him back. He felt that Angus would in some way think less of him if he knew he was a victim of sexual abuse. Tony did not tell anyone until he was in his 50s.

You do not need to reproach yourself if you did all you could to provide a comfortable, caring, safe atmosphere and yet a child could not disclose to you. Perhaps to your dismay he or she may eventually tell someone who is by no means so close or so caring. The reason is likely to be that, paradoxically, the victim loves or at least likes you too much to tell you.

It must be remembered that a child may not be able to tell because there is nothing to tell. It is possible for concerned adults to assume a child has been abused, after overhearing a chance remark, and then put the child's behaviour under a microscope magnifying every insignificant detail.

If the time and circumstances are right however, a child who really is a victim might start to tell you what happened. Sometimes the child or young person is obviously distressed and needs a lot of gentle reassurance. While it may be appropriate to say 'It's alright' it is not appropriate to say 'Don't worry, everything will be alright'. Unfortunately after disclosure everything is very far from alright and for a time the child's world may collapse around him.

Children may say they want to tell you something but you must keep it a secret. It is not okay to keep sexual abuse a secret. The abuser, as we know, may well exploit others; child molestation thrives on secrecy. Furthermore children usually tell because they want the abuse to stop and you may need to seek the help of other adults in order to stop it. You need to tell children that you can keep good secrets such as birthday surprises for a while but if they or another person is being hurt or upset then someone else who can help stop the hurt may have to be told.

Ask yourself why the child is asking you to keep a secret. Perhaps it is because it is the child's way of saying 'I have something important to tell you' in which case the reassurance that you are listening, taking notice and taking the matter seriously will be sufficient. It may be that the child fears everyone knowing his or her business; in this case you can give the assurance that only the people who have to know will be told.

The general rule is – *do not* promise to keep information to yourself but *do* make disclosure easier for children by reassuring them that they will be listened to and that you will only tell other people if you have to; even then it will only be other people who have to know in order to help.

Some children drop their voice to a whisper and you may find yourself continually having to ask them what they are saying. Ask them gently and without a hint of criticism. An exasperated 'How can I possibly understand what you're saying when you speak so softly?' is far from helpful.

Many children will need encouragement to go on with their account. One of the most effective ways is to repeat what they have said with a question mark in the voice. This shows the children that you are interested in them and are listening to what they are trying to tell you. It gives them a chance to think about what to say next. It enables you to avoid asking a leading question or making a comment that will divert them from their original intention. Sometimes however there will be an obvious question that needs asking.

*'I don't like staying with grandpa'*
*'Oh, why not?'*
*'I can't tell you.'*
*'You can't tell me.'*
*'No.'*
*'Could you try?'*
The child stares intently at a distant object.
Silence.
*'He er...er...*
Silence
*'Yes, he?'* said gently and slowly

*'He does rude things to me.'*
*'He does rude things to you?'*
*'Yes, he makes me sit on his knee.'*
*'He makes you sit on his knee?'*
*'Yes and then he rubs me.'*
*'Where does he rub you?'*
*'Between the legs.'*
*'Between the legs?'*
*'Yes.'*
*'How does he rub you?*
*'With his hand.'*

This combination of repetition and open questioning will help children continue with their explanation. Open questions start with words like 'who', 'what', 'where', 'how'. Leading questions such as 'Did he touch you between the legs', which only invite a 'Yes' or 'No' response, should be avoided

It is also essential not to assume the identity of the perpetrator. If a child says 'I am frightened to go home because he will start doing rude things' it is important not to leap to the conclusion that 'he' is the father and say 'So daddy has been doing rude things'. An anxious child may not hear this correctly or may not take the opportunity to correct you, so will continue to talk about 'he' meaning the lodger while you make mistaken assumptions about what the father has been doing.

Once the child has told you enough for you to suspect strongly that sexual abuse has occurred there is no need to keep gathering facts. It is the investigators' job to gather evidence and find out exactly what happened.

If however the child wants to continue to talk about events then try to carry on listening. There comes a time in everyone's life when we need to unburden ourselves to someone who will listen patiently and who will try to understand. This may be that time for the child and you may be destined to be the person the child has chosen, hopeful that you will be patient and understanding. He or she may still need a gentle prompt or helpful question in order to carry on.

Children's accounts are likely to be confused. Abuse may have happened at night when they were tired and only half awake. A few children, especially those involved in ritualistic sexual abuse, may have been given drugs resulting in altered perceptions. Children may be very unsure of what has been done to them, especially if approached from behind, have had their faces covered or are for whatever reason unable to see what is happening.

In cases where there have been repeated instances of abuse a child might have difficulty describing what has happened because one incident will merge with another. Occasionally events have been so distressing and upsetting that victims cannot remember or describe some of the worst aspects of the abuse.

Children frequently need help with the 'rude' words they cannot avoid using if they are to tell you what happened. They may try phrases like 'between my legs' or a word like 'thing' to refer to the penis. Here, sketches, dolls or books with illustrations of body parts can be useful. Stick people can be drawn and the genitalia sketched in – a small line for the penis, two small circles for the breasts, a small line coming out of the mouth for the tongue. Using an ordinary doll children can point to precisely where they mean.

Children should be encouraged to use the words for the genitalia with which they are comfortable. It is often acceptable to start by using euphemisms such as 'private parts or 'the bits you cover with a swimsuit'. You may then suggest that they tell you what they call the parts at home or what their friends call them. Some children may still be unwilling to use 'rude' words. In this case it is useful to say, for example when referring to the male genitalia, 'Doctors call this a penis, but a lot of people call it a willy – what would you like to call it?' If there is still no reply then you have to opt for one word yourself, 'Okay, so that I can understand what you mean I will call it a willy, is that alright?' The child may then more comfortably follow your lead.

### COPING WITH EMOTIONS

Despite the fact that most children's accounts are confused, a number of victims show very little hesitation, confusion or reluctance. Some will answer in a way that gives the impression that they are reading out a shopping list or talking about what they did during a particularly boring day at school. An unemotional account can be disconcerting and puzzling for the adult listener. Some people have refused to believe children who give a matter-of-fact story. They feel that such children must have been primed to tell a lie or have made up a story. Anyone however who works regularly with abused children will recognise that it is by no means uncommon for children who have suffered dreadful experiences to talk about them calmly.

This is because many abused children have been drained of emotion and so show no strong feelings when talking about the abuse. Others, like Sylvia Fraser, have separated off the person who is abused from their real self so that when talking of the abuse they do not feel directly involved. Many children are hanging on to their self-control and dignity to such an extent that they dare not show any emotion and so sound flat and unemotional.

### *Distress and physical comfort*

Although some children can give an impassive account there are those for whom disclosure is difficult and distressing. They may burst into tears, in which case let them cry. Do not feel you have to say anything. A period of silence is fine. But it may be helpful to make a comment like 'Its okay to cry, I guess you are feeling very upset' or if the child is struggling for control 'Its okay, just let go, we all need a good cry sometimes.'

A great temptation, when a child becomes distressed, is to give a cuddle. This may well be what is needed. It is comforting to be held securely. It is also a way of showing victims that they are not 'untouchable'. However some children may interpret any physical contact as a preliminary to sexual activities and might become afraid of your intentions. This is particularly true where a child has rarely been touched and cuddled except when being abused.

You may know a particular child sufficiently well to be confident that he or she would welcome a cuddle but in the case of children that you do not know so well it is useful just to put your hand lightly on their hand or shoulder. If they flinch and move away you know that physical contact is not welcome. If they seem reassured by the movement you can begin to hold both hands or shoulders and if they are still comfortable they can be drawn into a cuddle.

If you are a man and the child has been abused by a male perpetrator you will have to be very sensitive about touching.

Because the child is choosing to tell you, he or she must feel able to trust you, but suddenly sweeping the youngster into your arms or sitting him or her on your knee may be experienced as intrusive and interpreted as a sexual advance. You need to move slowly, patiently and gently at the child's pace. Even if you are a woman, possibly the child's mother, it is important to respond gently. Any sudden movement or emotional display of concern may confuse, overwhelm or frighten the child.

If the victim is crying you may find it hard to avoid crying too but it is important to save your tears until you are alone or with an understanding adult. Your tears will worry the child who may fear that he has hurt or damaged you and may then stop and even retract his account for fear of causing further damage. Children are often more caring and considerate of others than we give them credit for.

You may also feel like 'backing off'. It is hard to press on when faced with distressed children, yet they may need you to carry on asking questions. They may want to tell you more. A little gentle encouragement will not cause any damage. However, no child should be forced to continue, by using threats, entreaties or bribes. No child who is reluctant to answer a question should be asked it over and over again until eventually it is answered. Gentle probing – yes, but forceful interrogation – *no*.

### *Acknowledging and expressing feelings*

One of the most important tasks at this stage is to help children express and cope with their feelings about the abuse and about having disclosed. Instead of simply 'pumping' children for more information when you already have enough to know that the matter will have to be officially investigated, it is appropriate to turn to look at their feelings.

As the child's story unfolds it can be useful to ask at appropriate intervals 'And how did that make you feel?' If the child looks distressed then acknowledge the distress rather than ignoring it. 'I can see you are upset.' Some children are struggling to find the words and courage to tell you what has happened in which case it might be helpful to say, 'I understand how difficult this is for you.' If the child is obviously angry then you can say something like, 'I can see you are angry and you have a right to be angry with Uncle Joe, he should not have done that to you.'

As already mentioned in the previous section, it is important not to express your own anger even against the perpetrator because children, in a state of distress, may well think that you are angry with them. The statement 'He should not have done that to you' should be made calmly as if stating a fact rather than in tones of outrage and indignation.

---

### EXERCISE:

Try saying 'He should not have done that to you' in quiet, sympathetic, matter-of-fact manner. Then repeat it in an outraged way. Which way do you think would be more reassuring and comforting to a distressed child?

If possible find a partner and say the sentence 'He should not have done that to you' both ways as already suggested. Then ask your partner how he or she felt. Was the first quiet way more pleasant than the second angry way or vice versa? Swop roles so that you are on the receiving end – how do you feel?

---

The most important message to convey to children disclosing sexual abuse is to tell them, with conviction, that they were not to blame. Do not just tell them once, tell them several times. Kathy Evert, who was sexually and physically abused by her mother wrote:

> 'Listen, I figured something else out, too. No one, not one single soul, professional or not, ever told me 'Hey that wasn't your fault. You didn't do anything to deserve that' (Evert and Bijkerk 1987 p.24).

Contrast this to the experience of Sarah who was physically, emotionally and sexually abused by her father. As a young woman she went to live in digs. While there she met another lodger who, hearing of her experiences, said 'It isn't fair, why should it have happened to you.' This simple spontaneous statement had a profound and beneficial effect on Sarah who realised that her experiences were not her fault. She heard someone else confirm that she had not deserved to be exploited so brutally by her father.

You must make it clear to children who tell you about their abuse that they are in no way to blame for their mistreatment. They may feel guilty because they enjoyed some of the activities, accepted bribes or 'failed' to stop the abuse. Often they feel they must have done something wrong and deserve the treatment they have received. Whatever the case, they are not to blame.

A teenage girl who wears tight jeans or stays out late or a teenage boy who goes to a stranger's house may be rather naive or thoughtless but they are still not to blame. It is worth saying once more that responsibility rests with the perpetrator. This is the person with the power to take advantage of the victim's naivety, thoughtlessness or vulnerability. He or she makes the choice to abuse that power. We do not tell a rich businessman who has been mugged that he should not have been wearing such an expensive suit? We do not imply that if he 'flaunts' his wealth by wearing smart, good quality clothes then he deserves to be robbed!

Try to explain to the children concerned why they are not to blame. With younger children this might be in relatively simple terms 'You are very little and he is much much bigger than you', or 'He is cunning, he tricked you, he tricked your mum and dad and he has tricked other children as well', or 'Everyone likes presents, of course you liked the presents she bought you and thought she was your friend'.

With more sophisticated adolescents you could try drawing analogies. Ask them to think who would be to blame if they had asked an adult for a lift and he agreed then crashed the car because he was drunk and out of control. However reasonable or unreasonable the request for the lift was and however much they would have welcomed the lift and enjoyed the ride at first, it was the adult who had the power to drive and it was he who should have been in control but went out of control.

Abused children also need to know that they are not to blame for the consequences of the abuse and for the results of the abuse coming to light. If a perpetrator has made a child fear that his or her mother will become ill you can say 'If your mummy becomes ill and upset it is not because you told me but because of what your daddy did'. Similarly if a child is worried that the perpetrator will go to prison, you can explain 'It's not your fault if he goes to prison. It is his own fault. He should not have touched you and mistreated you in the way he did'.

Black children, it is to be remembered, may have an additional burden as they may feel responsible for having in some way betrayed their community and given fuel to white racists. Khadj Rouf (1991b) is black and was sexually abused. She writes of the responses of some white people:

*'Through deep black eyes I saw hatred.*
*I listen to open hostility*
*and the quiet comments*
*Of those who didn't realise that*
*I wasn't quite one of them.*

It is important that black children are helped to appreciate that they have betrayed no one. It is the perpetrator, black or white, who is responsible for any betrayals. The problem lies not with black abused children but with the perpetrators and with people with racist attitudes.

Time and again sexually abused children and adults have described intense feelings of isolation and of being the only child to have been abused or being part of the only family in which incest occurs. Khadj Rouf (1991b) again writes:

*'I was surrounded by people*
*but I was always alone*
*No-one knew what was inside my head,*
*Locked away, Secret.*

Abused children need to be told 'You are not the only child to have been abused'. Again, black children may feel doubly isolated. They need to know that not only are other children but other black children are sexually abused. Similarly, because until recently few men and boys have openly described being sexually abused, boys may feel very isolated and cut off from male society with its emphasis on not being a victim but on being dominant and powerful. They need to know that other boys are victims too.

You will need to reassure the child that she or he has done the right thing by telling you what has happened. It has taken considerable courage to do so. Something like 'I know you have had to be very brave, it isn't easy to tell about these things'. This again is very important for a boy who may fear above all else that people will think he is weak. Similarly black children need special reassurances that they have done the right thing and it is the perpetrator who has damaged their community, if any one has.

### OTHERS DISCLOSING

As already mentioned, abuse may come to light because the victim has told a friend or relative or because someone else finds out what has been happening. You may be told about the abuse by another child or an adult relative.

Whoever tells you, you should not, as already indicated, agree to keep the information secret. It is worth re-emphasising that child sexual abuse thrives on secrecy.

### *Children on behalf of other children*

If a child tells you on behalf of a friend or relative there are a number of issues to bear in mind. Firstly you need to determine, as far as possible, that the child is not really talking about him or herself.

Secondly, if the child disclosing is a brother, sister or a member of the same household and the perpetrator is also a member then the child should be viewed as a co-victim. Many of the destructive manipulations of the perpetrator will have affected all the child members of the household adversely. This means that most of the guidance relating to helping victims and enabling them to speak out will also apply to other family members. For example, avoid expressing anger against the perpetrator; the reasons being the same as those in relation to the victim.

Thirdly, the children concerned need to be congratulated for having taken a sensible course of action. They should be left in no doubt that whatever happens next is not their responsibility. It is not their fault if the perpetrator goes to prison or if the victim, their friend or brother or sister, is taken into care.

A nine-year-old girl, Karen, told her best friend, Louise that her father had begun interfering with her sexually ever since her mother started a new evening job at a local club. He had recently forced anal and vaginal intercourse upon her. Louise, upset by what Karen had told her, eventually confided in her own mother. Louise's mother, who was a local magistrate had quite rightly no hesitation in informing the police.

Karen's allegations were supported by medical evidence and by an admission by her father who was sent to prison. Karen's own mother totally rejected her daughter whom she believed had 'seduced' her husband. But Karen, her brothers and her mother blamed Louise for having told an adult. Karen became depressed, attempted suicide and ended up in a foster home. Louise was left with a heavy burden of guilt about having told her mother.

### Non-abusing parents or other adults

Adults who learn that a child is being abused and feel impelled to pass this information on may well be distressed. They need to be assured that they have done the right thing by sharing the information about the abuse.

Parents of victims will be particularly upset. They may feel guilty for having failed to protect their offspring. They may be overwhelmed with anger against the perpetrator, the victim or, as in Louise and Karen's case, against the informant.

Parents need to be allowed to express their distress. Often it is advisable to give them quite a lot of time and space in which to talk about how they feel. But it is also helpful to convey messages that only the perpetrator is to blame, *nobody else*. If the parents' feeling of guilt at having failed to protect the child is unrealistic they need to be told that parents cannot supervise their children all of the time. To be over-protective is a form of abuse in itself. Children have to be allowed increasing independence and parents have to take some risks.

Non-abusing parents should be encouraged to go to the investigative agencies themselves. The fact that the perpetrator may strike again, perhaps against another child has to be faced. However, many parents are understandably reluctant to expose their child to the rigours of a police investigation and they may need help and support if they are to report the matter to the authorities.

If, from what you are told, a crime appears to have been committed or a child is likely to be abused and the informant will not report the matter then you must consider very seriously contacting a child protection agency yourself, with or without the informant's permission.

## Perpetrators themselves

Occasionally the people disclosing are the perpetrators themselves. You must not give any guarantee of secrecy.

You may be a Samaritan or other counselling volunteer to whom the perpetrator has referred him or herself anonymously or you could be a priest bound by the confidentiality of the confessional. In such cases you will not be able to report the perpetrators to the authorities but you can help them to take a long hard look at their offending behaviour. Do not allow them to put the responsibility on other people. Do not allow them to make excuses for their activities. Do not allow them to minimise what they have done nor the effects on the victim, 'I didn't rape her, we only simulated intercourse'. Leave them in no doubt that their behaviour is compulsive, habitual, totally unacceptable and must stop. But they can only stop with a lot of will-power and help. They can be reassured that they are not monsters – just weak, selfish human beings whose behaviour is monstrous.

If you know the perpetrator's identity then you will be able to report the matter to the police or child protection agencies. This may feel like a betrayal but think about why perpetrators might tell you:

- *Reason one:* they might do so 'for fun', in other words they get sexual enjoyment out of reliving the events when describing them to you.

---

### EXERCISE

Think of a film or experience that has given you real pleasure recently. Did you want to recount what had happened to a friend? Think of exhilarating experiences that you have had in the past. Did you go over them in your mind afterwards and want to tell other people about the exciting time that you had?

---

You can re-create the experience to some extent by talking about it to others and in that way double the enjoyment. In a similar way sexual abusers can gain stimulation by describing the abuse to other people. If this is the reason the perpetrator is disclosing then he or she is sexually abusing you as well; misusing your kindness and ability to listen in order to gain sexual gratification. You owe him or her no obligation of loyalty in these circumstances. You are a secondary victim and just as the primary victim has the right to tell someone in authority, you too have a right and indeed, as an adult, a duty to inform an investigating agency that is the police, social services or NSPCC.

- *Reason two:* perpetrators may disclose simply to unburden themselves and feel better about what they have done. We all derive some comfort from getting things off our chest. However, in the case of people with compulsive behaviour (especially where the behaviour causes damage and distress to other people) the last thing we want them to feel is better about what they have done. They need to feel *worse* about their behaviour in order to prompt them to do something to control it. Simply listening to what they have to say and then responding with 'Don't worry about what you have done, its okay, don't feel upset' is simply a way of approving their behaviour and giving them permission to carry on.

  Perpetrators need to be told that their behaviour is unacceptable, they have broken the law and you have a duty as a citizen to report the facts to law enforcement agencies.

- *Reason three:* some perpetrators will disclose because they are desperate for help. As already mentioned, perpetrators are not monsters and it is possible to distinguish between their behaviour and them as people. We want them to feel bad about what they are doing and yet not too bad about themselves. So child abusers need to know that they are worth worrying about and helping as people but their behaviour is letting them down and cannot be ignored.

  Reporting them to the police or social services is really the only way of obtaining effective help. Unfortunately the law is a rather blunt instrument and in most countries, including Britain, treatment schemes for sex offenders are few and far between. In Britain most perpetrators are not prosecuted because of the difficulty of obtaining sufficient proof. But without a conviction sex offenders are unlikely to be referred for treatment because, in the eyes of the law, they have done nothing wrong and so do not need treatment. When a conviction is secured the offender may simply languish in prison for a couple of years. A fortunate few will be offered help and treatment which involves learning to understand and control their behaviour.

You cannot be certain when contacting the authorities whether or not the perpetrator will receive help. However one thing is certain, if you do report the matter the perpetrator may get help but if you do not then it is unlikely that he or she will be referred to an effective treatment scheme.

- *Reason four:* sometimes perpetrators disclose because their burden of guilt is such that they are seeking punishment. In such cases you would be meeting the perpetrators' needs by reporting them to the authorities. Punishment without help to overcome difficulties is a negative and destructive course of action. On the other hand there is a chance that the offender will be offered treatment as well as punished once the offending behaviour comes to light.

## Partners of perpetrators

If you are the partner, particularly the wife of an offender who has told you what he has been doing, it may be very difficult to report the matter. You may well be able to foresee enormous financial and emotional upheavals. It will take great courage to take matters further but unfortunately, even if your partner promises to stop the abuse, the compulsive nature of sexual offending behaviour means that eventually it will start again unless he is given effective help. One mother whose husband had molested their daughter as well as some neighbours' children wrote as though to her husband:

*We watched you go on as though 'reformed'! You kept your temper, helped with the washing up for the first time ever, and took up and read your bible whenever you came in from work.*

*Our daughter's peace of mind was increasingly shattered by your behaviour, as though nothing at all had happened. She couldn't eat, sleep or study. I asked you to leave us for a while until we sorted out our own feelings, but you refused, saying that you had 'stopped all that now'. I didn't know if I had the right to insist you left, but I needed space desperately to think.*

*If you cared at all about our daughter's health you would have gone, but you stayed, and continued to manipulate us and tried to soften us up. You finally, reluctantly, left us at the end of November. Oh! the peace and quiet, But you came back for Christmas, bringing presents, though mostly these were for yourself! (Corcoran 1987 p.108)*

The wife eventually sought help and was able to gain sufficient control of the situation to ensure that the children's wishes not to see their father again were granted and their needs for individual counselling were met.

Finally, you will not need reminding that child sexual abuse thrives on secrecy and that by keeping the perpetrator's activities secret, even when motivated by loyalty to and compassion for the offender, you will be helping to perpetuate this form of child abuse.

### REFERRAL TO INVESTIGATING AGENCIES

The person disclosing the abuse, in most instances, has a right to know that you will be reporting the matter to an investigative agency. In the case of victims it is important to explain that you cannot keep what they have told you a secret, you have to tell someone who may be able to protect them and other children from any more sexual abuse.

In the case of other adults or adolescents disclosing to you, you may try to encourage them to report the matter themselves. You could offer to accompany them to a police station or social services department. If they agree to report the matter but do not want you to come with them then you will need to find out whether or not they did contact the appropriate authorities. If they have not done so you will have to report the matter yourself. It is essential to give careful thought about what to do if the person disclosing to you is the perpetrator. It is important that the police are informed and able to investigate before the abuser can destroy evidence or intimidate witnesses.

Agencies which investigate child sexual abuse are first and foremost law enforcement agencies because most forms of child sexual abuse are against the law. Offences may range from rape and incest to indecent assault and indecent exposure. Forcing children to watch pornographic films is in many countries not a crime although it is abusive behaviour. However in Britain and in many other countries the possession and use of child pornography is a criminal offence.

State child protection agencies, such as local authority social services departments (in Britain) and certain voluntary agencies, are granted legal powers to investigate cases of child abuse. In England, Wales and Northern Ireland the National Society for the Prevention of Cruelty to Children (NSPCC) is the leading voluntary investigative agency. The Scottish equivalent is the Royal Scottish Society for the Prevention of Cruelty to Children (RSSPCC).

When reporting the matter it is important to give the authorities as much information as possible. You may be feeling very distressed but try to stay calm. If the victim is either with you or nearby it is doubly important to remain in control of your emotions. If, however no children are present and you break down in tears, allow yourself to cry for a while. What you are describing is painful and upsetting and there is absolutely no shame in showing you are upset if you become overwhelmed by the poignancy of the events that you must recount. Remember that the professional you are talking to will probably realise how distressed you must be feeling and will understand your reactions.

Very occasionally you may report the matter only to find nothing then happens. Sometimes this will be because the professional receiving the referral has simply forgotten to ensure that the matter is taken further or the referral has been lost somewhere in the system.

In some, hopefully increasingly rare cases, it may be that you have been unlucky enough to have referred the matter to a professional who simply does not believe that children are sexually abused and has therefore ignored you.

If you, the victim and/or the perpetrator belong to a black ethnic community and you refer the matter to a white social worker then very occasionally the worker will do nothing for fear of being seen as 'racist'. Alternatively the workers involved will have some stereotype image of certain forms of sexual abusive behaviour being 'normal' in some cultures. We can recall the school which had taken no action to protect an Asian pupil because the staff were anxious to find out if incest 'was acceptable in Punjabi culture' (Ahmed 1989).

One Asian colleague described to me her frustrations in trying to convince her white colleagues in her local social services department that an Asian girl was indeed being sexually abused by her father and was in need of statutory protection and counselling help. For white workers there is one 'safe' approach which is not to intervene at all because no intervention means no racist intervention.

In some cases the character or status of the perpetrator ensures that investigative agencies will ignore the referral. Obviously powerful or wealthy men may intimidate local professionals who simply will not risk acting against them. Sometimes the perpetrator finds other ways of disabling investigative agencies. One man who was abusing all the children in his family befriended the key male social workers in his local social services department. When the eldest girl accused him of abusing her they felt that he was their mate and he would never abuse children. They convinced themselves that the girl was lying because she had already accused her uncle of abusing her. It took a lot of effort on the part of female social workers and disclosures by all of the other children in the family before the male managers and workers would take action against the father.

If, for whatever reason, the agency to which you reported the abuse takes no action then you must either insist in taking up the matter with a more senior person in the agency or refer it to another investigative agency. Therefore if a referral worker from your local social services or child welfare department does not seem to be doing anything you should then ask to speak to his or her senior or report the matter to the local police. Keep reporting the matter until eventually someone does take you seriously.

# Six

# Continuing to help

Once the case has been referred to the investigative agencies, events may move very quickly and become confusing and often distressing.

KEEPING IN TOUCH

It may be that you have no further contact with the victim or person who disclosed. You may be a teacher, secretary, dinner-time helper, school crossing warden (lollipop person) or caretaker at the child's school. The child is suddenly taken into care and moved to a new school. There seems to be little more that you can do, apart from look after yourself – there is more about this in the final comment section.

There is however, something more that you can think about doing even when the child suddenly disappears out of your life, especially if he or she chose you to disclose to. Children or young people who have been abused often feel that they have done something wrong and that they are 'dirty' and unworthy of respect. They may well imagine that there is no way you would want to have anything to do with them after learning how 'rude' they have been. They may also fear that the information that they gave to you has in some way damaged or destroyed you.

If, after the disclosure you simply disappear out of the child's life then he or she has no way of knowing whether or not you are surviving and whether you still like and respect him or her.

It might be inappropriate and impractical for you to visit but you may be able to make contact via the telephone or send a card with your best wishes and kindest regards. Keeping in touch even indirectly can be very important and helpful. You should consult with the child's social worker before establishing contact but do not be put off if the worker seems too busy or does not realise the significance of your contact with the child; for the youngster's sake be persistent.

It could be that you are a parent, grandparent or other person who is close to the victim. The fact that the child chose to confide in you means that you must be trustworthy as far as he or she is concerned. Because of this it may well be appropriate for you to accompany the victim through a large part of the investigation.

This is likely to be a difficult experience for both you and the child. Several different professionals will be involved and you will probably not be aware of everything going on behind the scenes. You will feel confused and bewildered as will the child. Some things might seem to happen very quickly while at other times you will be kept waiting and events will seem to progress slowly.

These next sections should give you some insight into what is likely to happen and what you and the victim have a right to expect. Unfortunately, resources are often short, workers poorly trained or over-loaded and some interventions misguided. When the investigative process falls very short of the out-line of good practice indicated here, you may come to the conclusion that, in the interests of the victim and other children, you have to voice a complaint. Most agencies have a complaints procedure which you have the right to set in motion. On the other hand it is also worth remembering that the individual workers are all too often doing the best that they can in almost intolerable conditions of stress and inadequate resources. They may have to chose not the most beneficial course of action but the least harmful one; a choice between two or more evils. It is also to be remembered that most decisions are taken by several people who jointly have a broader perspective than you might have. The decision to complain and the way in which you do so must take into account all these factors.

## Following procedures

Different countries and even different local authorities have their own particular way of responding to allegations of child sexual abuse. In Britain, each local authority will have a set of procedures for the investigating workers and other professionals to follow.

If you are a professional yourself then you need to ensure that you are following the correct procedures for your agency. This is important because the procedures were designed to achieve a balance between protecting abused children and respecting the rights of their families. The procedures will also offer some protection for you. If you follow them correctly you are less likely to run the risk of being charged with negligence or with unprofessional conduct.

Should you be a volunteer it is worth discussing what to do with your supervisor, a member of your management committee or volunteer coordinator. There may well be an agency policy which you can follow. Again this should act as a safeguard for the victims, their family and yourself.

INTERVIEWING CHILDREN

When the victim is a small baby or a pre-verbal toddler then the evidence of sexual abuse will be the infant's medical condition including damage to the genitalia and symptoms of sexually transmitted diseases. The baby may also show some unusual behaviour such as opening the legs wide or showing tenseness amounting almost to paralysis when the nappy is removed. Workers investigating allegations will want the child to be medically examined and will need to observe the child closely. These observations and examinations should be carried out in a way that causes the infant little or no distress.

An older child will be interviewed, often jointly, by a police officer and a social worker. If the interview is recorded on audio or video tape then the child should be told that this is happening.

In England and Wales, children whose evidence might be used in certain criminal proceedings can be spared the ordeal of recounting their evidence (in chief) in court if there is a satisfactory video recording made of an interview in which they give an account of their experiences. They must however be available and able to be cross-examined. The basic legal principles of this are laid down in the Criminal Justice Act 1991.

A guide for interviewers using video equipment under the terms of the 1991 Act has been provided by the Home Office and Department of Health called a *Memorandum of Good Practice 1992*. Although specifically designed for video interviews and containing some technical details, the general advice given in the *Memorandum* is also applicable to any formal investigative interviewing of a sexually abused child.

Children being interviewed must be helped to feel comfortable. The adults involved should be introduced to them and their roles explained. Children have a right to know what is happening and they must not be left confused and frightened. Their physical comfort can be addressed in such a way that they know that they can ask to go to the toilet and should not be interviewed when hungry, thirsty, cold or tired. The *Memorandum of Good Practice* exhorts practitioners to consider the needs of children with disabilities particularly wheelchair access or a loop system for the hearing impaired. There must be appropriate toilet facilities for wheelchair-user children.

Having given due attention to their physical comfort, the emotional comfort of youngsters needs to be addressed. Children should be spoken to gently and with respect and consideration. They must not be bullied, threatened or bribed with promises of rewards if they 'tell'. I have watched, with mounting horror, a true life video of an interview of a small boy conducted by a well-built male practitioner who persistently verbally bullied the child and at one stage, when the boy started to run around the room, thundered 'Just you come here, sit still and tell me what happened or I'll give you a good bloody hiding'. The threat to hit the child was made repeatedly. The mother, who was in the room but probably in a state of shock, was evidently unable to intervene.

Nowadays so extreme an example is unlikely but if you witness any threat or bullying then you have the right to intervene directly. It may be difficult to challenge the interviewers and stop the interview. If necessary, withdraw and ask to see a senior officer urgently.

During an introductory phase the workers will endeavour to

establish a rapport with the child. Then the child should be allowed to explain what happened in his or her own words with perhaps some help with words for sexual parts or activities, as explained in the previous chapter. Leading questions or ones which can be answered with a nod or shake of the head should be avoided.

Investigators will probably be looking for evidence which will be of value if the offender is prosecuted. They will therefore need to be sure about who the alleged perpetrator is. Some children refer to two or more men as 'Daddy'. Other children may know several people with the same name. For example, some families have traditional names so that Ebeneezer Entwistle may be the name of the grandfather, uncle, father, cousin and older brother. Similarly, there might be two Mrs Smiths teaching at their school.

Investigators will also be looking for precise details of the abuse. They will want to know exactly what the perpetrator did because the charges that can be brought against the offender may depend on the nature of the abuse. They will want to know precisely what time and where certain offences were committed so that they can check if the alleged perpetrator had an alibi at those times or had the opportunity to commit the crimes of which he or she stands accused.

As already mentioned, children can become very confused about the sequence of events particularly if they were molested at night when half-asleep or if the abuse happened so often that one incident merges into another. This presents a dilemma for specialist interviewers. Given our present systems, the victim and other children can best be protected if perpetrators are found guilty and have to face what they have done. For that reason interviewers have to collect precise details. On the other hand the victims will probably find it painful to have to be repeatedly questioned about such details.

Two of the most destructive questions to ask children are, why they did not resist the abuse, and why did they 'allow' it to continue. Good interviewers will recognise that perpetrators use whatever powers they have to prevent their victims from resisting and from telling someone about the abuse. So the interviewer should never ask 'Why didn't you say No?' or 'Why didn't you tell someone the first time'. Instead the skilled professional will ask 'What did Uncle Pat do so that you couldn't stop him?' or 'What did Aunt Jane do or say to prevent you from telling someone?'

Questions always have to be formulated to indicate that it was the perpetrator who was responsible for the abuse and not the child. Therefore, when wanting to find out if the child was made to masturbate the offender, the questions 'Did you do anything to daddy?' or 'What did you do to daddy? must be avoided. Instead the child should be asked 'Did daddy make you/ask you to do anything to him?' or 'What did daddy make you do to him?'

Children may become upset when having to describe the abuse. The investigators might have to press on despite the distress in order to gain the information they need. However they should acknowledge with the child how difficult it is to describe such events. They can also give the child a little space in order to recover or express distress. Sometimes offering children a drink or simply allowing them to cry for a while will help. The investigators must not carry on with their questioning while ignoring the victim's discomfort.

Interviews should not last too long. Some investigators insensitively carry on questioning a young child for several hours. Other investigators in an attempt to gain a disclosure will continue to put pressure on a child who is unwilling or unable to talk about his or her experiences or who may not in fact have been abused.

Skilful interviewers will respond sensitively while managing to obtain information and, despite the fact that these are not therapeutic interviews, they will also help child victims cope with their feelings.

The children's sense of anger, confusion, fear, guilt, shame or distress should be met with an understanding response. The interview can be sprinkled, whenever appropriate, with statements such as 'You have a right to be angry with Auntie Pat. She hurt you'. 'We know that you have done nothing wrong'. 'It must be very hard for you to have to remember all these things, I appreciate how upsetting it can be.'

Abused children may have learnt, from their abusers, words and phrases which are particularly offensive and yet children have to use these phrases to describe what the abuser said or did. Even people who consider themselves broad-minded and not adverse to the occasional earthy expletive may well be shocked by the explicit nature of some of the children's comments.

If you remain in the same room with the child throughout the interview then you must stay in the background and let the interviewers get on with their job. You must not answer for the child. Nor should you intervene even if he or she appears to be distressed. If you do not feel comfortable with what is happening then remain quiet and calm but raise your concerns with the investigating agencies afterwards. The exception to this is that you would be within your rights to intervene immediately if the interviewers use threats against the child, swear at or hit him or her or use any form of humiliation or intimidation.

## *Anatomical dolls*

Children may be asked to demonstrate the activities using dolls, sometimes these will be 'anatomical' ones. These are sets of rag dolls, usually representing at least one adult male, one adult female, one boy and one girl. Their mouths can open to reveal a tongue and they are endowed with a penis or a hole for a vagina, nipples and – in the case of females – breasts, a hole for the anus, a navel, pubic and underarm hair for the adult dolls and separate fingers.

Thought should have been given to the colouring of the dolls, it should not be assumed that representations of blonde, blue-eyed characters are universally acceptable to all children, whether black or white. Similarly, careful consideration should be given to the appearance of the dolls where the child or significant others in the child's circle have a visible disability.

The anatomical dolls can help children to demonstrate clearly their experiences. Some defence lawyers, in an attempt to discredit what is a very useful tool for helping children describe what has happened, have tried to maintain that non-abused children will automatically put a penis into a hole in another doll in much the same way that children will fit jig-saws together. This is somewhat far-fetched as anyone who has witnessed a child handling these dolls will know. Furthermore recent research (Sivan et al. 1988, Glaser and Collins 1989) has shown that non-abused children are very unlikely to demonstrate sexually explicit activities when presented with the dolls.

The Cleveland report (Butler-Sloss 1988) recommended that the dolls are not used as the first stage method of evaluation. However both the report and *Memorandum* acknowledge that used by trained professionals they are a useful adjunct. I interviewed a 10-year-old girl who had already given details to the police of indecent assault against her by a male relative. At a later stage she said what made her really angry was 'the other thing' that the relative had done. I asked her if she would like to tell me what that was. She looked embarrassed and said that she was unable to do so. I asked her if she could show me. She agreed so I introduced the anatomical dolls, whereupon she showed me clearly and explicitly anal penetration. I checked with her whether she really meant the adult male doll's penis to be inserted into the girl doll's anus and she was emphatic that this was correct. Although she had been able to tell us of inappropriate touching there was no way initially that she could find the words to tell us about the anal intercourse.

When a child does show explicit activities using the dolls it can be a vivid but distressing experience for any onlooker. Somehow you will have to contain your emotions if this happens until the child no longer needs you to be calm and until you can express them safely.

The anatomical dolls can in fact serve as a protection for suspected perpetrators. One colleague who was involved in a potential incest case many years ago recalled that when questioning the daughter, the investigators has to establish whether or not the father had had intercourse with her. The child was too young to be explicit. It was important to ascertain whether or not the father had an erection. They eventually asked the girl if the father's penis had been 'big'. The little girl replied in the affirmative because it seemed big to her. The father was sent to prison for several years. As an adult the daughter was full of anger, guilt and remorse because she realised that her reply had been misinterpreted and her father had never had an erection. Had she been able to use anatomical dolls she could have contradicted by demonstration the suggestion of the erect penis and her father would have been charged with a lesser crime and would probably have received a more lenient sentence.

In another more recent case it was not clear to which 'daddy' a four-year old was referring. He had a natural father and a step-father. He spent periods of time with both and called both 'daddy'. He was given the dolls in order to clarify what he was saying. Before he played with the dolls he insisted on rummaging through a bag of dolls' clothes until he found a vest. He dressed the adult male, referred to him as the 'daddy-with-the-vest-on', showed him mounting the boy doll and rhythmically simulating intercourse. The step-father always wore a vest or a vest-like T-shirt while the natural father did not do so. Although not conclusive evidence it gave a useful indication of the identity of the more likely abuser.

Despite being provided with the dolls, some children cannot demonstrate clearly exactly what has happened because they are very confused about their body. They are not sure which 'hole down below' was penetrated and they may be uncertain whether full intercourse or not took place. Abusers often cover their victims faces, engage in activities underneath bed clothes or in the dark or approach the child from behind. Confusion is not to be equated with lying.

### Other considerations

Other toys may be used depending on the age of the children.

Black children should not be presented with nothing but all white figures. It is more appropriate to have a range of figures, dolls and pictures representing black, Asian and white people and some with disabilities. Similarly, all children should be presented with toys suitable for both genders rather than the interviewers selecting what they believe are gender appropriate toys, such as cars for boys and dolls for girls.

Throughout the interview the workers should be sensitive to the victims' needs and should use age-appropriate methods. A small child for example will not want to sit upright at a full-sized table but may wish to sit on the floor preferably on floor cushions. The interviewers should be prepared to descend to the floor too.

Ideally, the investigating agencies should give some thought to the gender of the interviewers. A girl who has been abused by a man or even several men should not be ensconced in a room with two men, albeit professional ones, and be expected to dwell upon sexual matters. On the other hand teenage boys generally and younger ones from some traditions and cultures would find it difficult or even impossible to talk to women about intimate sexual matters.

The adoption of video interviews for evidential purposes has resulted in increased anxiety for the interviewers. In addition, facilities, training and experience are patchy.

Some colleagues have reported feeling unduly constrained and believe that they have a 'one-off' chance to obtain a disclosure which inevitably puts them under pressure. The *1992 Memorandum* states:

> *In no circumstances should a supplementary interview for evidential purposes be conducted by members of joint investigation teams unless they are fully satisfied, in consultation as necessary with the Crown Prosecution Service, that a supplementary interview is needed (p.23).*

and:

> *It may be important to be able to demonstrate that the child was not prompted or coached between interviews. It will be difficult to keep a proper record if the interview is spread over more than one day, and it is therefore strongly recommended that interviews are conducted on one day if at all possible (p.12).*

The intention behind these recommendations are laudable. The idea is to avoid subjecting children to repeated interviews and to ensure that the evidence that they give is seen to be uncontaminated. But my experience of children's revelations about the abuse is that it is a messy business with the youngsters giving additional information over time as they remember more details or feel increasingly secure. The more traumatic and long standing their experiences, and therefore possibly the more serious the crime against them, the less able they are to give an immediate coherent account. They are much more likely to disclose gradually over months or even years. This is also reflected in American research which showed children tending to make vague disclosures at first but becoming more specific later 'disclosure is a continuous process...some aspects of abuse may not be revealed until months into therapy' (Gonzalez et al. 1993).

The need to obtain video evidence is also influencing investigators' attitudes to the role played by non-investigative lay or professional people acting as a child's supporter, which may be less welcoming than before. The *1992 Memorandum of Good Practice* states:

> *Limiting the number of people present at the interview should lessen the possibility of the child feeling overwhelmed by the situation and uncomfortable about revealing information...* *However, such considerations may be outweighed by the benefit of having a supportive accompanying adult available to comfort and reassure a very young or distressed child, particularly if the child requests it. In such cases the accompanying adult will need to be clear that he or she must take no part in the interview (Home Office 1992 p.13).*

### After the interview

You may have witnessed the interview either because the child wanted you to stay in the room and you were able to do so or because you were able to watch through a one way screen or by a video link. If you have done so then, after the interview, you can praise the child for the way he or she coped.

Also after the interview you may be in a position to reinforce messages which indicate that the victim is not to blame, has nothing to be ashamed of and is not responsible for any of the consequences. You may also be able to remind the child involved that they are not the only ones to have been sexually abused. Again, children may need physical comfort and a demonstration that they are not 'untouchable' – although any such comforting has to be undertaken with great sensitivity. It has to be remembered that some sexually abused children can misinterpret any attempts by an adult to make physical contact.

Sometimes children want to talk about the interview immediately afterwards; sometimes they need a period of recovery and reflection but then later wish to talk through how they felt. Be prepared to listen whenever the youngster wants to talk about the it.

If you believe the interview was mishandled then you may be able to rectify matters by contradicting the messages given by clumsy interviewers. For example, if the questions asked implied that the child was to blame, you may be able give the reassurance that the victim is never to blame. If the interviewers gave the child no chance to express feelings then you can help him let off steam, perhaps with the question 'How are you feeling now?' 'How was the interview for you, you looked a bit upset at times?'

It might also be worth taking up issues of concern with the interviewers and their managers, preferably informally to give the workers the opportunity to explain their actions and you the chance to share your perspective. It may at times be necessary to resort to the official complaints procedures. Bad practice will only be improved if objections are raised.

MEDICAL EXAMINATIONS

In many, although not all instances where children are thought to have been sexually abused they will be medically examined. If you have a close relationship with the victim it may well be helpful if you stay for part or all of the examination, although this should be with the agreement both of the child and the examining professionals.

The examinations can be very upsetting and adult survivors who were medically examined as children frequently say that they felt that they were being re-abused during an intimate examination.

### *Environment and the child's comfort*

There are a number of measures which can be taken nowadays to minimise children's distress. Every effort should be made to ensure that they are made to feel relaxed and comfortable. They should be told what is to happen and why, in a way they can understand and in as reassuring a manner as possible.

There is usually no need for children to be stripped and stand around naked or nearly so. If the children have to take all their clothes off they should be covered with sheets or a gown and only the part of their body being examined should be uncovered.

The examination should take place in a private, warm, comfortable setting and not in a police station unless it has a special suite for the purpose. Unfortunately, sometimes there are no proper local facilities or insensitivity abounds. It was not so long ago that I accompanied a 12-year-old girl who had made allegations against her step-father. She had also managed to smuggle out of the house a photograph of her step-father touching her sexually. She was sensitively interviewed in my presence by a specialist police woman. She was then taken to the local police station and left in a bare interview room with nothing but a chair and an examination couch. A young police women told her to take all her clothes off and then left. There was neither gown nor screen available.

It is preferable for an examination of a girl to be undertaken by a female doctor particularly in cases where the original abuser was male. Generally, there are too few female doctors for this to happen in every case. However there is no harm in making a fairly forceful request for the child to be seen by a female doctor if you feel that this would be in the child's interest especially if also requested by the girl. It is essential for the investigating agencies to consider the gender of the examining doctor when dealing with children and young people whose culture and religion are particularly averse to intimate examinations by members of the opposite sex.

### *Consent to the examination*

In many countries and certainly in Britain under the Children Act 1989 children and young people have the right to refuse a medical examination. Older children have to consent to the examination and that consent should be 'informed', which means that they should understand to what they are agreeing and are aware of any possible consequences. They should also agree freely, that is they should not be pressured or coerced. Consent can be given orally or in writing. In most cases parental consent is required if the child is too young to give it. There are instances where a small child is deemed to be in need of the examination but the parents refuse. In these cases the doctors and social workers have to decide whether or not to institute legal steps to ensure that the examination is undertaken.

There are many very good reasons for having a medical examination which should be explained to any child old enough to comprehend the issues and to parents of abused children. Attempts should be made to allay – but not to ignore – a reluctant child's fears. This should not however amount to coercion.

If you are the victim's parent then again you would be well advised to allow a medical examination providing that the investigating professionals feel it is necessary and providing that it is being carried out in a manner sensitive to your child's feelings and needs.

### *Reasons for a medical examination*

One reason for an examination is to check whether the victims' allegations are supported by physical signs. Children subjected to frequent and/or recent vaginal or anal penetration may well have some of the medical signs already mentioned such as a red clitoris with a torn hymen or anal dilation with bruising, swelling and fissures of the anal margin. These findings can indicate that the child has been abused but may not identify the abuser. In a few cases where the abuse has been very recent, findings such as semen on a little girl can give a strong indication of the identity of the perpetrator.

A medical check can ensure that there is no internal damage in cases where there was penetration by the abuser. Even when there was no penetration, both girls and boys may welcome the message that no harm has been done. Adolescent girls may benefit from the assurance that they are not pregnant. If they are found to be pregnant they will then need to be told in order to make decisions about the expected baby. In these cases they will need very sensitive counselling and help.

Some younger girls may believe that they can be made pregnant by non-penetrative activities so they too may need the reassurance that they are not going to have a baby.

In some cases, injuries or sexually transmitted diseases requiring treatment are found through the medical examination and can then be treated.

A general examination can also reveal signs of physical abuse or neglect. In a number of cases, children are subjected to multiple abuse at the hands of their carers. In other cases, children who are physically abused and/or neglected are vulnerable to paedophiles who will offer friendship to lonely, miserable children in return for sexual favours.

Sometimes children's general condition may need to be checked if they are to be taken into care. A general examination will protect the parents or original carers in the event of a child being injured in the substitute home and, conversely, substitute carers will be protected from accusations of abuse if any injuries are discovered before the placement starts.

### *The examination itself*

At the beginning of an examination the doctor will probably want to obtain some background information. He or she will then give the child a general examination, followed, if necessary by a check of the genitalia. In some cases swabs will be taken. The doctor may need to insert a finger or an instrument called a speculum. Photographs of any injuries or medical abnormalities may be taken.

The child should be relaxed and not have to be held down screaming. Small children can often be examined on a parent's or trusted adult's knee. Children should be told what is happening and as far as possible be allowed to help. They may for example be able to take their own swabs (Bamford and Roberts 1989). As far as possible they should feel in control of events.

Occasionally children are examined under general anaesthetic. This is usually only in the case of children with internal damage who may have to be seen by several different specialist doctors – police surgeons, paediatricians and gynaecologists.

### Who undertakes the examination?

Although an initial or general medical examination may be undertaken by a community medical officer, school or family doctor, police surgeons will usually undertake the more intimate medical examinations. These are general practitioners who undertake special training in order to examine people against whom a crime has been committed. They build up an expertise in the sort of injuries associated with assaults and other crimes. They are also experienced in collecting medical evidence which is helpful to the police in their investigations and they know how to present that evidence in court.

Paediatricians are doctors who specialise in injuries, illnesses and medical conditions in children. They are normally based in hospitals. They will probably be asked to see children whose injuries are such that they require treatment.

Gynaecologists specialise in examining and treating female patients who have problems relating to their reproductive system. They will therefore become involved in cases where a girl may have suffered damage to her reproductive organs and is likely to need specialised treatment.

## *Final comment on medical examinations*

A major inquiry into the management of child sexual abuse cases held in Cleveland, England in 1987 recommended that 'Children should not be subjected to repeated medical examinations solely for evidential purposes' (Butler-Sloss 1988 p.245).

Some children have to be seen by several doctors because they are found to have a medical condition, damage or disease which has to be looked at by several different specialists. However, children should not be examined repeatedly solely because, in the event of legal proceedings, a host of solicitors representing different parties each wants to find a doctor who will support their client's story.

A final point is that the child or young person should be told the outcome of the medical examination in a way that they can understand. Fear of the unknown is the worst of all fears and if children are medically investigated they may think that there is something dreadfully wrong. Not only should the reasons for the examination be explained carefully beforehand but they must be told the results. In all the turmoil of the investigation the professionals closely involved are sometimes so busy communicating with each other and the parents, that the youngster is left in an anxious state of unknowing.

Again if you are close to the child and have been present during the examination you may be the best person to explain the outcome although this would only be undertaken in consultation with the medical staff involved.

### OTHER CHILDREN

Some perpetrators may abuse and re-abuse one readily available child. But after a while they realise that their 'target' child is beginning to resist or grow out of their preferred age range, so they begin to groom and abuse a new child. Other perpetrators find that they can best satisfy their needs by having several children in their power and will abuse whichever one is most available. Some gain particular gratification from sexual 'games' which are best enjoyed simultaneously with a number of children. Whatever the perpetrators' predilections, they will have abused, or be abusing more than one victim.

It may be that there are no other children being abused by a particular offender at the time of disclosure. For example, a father may be abusing his youngest daughter. His other victims may be his older daughters and his own sister, all of whom are now adult. However, such cases are probably in the minority and part of the investigation has to be the search for the perpetrator's other child victims.

Here it is worth clarifying that the distress and pain of adult former victims should not be ignored. You may be in a position to help any adults whose abuse has come to light because of a child's disclosure. However, the investigators will have to focus most of their attention on potential child victims rather than adult former victims because, in many areas, investigating and child protection agencies have a prime responsibility for children. They invariably have to function with inadequate resources and have little to spare for any adult survivors.

The investigators will probably want to interview all other children whom they feel might have been molested. In cases of abuse by a family member they will need to see all children in the household. The investigators might also request that these children be medically examined if they feel that there is a likelihood that they are or have been victims.

This can be very distressing for parents, particularly if they feel that younger children should not be told about disturbing events. However, not to share information with other youngsters in the family is a grave mistake. Children invariably know that something is amiss and the truth is always easier to cope with in the long run than are lies, secrets and being kept in the dark

### Viv's story

In the early days of my work I met a young parent who was physically abusive to her own children. She was evidently full of anger and mistrust. My colleagues and I worked with this woman whom we will call 'Viv'. We gradually learnt about her childhood.

Viv was the middle child of five. Her mother died when she was about nine and her eldest sister twelve. For three years her widowed father looked after his large family well. Suddenly all the children were taken into care. The explanation given was that their father could not cope with them.

Viv, who was by now 12, was angry and perplexed. It had been obvious to her that not only Viv herself but also all her brothers and sisters were well-clothed and fed and their house was always clean. Neighbours and family friends used to say how well her father cared for them all. She sensed that the adults around her were not telling her the truth. She felt resentful, distrusting and betrayed.

Viv also experienced a huge burden of guilt because she felt in some ways she must have done something wrong. She constantly told herself that the family would not have come into care if she had done more to help her father, if she had never been naughty, if she had looked after the younger children better, if, if...

As an adult she learnt that the real reason for her removal into care was her father's sexual abuse of her eldest sister. This revelation added to her anger as it confirmed her suspicion that the adults who were supposed to be interested in her welfare had lied to her. However, she was relieved to know the truth at last and to know that she had not done anything wrong.

Viv should have been told the truth as a child. She could have been told in ways which she could understand and she should have been helped to come to terms with her loss and distress at the time. Of course it would have been painful but no more painful than being taken into care and being left with such a burden of mistrust, guilt and anger.

Where the abuser is not a family member, other children may still have to be interviewed and medically examined. Recalling the case of Lisa, after she disclosed, other children at the English teacher's school had come forward to say that he had molested them. One pupil had already been expelled for making 'false' allegations when she had told the headmaster that this teacher had raped her. Eventually the weight of evidence from several young people became overwhelming and he was found guilty on a number of counts and sent to prison for a substantial period.

Whatever the case, it is worth repeating that children must be given the truth in terms they can understand. They must be told who is interviewing them and why, and if they have to be medically examined they have to be told why. If they are not given the truth they will inevitably imagine that they have done something wrong or that there is something wrong with them. After any medical examination they should be informed of the outcome.

It is worth adding that while children must be told the truth, they do not need to be made aware of all the brutal facts. If for example a teenage boy rapes his sister, younger siblings can simply be told: 'Jimmy did something very rude to your sister, something that she did not want him to do. Perhaps he did something to you that you did not like.'

The follow up to this will depend on the children's reaction as well as their age and understanding. The given explanation might be enough but, in other cases, children may need to be provided with additional details. 'Jimmy hurt your sister and we have to make sure that he has not hurt you.' The younger children, however, do not need to be told explicitly that the sister had been raped at this initial stage. Nevertheless, as they grow into adolescence they may need to know the exact details. If subsequently they ask, they should be answered truthfully but sensitively.

Finally if you have any doubts about sharing what has happened with other children who could possibly be directly or indirectly affected, remember that child sexual abuse thrives on secrecy and on 'not telling'. A secret shared is a danger halved.

### OTHER ADULTS

The investigators will also wish to interview the victim's parents. Exactly when and how this happens will depend on whether or not the parents are suspected of abusing the children. In cases of non-family abuse, the parents will probably be closely involved in the process.

In the case of family abuse the investigators will have to balance the rights of the parents with the need to gain evidence. There may be evidence in the victims' house such as photographs, 'sexy' clothes worn by the children or home videos showing explicitly abusive acts. If the parents are alerted to the suspicions of the investigators they may have time to destroy evidence or intimidate the children before the investigators can pursue the allegations.

The alleged perpetrators, whether family members or not, will be interviewed as soon as possible. Many perpetrators are very articulate and plausible. Often they will have planned for the possibility of the victim disclosing and will have a well-rehearsed story to convince everybody of their innocence. On the other hand, a number of offenders will be glad to have been caught and will want to 'confess all'.

In some instances the police will have to interview a number of innocent people in order to exclude them from their inquiries. In the case, for example, of attack by a stranger, where the victim was able to give a reasonable description or where witnesses saw a person acting suspiciously, the police may have to interview all people of a particular appearance driving a certain type of car in the vicinity of the attack.

When interviewing non-abusing parents, the investigators will assess how far the parents can be relied upon to protect the child from further abuse and how far, if at all, they contributed to the abuse. In some cases, such as that of Lisa, the parents are deemed to be the victim's main supports and protectors. In other cases apparently non-abusing parents are seen to have added to their child's vulnerability by perhaps showing so little affection that the child has sought this from the perpetrator.

The investigators will wish to interview any other adults to whom the child disclosed. They will want to find out exactly how the victim behaved. If you picked up signs and symptoms of abuse, the investigators will want to add these to the general picture that they are trying to build up of what has happened to the child and what effect this has had. Finally former victims of the abuser, who are now adults, may also be interviewed.

### COMMUNICATION AND CONSULTATION

In the past, and even in the present day, children have been reabused because the various agencies and people involved have not shared information and concerns. Good communication and consultation are essential parts of ensuring the well-being of vulnerable youngsters. Throughout and after the investigation, the various leading workers should be communicating with the children, the family and with their volunteer and professional colleagues.

As well as interviewing key witnesses, the investigators will need to gain additional written and verbal information in order to build up a precise picture of what has happened. They will also have to notify other professionals and interested parties so that they can respond appropriately. Often this communication will be informal, by telephone, verbal exchange or letter.

On other occasions the communication will be more formal through official letters, court orders and other relevant documents. One of the conventional methods in Britain is through the case conference which will usually be called if the abuse occurred within the family. They are rarely held when the perpetrator is neither a family member nor part of the household and the parents can provide appropriate protection. But the procedures vary from area to area.

## Case conferences

Once the investigators have collected as much information as possible from key witnesses they will ask for a case conference to be held.

If you are a professional, such as a teacher or health visitor, then you are likely to be asked to attend the case conference. The presence of volunteers such as Homestart workers might be requested but they do not usually have a right to attend. If you are a parent you may be invited to the conference although this depends on local policy and other circumstance. More distant relatives and friends are not usually permitted to be present.

The victims themselves are often excluded and may not wish to attend if the parent abusers are participants.

The fact that abusive parents may be in attendance while the victims are prohibited from taking part can often skew the discussion in favour of the adults. The perpetrators are able to exercise their power and elicit sympathy for themselves. The theory is that the social workers, class teachers and others in touch with the victim can represent them. If you are in this position then it is important to advocate for the children concerned. Be prepared to challenge anyone who tries blaming the victim or uses phrases such as 'she is a very sexually provocative little girl'.

It is an intimidating experience if you are not used to attending case conferences. Often there is an 'in crowd' of professional specialists who all know each other. Should you arrive early you are likely to have a courteous and helpful greeting by reception staff. But then, if your luck runs out, you could find yourself conducted to the conference room where you are left waiting in silence, feeling ignored and slightly intimidated by other conference members who are chatting to each other about assorted mutual concerns and are obviously confident and at ease. On the other hand, if you arrive late, you are likely to feel even more uncomfortable as inquiring or hostile eyes are turned in your direction.

No two case conferences are alike and much depends on the skill of the chairperson who is likely to be a senior representative of the social services department. After the introductions, people are invited to give information in roughly chronologically order. You have been invited because you have something important to contribute. Wait until asked by the chair to contribute but, if after everyone else had had their say, you have been given no opportunity then you must attract the attention of the chairperson before the conference moves from an information sharing stage to general discussion and formulation of recommendations.

In order to decrease the embarrassment factor, ensure that you are well organised. If you are taking along a large file make sure you can gain access to the information you need quickly. There is nothing more likely to lead to mortification than to have your papers fall out all over the floor leaving you to grovel at everyone's feet as you try to pick them all up quickly. Almost as humiliating is to find everyone else staring at you in an interminable silence while you thumb backwards and forwards through your file desperately trying to find that all important letter or remarkably pertinent extract from a report.

The early part of most case conferences is usually quite formal. Once all the information has been shared then a general discussion about the implications is often slightly less formal with contributors exchanging views without constantly doing so through the chairperson. Having said that, in some areas the conference will remain formal throughout. You will need to follow the lead given by the chair and other participants. Towards the end, the chairperson will summarise the findings and discussion and identify the recommendations. These form the basis of a plan for the future management of the case and should identify who does what and when.

If you have never or have rarely attended a case conference before, the following check list might be helpful:

Do NOT

- arrive late but, if you do, just apologise briefly and settle down as quickly and quietly as possible.
- interrupt other people; only do so if you have to correct an important factual mistake such as a child's age.
- make sweeping generalisations or judgemental statements such as 'She's such an awful mother'.
- include irrelevant material and keep wandering from the point.
- include rumours and scandals unless they are really essential.
- talk about other cases.
- feel so overwhelmed or intimidated that by the end of the conference you have made no contribution.

Do

- prepare beforehand the information you are likely to be asked to contribute – you may be required to submit a formal report.
- sort out your written records.
- arrive on time.
- introduce yourself clearly when asked to do so.
- listen carefully to the chairperson and other contributors.
- wait until it is your turn to contribute.
- ensure that you give your information before the general discussion stage.
- speak very clearly and audibly.
- avoid jargon and briefly explain any technical terms or unusual acronyms.

If you are not asked to attend but have a point of view which you wish to express then you should write a letter to be read to the conference. Similarly if the children have an opinion which everyone is ignoring you could encourage them to write a letter or record their views on a tape to be presented to the case conference.

### Child protection registers

The case conference is designed to pool information and come to some important decisions such as which roles the various professionals should take. It will also make recommendations about legal action and about placing a child's name on a Child Protection Register.

Many parents will be distressed to find their child's name on a register, but it should be remembered that this is often the best way in which resources to help the child can be released. It does not necessarily mean that the parents have failed or done something wrong. Instead it means that a child is recognised to have special requirements. The name should be removed from the register once the child or young person no longer requires intervention or resources.

## Core groups

During the conference a core group of professionals will be identified. They will be in a position to help the child and monitor his or her welfare. The individuals in the group are responsible for the broad management of the case in the future.

The group will meet regularly and in most cases the parents are seen to be working in partnership with the rest of the group. This means that they are usually invited to the group deliberations. The children are sometimes permitted to be present. The meetings are still official and should be chaired and minuted but have a less formal ambience than the case conference. If the core group run into difficulties or if there are significant new developments a full case conference may be convened again.

Again it has to be stated that if a child has been sexually abused by a stranger or a non-family member then a case conference, registration and core group may not be felt to be necessary. This will depend on local policy and the exact circumstances of the case.

# Seven

# Keeping children safe

There are a number of different ways in which children can be kept as safe as possible. The first priority is to separate any child who is known or believed to have been abused from the source of danger. Then the immediate separation must become a long term arrangement. To ensure protection in these situations legal means often have to be used. Victims also need to know how they can make a contribution to protecting themselves from being reabused in the future. Other children and young people, associated with the abused child, who could become substitute targets must also be kept safe.

Finally, because primary prevention is better than cure, this section looks at ways in which children can be helped to reduce their vulnerability and helplessness and so contribute to their own protection.

### SEPARATION FROM THE SOURCE OF DANGER

The immediate concern of the investigating agencies will be to ensure the children's safety. Having identified the probable perpetrator they will then have to ensure that this person is not in a position to intimidate or re-abuse the children. Sometimes the investigators have to err on the side of caution and an innocent adult might find him or herself under suspicion. This is particularly true in cases where a young child is the victim with clear medical signs but without the ability to identify the abuser. In these cases the finger of suspicion is often pointed at fathers and other male caregivers.

## Under suspicion

If you or your partner are wrongly suspected it is important to try to remember that the investigators have to be over, rather than under, cautious. If you live in the household of the victim it may be in the child's interest for whichever of you is the suspect to leave the household until the investigators are satisfied that the child has not been molested by either of you.

You will feel angry, indignant and distressed not to mention fearful. But try to remain calm and understand the investigators' dilemma. They must be able to guarantee the child's safety. If a suspected perpetrator refuses to leave the house then in most cases the investigators have no option but to remove the victim and any other children in the household from the potential source of danger.

## Removing the perpetrator

Occasionally the perpetrator is removed by being arrested. There may be sufficient evidence to keep the offender in custody or have bail conditions which ensure that he or she remains out of the household. However in most cases there is little that can be done if the perpetrator is determined to remain in the home and the non-abusing parent allows this to happen.

In one case, typical of many, a man was convicted of sexual assault against his step-daughter and put on probation with the condition that he lived away from home. He rented a flat and moved all his possessions into it. However he continued to visit the family home and stayed not only overnight but for as long as he liked. His wife maintained that the visits were mere fleeting ones. His step-daughter became increasingly fearful and distressed and we eventually had no option but to accede to her request and remove her from her family home.

## Removing the children

Although the ideal is for the wrong-doer to leave, experiences like the one just described often compel protective agencies to remove the children, especially in the early stages of the investigation when victims can be intimidated and forced to retract.

When the abuser is living in the home, it may be decided that all or most of the other children in the household have to be removed as well. This is because they could already be victims but have not been able to disclose and might now be coerced into total silence. On the other hand if they have not been abused then they are at risk of becoming new targets after the original victim has been taken out of the home.

In England and Wales statutory removal was usually effected by means of the controversial place of safety order until the introduction under the 1989 Children Act of emergency protection orders. The place of safety orders which allowed a child to be taken or to remain in a safe place could be granted by a magistrate for up to 28 days and the parents had no right of appeal for the duration of the order. They were criticised in the Cleveland Inquiry Report 'For a number of reasons the place of safety order does not sufficiently meet the needs of the child at risk' (Butler-Sloss 1988 p.228) Emergency protection orders are only granted for eight days although they can be renewed for a further seven days. There is a right of appeal after 72 hours.

Many victims feel they are being punished by being sent away. The perpetrator could well have used the threat 'If you tell anyone you will be sent to a home'. Sylvia Fraser's father tried to intimidate her by warning 'I'll send you to the place where all bad children go. An orphanage where they lock up bad children whose parents don't want them any more' (Fraser 1987 p.11). The fact that the perpetrator's dire warnings come true only serves to increase the power and infallibility of the abuser in the victim's eyes. The child might feel 'If he is right about my being sent away, maybe he will also be right about all the other things he said – my kitten would die, I'd make mum ill, everyone would hate me'.

The other children in the family sometimes blame the victim if they have to be removed from home. If victims themselves, they may have chosen not to tell because they prefer the security that even an abusive home represents. If they were not mistreated nor witnessed anything untoward they are likely to resent and disbelieve the victim who can become an outcast, sensing that whatever love and warmth there was at home has now been lost.

### Staying at home with safeguards
In some cases it is fondly believed that the source of danger can be eliminated by controlling the abuser's behaviour without

removing either child or perpetrator. Both remain at home but safeguards are instituted. This is often thought to be the best solution. The perpetrator is happy to accept the safeguards and it avoids the trauma of the children being removed. However, the more we learn about the power, persistence and deviousness of perpetrators the more we have begun to realise that this is rarely a satisfactory option.

The safeguards often impose an unacceptable burden on the youngsters involved. They are not about the controlling of the perpetrator's behaviour but that of the children. Conditions have included:

* the children having to wear dressing-gowns over their night clothes except when they were actually in bed – this condition, incidentally, was imposed just before the summer weather developed into a soaring heat wave;
* teenage girls not being allowed to wear short skirts or tight clothes in their own homes;
* children or young people having to lock their bedrooms at night;
* the mother having to chaperon the children constantly;
* a daughter only being allowed to take a bath when the father was out of the house.

Often these conditions are laid down in a formal written contract, the offender agreeing not to abuse as long as the conditions are kept. This gives the offender a truly wonderful opportunity. If the children or non-abusing parent, weary of being so restricted, deliberately or even inadvertently 'break one of the rules' the perpetrator will seize the opportunity to abuse the child and then cast the blame on the victim or non-abusing parent. The offender is also likely to manipulate the situation so that the conditions are broken by the children.

Perpetrators left at home may also use particularly subtle means of punishing children for telling and may force them to retract. We have to remember that sex abusers are adept at knowing how children think and feel and can manipulate youngsters' deepest emotions.

In some cases the family is able to make satisfactory arrangements to protect the children at least in the short term. For example, if an elder teenage brother is the perpetrator the parents may arrange for him to stay with grandparents who live some distance away.

When a family member is not involved, the child can usually stay at home and be given protection and comfort by the parents. The exceptions would be where:

• the perpetrator, though not a family member, was a part of the household and could not be forced to leave;
• the parents were inflicting other forms of abuse on the child;
• the parents were fully aware of the abuse and were allowing it to happen by, for example, prostituting the child for financial gain.

SUBSEQUENT LEGAL ACTION

## Criminal proceedings

One of the main concerns of the investigating agencies will be to catch the abuser and curtail his or her activities. There are some cases such as children abusing children, an adult perpetrator with diminished responsibility or an elderly person suffering from senile dementia where the police feel it would not be in the public interest to pursue a prosecution and so the criminal legal processes are halted.

In some cases the authorities know that a child or young person has been abused from the child's behaviour and medical condition but the identity of the perpetrator is not known. This is especially true in the case of young children with limited verbal skills or older ones who have a disability which prevents them from communicating details of the abuse. Again the criminal legal processes may not be worth pursuing.

In the majority of cases, the investigating agencies believe that they know who the perpetrator is but there is insufficient evidence to secure a conviction. In criminal proceedings a person is presumed innocent until found guilty and the burden of proof is on the prosecutors. Guilt has to be 'beyond reasonable doubt'.

This can cause some confusion because a family court may grant an order to protect a child on the grounds that it has been demonstrated that the youngster has been abused. However in civil proceedings and family courts the case is judged on the 'balance of probabilities'. The focus is on the welfare of the child and if it seems more likely than not that he or she has been mistreated then the court can agree to legal sanctions to protect the child. Furthermore in the family courts it is sometimes not essential to establish exactly who harmed the victim.

In contrast, in criminal proceedings it is imperative to identify exactly and beyond reasonable doubt who is guilty of the offence, because the primary objective is not the protection and welfare of the victim but the future, in terms of treatment, punishment or control of the offender.

This often leads to a paradoxical situation where a case of abuse against a child is 'successfully' proved in a civil court but is not proved in the criminal court. Usually the proof needed to secure a conviction is inadequate.

The reason for this is because sexual abuse is something which occurs in secret. Usually the only witnesses are the victim and the perpetrator. The victim is usually a young child and the perpetrator an adult male. The law's attitude to women and children is generally to regard them as unreliable witnesses on sexual matters.

*Problems for child witnesses*

The roots of the problem are to be found in the general domination of men in most of the world's cultures. Basically laws world-wide are made by men in order to protect men, particularly in sexual matters. In Pakistan for example if a female child or woman complains of rape, she may be charged with adultery. In 1994 for example, two sisters aged 8 and 14 were awaiting trial charged with 'zina' or adultery with their father. If found guilty they face a minimum of 10 years in prison and 30 lashes (Evans 1994, Goodwin 1994).

In her truly brilliant expose of the British judicial system and its discrimination against women Helena Kennedy paints a colourful but all too accurate picture of what is happening in courts:

> *In the handling of sexual abuse cases, social workers, predominantly female, are accused of hysteria, lack of professionalism and distortion of evidence... We want our rapists, wife batterers and child abusers to have mean mouths and eyebrows that meet. If the men in the dock do not conform*

*sufficiently to the stereotype of the deviant...they are more able to*
*resist allegations. (1992 p.99)*

Sigmund Freud also helped to feed the view that children and women are unreliable witnesses. At the end of the nineteenth century he was treating people, especially young women, suffering from the medical condition 'hysteria'. The assumption was that this was caused by long forgotten psychological trauma. The treatment was to use psychoanalysis to recall the trauma, thereby ensuring that it was no longer repressed. Time and again Freud's female patients recalled being sexually abused by their fathers or other male relatives.

Freud and more importantly the medical establishment of the time could not accept evidence of such widespread incest and sexual abuse – rather as today we cannot accept the evidence of widespread anal abuse discovered in Leeds and Cleveland by Doctors Hobbs, Wynne, Higgs and Wyatt nor the increasing evidence of ritual abuse. Freud at first believed what he heard but later felt impelled to build a theory that young children fantasised about having sex with their parents. Any little girl, the theory implies, who accuses her father of incest is really just making it up, since all little girls dream of having sex with their fathers. In the cool light of day this seems the most extraordinary theory for which there is scant evidence and yet it was welcomed as a way of explaining an unpalatable truth.

This has left us with a legacy of scepticism when children accuse adults of sexual abuse. It is far less painful to believe that a child is simply making things up, and so we have colluded with the theories that children fantasise. Nowadays when children or adults recall abuse, many of us can comfort ourselves with the concept of the 'False Memory Syndrome'. Proponents of this claim that therapists plant spurious memories into the minds of their clients. The courts, inherently conservative, male-dominated institutions, are some of the last places likely to abandon such comforting theories.

Generally courts are unfriendly places to children. They are not designed with the youngest citizens in mind. There is nowhere for them to wait comfortably until being called. Often they have to face their abusers in court and may well encounter them while waiting to be called. Cross-examination is designed to test a witness but is frequently used to undermine children's confidence which, especially in an abused child, is so very fragile and so very easily undermined.

Children are expected to give a clear, consistent account of distressing events which touch the deepest, most painful emotions. Many children are abused more than once and events naturally become confused. They do not have the same command of language as do barristers. In the witness box they must stand alone and exposed in a world which is intimidating and alien for most adults and is all the more so for children.

It is hardly surprising that most children break down in the witness box however competently and clearly they may have explained events to the police and social workers. This is why state prosecutors and parents alike are unwilling to expose children to the additional trauma of appearing as witnesses in sexual abuse cases.

In a number of countries attempts have been made to make the court a little more friendly to children. In some instances the child need not give a full account directly to the court; instead the original investigative interview is recorded on video and the tape used in court. However the children still have to be available for cross-examination, which means being questioned about what they said on the video recording.

In England and Wales, at the judge's discretion, life can be made easier for children. He or she can make the court less formal by agreeing to the removal of wigs and gowns. In some cases young children have sat on the judge's lap or in a chair close-by. A supporter can be allowed to sit or stand with the child. To reduce the number of strangers the court can be cleared of the public and press, although this can present problems. In one case recently a colleague told me that when the court was cleared the mother who throughout the investigation had believed and given support to her daughter had to leave the courtroom along with every one else.

In some instances, again at the judge's discretion, witnesses can be screened from the defendant. Some Crown Courts also have a video link so that the child can sit in a room near the courtroom and speak to the judge and lawyers through a television screen. This means that the young witness does not have to stand in open court and cannot see the abuser. Not all Crown Courts have a link but it is possible to move a case to a court with one. If a child is to be a witness there should be discussions with the Crown Prosecution Service to identify what provision can be made to make the ordeal for the child more comfortable.

There is however another obstacle in the way of children appearing as witnesses. Adults are able to rehearse their evidence and refresh their memories before giving evidence. Generally children are prevented from doing so because defence lawyers will maintain that they have been 'coached'. The argument is that children are more suggestible than adults and a parent or social worker can subtly persuade a child to make evidence against an abuser sound more convincing. In fact there is absolutely no evidence to support this view but it has been used to good effect by defence lawyers.

### Other evidence

Not only can the victims rarely be used as witnesses because they are too young, distressed, intimidated or confused but in recent years all the other corroborative evidence has been challenged. The Cleveland controversy in Britain in 1987 revolved round the soundness or otherwise of medical evidence. This has forced doctors to be circumspect when giving an opinion in sexual abuse cases and has led courts to view medical evidence with suspicion.

Confessions by defendants are also regarded as unreliable in view of a number of notable apparent miscarriages of justice in Britain (mostly relating to terrorist activities) in the 1980s.

Even if the perpetrator is convicted there is a strong chance, if male, that the sentence will be light because many male judges appear to be sympathetic to the excuses made by the perpetrators. Mitigating circumstances have included the fact that a wife was pregnant and so the only sexual outlet for the male offender was her 14-year-old daughter! Another judge expressed the view that an eminent paediatrician collecting child pornographic photographs was like someone collecting cigarette cards. Other judges have felt that the victim contributed to his or her own abuse by accepting a lift from a stranger or by wearing certain types of clothes.

### Giving evidence

It could be that one of your roles in protecting the victim is to act as a witness probably in a civil case but possibly in criminal proceedings. There are a few hardy souls who enjoy giving evidence, they enjoy the drama, being centre-stage and verbal duelling with cross-examining lawyers. But for most of us having to appear in a witness box is an ordeal. Going to the dentist holds no terror after having had to cope in court.

There are a few ideas which might help. There are ways of helping yourself long before you enter the witness box. Firstly you will probably have given some form of written statement or affidavit. It is important that you are careful about what you write. Be certain that you can justify each statement. Ensure it is truthful and factual rather than being a vague impression, an assumption or your opinion. For example, if you say a bedroom was untidy, that is your opinion. Instead you need to give factual details such as the piles of clothes on the floor and unwashed sheets strewn around the room.

You need to read through your statement and refresh your memory. Dress in neat, 'sober' but comfortable clothes. It is nowadays acceptable to wear traditional clothes such as the *kemise* and *shalwar* if that is your usual dress. You are however likely to be ejected in court if you turn up in a bikini or frayed jeans and designer stubble. It makes sense to create a favourable impression in court because you will be in a better position to act in the interests of the child. If possible try to familiarise yourself with the court. Visit it a few days beforehand and find out where the parking spaces, bus stop, toilets and refreshments are. On the day if in doubt ask an usher who is usually dressed in a black gown.

Once in the witness box affirm or take the oath as confidently as you can. You will be able to read it from a card. If you do not have a religious faith you will probably be most comfortable reading an affirmation. If you wish to take the oath but are not of the Jewish or Christian faith you need to contact the court beforehand because your own holy scriptures may not be immediately available. Similarly if you are sight or hearing impaired provision can be made if you give the court advance notice of your requirements. Generally, the usher will tell you what to do so there is no need to worry.

After the oath or affirmation turn towards the lawyer asking the questions then reply to the magistrates or judge. If necessary face the judge all the time. It is important not to answer questions while turned towards the lawyer. Speak slowly and loudly. You will notice that the judge or magistrates are trying to write down what you are saying so that it is important to give them time to catch up.

Your own solicitor or the barrister for the party which called you will ask you to clarify your written statement. You will then be cross-examined by the lawyers for the other parties. In some child care cases these have numbered nearly a dozen, but more usually it is two or three. Then your lawyer might ask you to clarify some points and the judge or magistrates could also ask you a few questions. Finally, your lawyer should obtain permission for you to 'stand down' or 'be released'. If you are released you can go completely but if you are only stood down then you should check before going because you may be recalled.

If the cross-examining lawyer starts to ask you difficult questions or makes personal attacks try to remain calm. Personal attacks indicate that the lawyer is losing his or her case and because your evidence cannot be demolished he or she is trying to discredit you instead. Do not get offended or angry, just smile to yourself because you know you are winning the exchange. If however the attacks are racist, sexist or in other way discriminatory do take the matter up with your own solicitor afterwards and, if appropriate, lodge a formal complaint.

### Civil proceedings
There are a number of ways in which the longer term security and welfare of children who have been victims of abuse can be secured through action in civil (non-criminal) courts.

### Protective court orders
Civil proceedings are often used by the social services to protect abused children. Emergency Protection Orders have already been discussed. In addition, the police have powers to protect children in emergencies. An Assessment Order may be used when there is no dire emergency but where the child may be suffering or is likely to suffer 'significant harm' and the necessary assessment cannot be made without an order.

Children could be placed with substitute carers either in a residential or foster home under a care order if they have been abused in the family and if the perpetrator remains in the household or non-abusing parents have shown that they are totally unable or unwilling to protect their offspring. A care order can last until the young person becomes an adult at 18 years but they are often discharged earlier.

Abused children can also be protected under the 1989 Children Act by Section 8 Orders which are a flexible package of orders such as a residence order which determines with whom a child should live. Additionally a child may be protected by a supervision order. Unfortunately courts have been all too ready to leave the perpetrator in the household with social workers trying to monitor the child's welfare under a supervision order. We now know that this is often unworkable because of the power and skill of child sex abusers especially where they are adult males in a father role to the child. The perpetrator will simply re-double his efforts to groom the child and ensure that his victim is unable to disclose again.

In some circumstances children can apply for an injunction to prevent the abuser from molesting them. In practice this is not used very much possibly because there is often a delay between the actual abuse and the child taking action and disclosing.

### Compensation and financial security

In Britain the victim of any crime can be awarded compensation by the Criminal Injuries Compensation Board which is a committee of eminent lawyers. The award is not dependant on the securing of a conviction. Instead the Board must be given proof that a crime has been committed and that, as a result, the victim has suffered damage.

It is important that non-abusing parents or guardians or social workers make claims on behalf of children or show older children how to make a claim within the time limit if they believe that they have suffered damage as a result of unlawful sexual abuse. There are steps being considered to make the time limit less of an obstacle for sex abuse victims.

If the abuser has been clearly identified and has assets a victim may obtain redress by way of damages under the law of torts. A conviction in the criminal court does not have to be obtained. Again parents or people responsible for an abused child are well advised to discuss this possible claim with a solicitor.

HELP FOR THE VICTIMS AFTER THE INVESTIGATION

There is a great temptation to 'leave well alone' after the investigation and allow the child to forget and get on with his or her life. However most abused children will not easily forget the abuse. In many ways they are like bereaved people who cannot simply forget that a loved one has died. They will be full of feelings which will not fade away just because no one talks about what happened.

There are a number of ways in which people coming into contact with sexually abused children can help. How far, will depend on a number of factors such as your relationship with the victims and their family, how well you knew them before disclosure and investigation, the role of other people helping and the children's age and developmental level.

## *Counselling*

The idea of counselling a sexually abused child sounds a rather daunting prospect which, some would argue, should be left to a specialist counsellor. However I use the term very broadly and define it as a process of exchange of information and views leading to a change in behaviour and/or opinions in the person being counselled. In the case of children, and indeed with adults, communication need not be restricted to an exchange of words. Children can make effective use of a wide range of objects, toys and materials in order to clarify what it is that they want to convey.

In some cases children will be referred to a specialist counsellor or therapist. However such resources are very scarce and can only be provided for a very small percentage of abused children. Even these children and young people may benefit from supplementary informal help.

Others will only have help that the concerned adults in their life are willing and able to give them. For some it has been a chance caring remark by a respected adult that plays the greatest part in healing a damaged and distressed young person, such as the remark by an older woman 'It isn't fair, why should it have happened to you?' which was such a significant help to Sarah, the victim for many years of abuse at the hands of her father. (Doyle 1990 p.117)

Abused children are also helped by hearing consistent messages not just from one person such as their mother or a

**Figure 4: Messages which can release a victim of child sexual abuse**

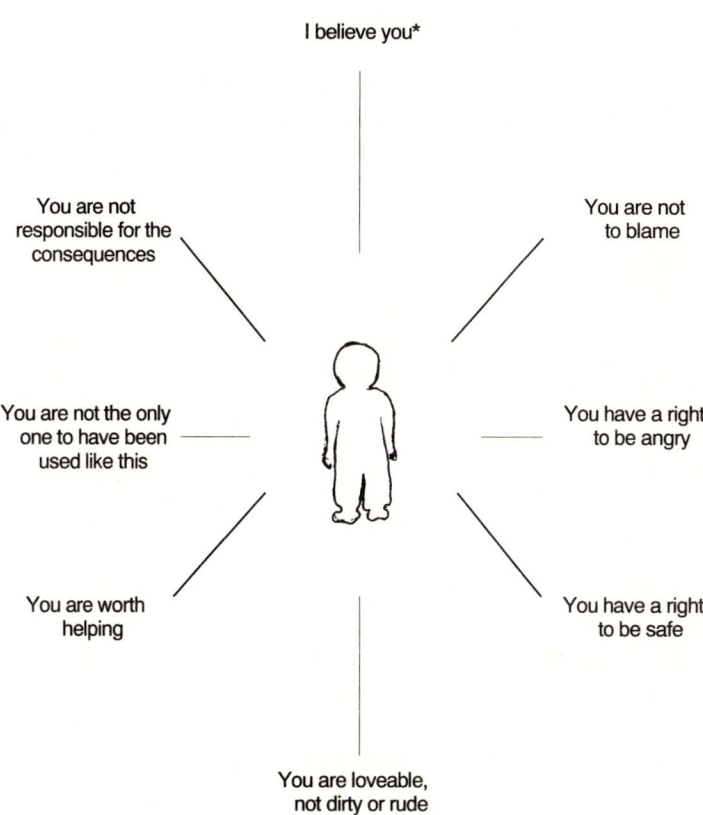

I believe you*

You are not
responsible for the
consequences

You are not
to blame

You are not the only
one to have been
used like this

You have a right
to be angry

You are worth
helping

You have a right
to be safe

You are loveable,
not dirty or rude

\*   The meaning of 'I believe you' is an acknowledgement that the child is telling you the truth from his or her perspective, even if the reality is slightly different. For example, if a youngster says of the abuser 'He didn't hurt me' when you know from her injuries that he must have done, the message is 'I believe you are sincere in what you are saying and I understand that is how it seems to you now.'

special counsellor but by as many people as possible. They need for example to be told they were not to blame by anybody and everybody who has a chance to say this to them. Figure 4. summarises the messages of healing that should be conveyed to all abused children.

---

### EXERCISE

You are wearing some new clothes. You are not sure if they really suit you. One friend comments 'You look very nice'. How would the comment make you feel.

My guess is that it would probably please you but not convince you that your new clothes looked really good – your friend may just be being kind or may have a rather idiosyncratic taste in clothes.

Now imagine several people – some very close to you such as your parents or partner, some friends, some casual acquaintances all make favourable comments about your new clothes.

My guess this time is that you would be well on the way to being convinced that the clothes really did look attractive on you.

---

In a similar, but more important way, abused children can be convinced that they are attractive people who do not need to feel guilty or ashamed, who have a right to feel angry and distressed and who are worth helping. They also need to know that they are not the only ones to be sexually abused. Children who have disclosed need to be told again and again that they did the right thing by telling and are not responsible for any of the consequences of their disclosure.

It may be that you can seize a chance opportunity. You might for example be a neighbour, relative, Homestart volunteer, family solicitor or health visitor. You are having a chat with the mother of a 5-year-old girl molested by a local paedophile. The girl happens to be playing in the same room. The mother comments 'I'm glad that pervert was sent to prison'. You can respond with words to the effect of 'He deserved it. It was his fault. The children were not to blame, they were too little'. You are aware that the little girl has stopped playing and is listening so you can turn to the child 'He was a naughty man wasn't he?' He has been naughty to a lot of children, all as nice as you are'.

At other times you may be able to spend quite a lot of time communicating with the victim. You may be a parent or foster parent, a voluntary counsellor or in a job working with children such as a teacher or youth leader.

In these cases you should not force a child to talk about the abuse but you may be able to give them a natural opening to do so especially if the child is showing signs of distress. You must then be prepared to listen, to listen with care and understanding.

Sometimes you can simply start with a casual 'Hi, how are you'. At other times you may have to be a little more direct. 'You look really unhappy' or 'You seem to have been really angry these past few weeks. I'd like to help you and if you can tell me what's wrong I'm here to listen'. The child could well respond angrily 'Leave me alone, I'm fed up with f....ing do-gooders interfering'. Remember the child has been hurt and has a right to be angry. Just say calmly 'Okay but I really am here for you if you want a chat anytime'.

On other occasions children will be grateful for someone prepared to listen and will unburden themselves, sometimes quite a long time after the abuse stopped. Try to find a safe, secure environment when you have time to spare. Give them control of the session – within the bounds of safety. If you are on your own with a child, focusing on sexual matters and you are in control, then you are just recreating the abusive scenario. So in order to change the situation from a potentially abusive one you give the child the power to come and go as he or she chooses, to determine what is talked about and to use whatever materials are helpful, although you can suggest possibilities if the child becomes stuck – 'Why don't you show me in a drawing – I have a pen and there is some paper here'.

*The needs of black children*: black children have some distinctive needs. They may find it difficult to believe that they are in control if their counsellor is white. It is helpful for black children to spend time with black counsellors who understand their perspectives. However black children should not be denied the opportunity to talk and if they chose a white person to share their experiences with then their choice should be respected.

In the case of black children, the use of play materials which only represent white people is unsuitable. Animal figures, cuddly toys and puppets may be free from representations of culture or gender. However there are also specific materials with which black children can identify and these should be used whenever possible. The books and writing of Kadj Rouf (1989a, 1989b, 1989c) are particularly valuable. Increasingly the materials being produced take account of the needs of black children and those with disabilities.

### Expressing feelings

Allow abused children, whether black or white, to express feelings, cry or throw things in anger – although in the interests of safety you may suggest throwing a cushion and not a large glass ornament. Help them to feel good about themselves. They are worth listening to and helping, so tell them they are. Let them know that what has happened is not their fault. Whatever they are feeling is understandable and felt by other children who have had similar experiences.

There are two things to be wary of. The first is promising to keep secrets. The child could give you additional details which indicate that other children have also been abused; if so it is likely that you will have to let the authorities know. Also think carefully before telling a child about any abuse to yourself or someone close to you. This can be helpful occasionally but can also make the children feel that they should be helping and comforting you. They do not need the burden of someone else's pain as well as their own. There is no hard and fast rule about when to share experiences but you should only do so with great sensitivity and care. If you decide it will be helpful then only give the essential details.

As mentioned earlier, you also need to exercise caution when using touch to comfort a distressed child. It can be exactly what the youngster needs and is a concrete way of demonstrating that people who have been abused are not contaminated or untouchable. It can however be threatening to others.

One important point to remember is that abused children are in a state of grief and loss. They have lost their childhood, their faith in the goodness of other people, their self-esteem and the ownership of their bodies to name but a few of the losses. If you have any skills in counselling bereaved people then you will find that you can transfer the knowledge of the processes and emotions of grief and mourning to good effect in helping sexually abused children.

### *Reliving the past*

Abused children may need to talk about the past in order to view events in a new and more constructive light. It can be distressing for them to recall what has happened but helpful to find someone who will re-interpret events in a way that leaves them feeling less guilty and ashamed of what happened.

Children may also want to act out events and change the ending of the story. So they will want to play at being approached by the molester but this time killing or scaring away the molester before they are attacked or tricked into sexual activities. Sometimes this may be through a fairy tale. They may become a prince or princess, a baby or a small animal and the molester a monster, witch or wild animal. You may be given the role of the molester or the victim. Always let the child dictate the script by saying 'What happens next?' 'What does the witch do next?' 'What does the little mouse do now?'.

This can sometimes be difficult for the helping adult. Jessica, a 5-year-old girl, who had been ritually abused continually played the same scene. In it a good mother became a witch who snatched the baby daughter. The baby would be taken in a van to a place with a table where she would be given a drink. Lying on the table her stomach would be cut open with a cross-shaped incision and then the blood would be drunk. Jessica acted out this scene over and over again. When she was not playing this she was cutting up dolls, giving everyone 'poison' to drink and repeating incantations. She also wanted to repeat some of the sexual activities by touching the adult present. This meant that although she was in control of the session she had to be told that there were a couple of rules to the game – no touching private parts and no hurting people.

Children often return to the emotional age they were when the abuse first started. This can be very difficult for parents, other carers and teachers to cope with. If the abuse started when the child was a baby it might be disconcerting to find you have a 7-year-old boy who wants to suck his thumb, loses bladder control, refuses to eats solids and cries and whines incessantly. Try to be patient and to understand that this is the beginning of a healing process. The child has lost those years to fear and betrayal. He needs to go back and live them again in safety and security. Children in this state will 'grow up' in a matter of weeks or months. They will pass through various developmental stages so that a 10-year-old girl who goes back to babyhood will, after a while, behave like a toddler – tantrums and all! she will then pass through the preschool emotional stage and eventually emerge as a more self-assured, happier 10 or 11-year-old than before.

Adolescents originally molested at, for example, the age of six may lose all interest in boy or girl friends, rock music or teenage fashions only to start playing with toys. They may prefer to dress in rather childish clothes and will be distressed by the physical changes of adolescence. There is the possibility that girls in particular could diet in order to keep a skinny, childish figure and run the risk of developing anorexia nervosa.

Do not make fun of a child who is regressing. Help them to enjoy life, indulge their preferences for a while and let them feel comfortable about themselves. If, however, a child seems to be stuck at a stage for a long time it might be worth considering specialist assistance.

Just as bereaved people need time to grieve but should eventually be able to move on, so abused children will need space and understanding to work through what has happened to them but if they seem unable to come to terms with what has happened they may need specialist counselling or psychotherapy.

### Protection for the future

Children who have been sexually abused might be made more vulnerable to further sexual exploitation. Abused children may feel that adults have a right to abuse them or that they only have value as sexual objects. Some children have become sexualised and seek out sexual experiences. Those abused by a close relative sometimes believe that the only way love is expressed is through sexual favours. Children abused by people outside the family might have had to seek affection from outsiders because there is so little love for them at home.

Even very much loved and well-cared for children or young people may be confused about the rights they have to protect their own bodies and demand respect and privacy. The offender is likely to have given them the message that abusive sexual activities are normal and they have no right to resist and are 'abnormal' if they do so.

This means that abused children need, first and foremost, to know how their body works, why certain parts are private and which activities involving the private parts are acceptable and which are not. It is usually okay when they feel they can talk about the activities; so a doctor looking at a boil on their bottom is alright, it might be a bit embarrassing but it does not have to be kept secret from their mum and dad.

Children need to know that they do not have to be polite to adults all the time:

- if a stranger approaches them they should ignore the person;
- if any adults or older children talk to them about rude things or try to touch them in a way which makes them feel awkward then they have the right to tell them to stop and go away;
- they can run away from anyone they feel is a threat however impolite they have to be. They should then tell someone about what happened.

Abused children need to be put in charge of their bodies as much as possible. They should learn that other people should not be allowed to touch or kiss them if they do not want this. Sexually abused children should not be subjected to corporal punishment under any circumstances. We cannot teach them that their body is to be respected if we then use their bodies to inflict physical pain and humiliation.

Nowadays, there are some very good materials and books to help protect children from sexual abuse. One word of warning though. Some of the materials tell children that if approached they should say 'No'. If children are left with this message *on its own*, the guilt of abused children can be compounded. They are told to say 'No' and yet did not want or manage to do so. In children's straightforward logic, they did not do as they were told so they must have done wrong. It is therefore very important to emphasise that children have a right when in possible danger to say 'No' and yet there are times when they are prevented from exercising that right. Sometimes they do not realise there is anything wrong until it is too late to object. At other times they may be too small, too fond of the perpetrator or too frightened to resist.

It is possible to explain the cycle of abusive behaviour – described in the section on perpetrators – to children who have been abused. Even 6-year-olds can understand that they were tricked. The grooming process can be described to them very simply and they will recognise the process as it related to themselves. This will again emphasise the fact that although they have a right to say 'No' to anyone, even an authority figure, who wants to touch their private parts in secret, it is not always easy to do so.

However adults must recognise that to be consistent they should avoid smacking sexually abused children especially on the bottom and they should also endeavour not to force a child to have an intimate medical examination or treatment if he or she objects. This may require creative thinking on the part of the doctors and adults concerned. As mentioned, one way around the problem could be to allow children to take their own swabs or treat themselves; they could, if necessary, be shown how to put cream on their vaginal or anal area.

### PROTECTING OTHER CHILDREN

While the focus of the previous section has been on victims, other children need to be helped and protected.

### *Brothers and sisters*

Of particular concern are the brothers and sisters of abused children who were not themselves abused at the time of disclosure. Their protection is a priority if the abuser is or was a family member.

Siblings can feel very guilty about what has happened. Some believe that they should have protected their brother or sister. They might have known what was going on yet were too frightened to tell anyone. Non-abused siblings who, on finding out what was happening, disclose could well be made to feel guilty about the consequences, particularly if their father is sent to prison or the children have to leave home. In such cases they need to be helped to realise that the only people who are in the wrong are abusers themselves.

Siblings may also be in a state of loss, perhaps of a parent, of family living standards, of self-esteem – especially if the family has been pilloried and stigmatised – and of security. Some are full of anger which might be directed against the victim, their parents or against protective agencies. Again they need help coping with anger, with grieving and with coming to terms with their losses. This means that even if you do not know the victim but are in contact with the brothers and sisters of an abused child you might be able to provide a friendly listening ear or a shoulder to cry on.

Turning more specifically to protection, sometimes the victim is removed but the siblings are left in the home with the abuser in a mistaken belief that he or she will not touch the remaining children.

We must remember that child sexual abuse is a compulsive behaviour. It has been likened to an addiction. Think of alcoholics. Their preferred tipple might be whisky. So you remove all the whisky bottles from the alcoholics' reach. Will that really solve their drink problem? My guess is that they will eventually find that brandy is an acceptable alternative. If you are a chocoholic your real penchant may be milk chocolate bars however if they suddenly go out of production I bet that plain chocolate bars will eventually prove to be a satisfactory substitute.

Similarly a man who has abused his 7-year-old step-daughter might prefer little girls aged between about four and 10-years-old. However, once the step-daughter is removed he will look for an alternative. It may not be safe or satisfactory to abuse any girls outside his family so he could turn to his 5-year-old son for sexual satisfaction instead. Some people believe that if a man has abused his step children he will not interfere with his natural children. *Rubbish*. Natural children do not have some form of magic ring of unavailability around them. They are children and ultimately as far as a considerable proportion of perpetrators are concerned a child, is a child, is a sexual object.

Children, ideally, should not be left in the home of a known perpetrator but the reality of life is that sometimes this has to be allowed to happen. In such circumstances the children should be told that they have a right to say 'No' to any advance that makes them uncomfortable. If possible the perpetrator him or herself should give the children, in front of witnesses, permission to tell someone if he or she ever tries to molest them. If the perpetrator refuses to do this then the non-abusing person should give the children permission to tell in front of the perpetrator. If possible this should be recorded on tape or in writing.

The onus for controlling behaviour must be on the perpetrator and not on the children. This means that there should be no restrictions on their behaviour – beyond the normal restrictions applied to any child. If children want to play in the garden in summer in swimsuits then they can do so. If that provides a sexual stimulation for an abusive step-father then that is his problem. The potential offender must control his own behaviour and inclinations rather than impose unwarranted limitations on children.

### Protection for all children

Child molesters exist both within and outside families. Because of this all children should receive protective education. Most schools and parents teach children not to talk to strangers. However a number of 'danger stranger' programmes are worse than useless; they are dangerous because they mislead children.

Children often think that a 'stranger' must be an ugly man. At times children are not taught to be on guard against women or good looking, charming men. They tend to think that friendly people who know their name cannot be 'strangers'. Yet child molesters are adept at finding out names. Children often have them displayed on bags, jewellery or T-shirts. Some schools imprudently insist that their pupils' names are on the outside of parts of their uniform, my own secondary school did! Parents would be well advised to ensure that their children do not have their name on anything which a potential molester could spot. They should also warn children to ignore anyone that they do not recognise even if the person knows their name.

There are however some very good preventative programmes. One of the best in Britain is the Kidscape Programme founded by Wendy Titman and Michelle Elliot. This includes the concept that children have rights – to breathe, to eat, to go to the toilet, to be safe. The programme examines the way children can protect themselves from bullies and then moves along the spectrum of danger and exploitation to child sex abusers including relatives. The programme also encourages children to distinguish between good and bad touching and to trust their feelings. If they sense an unsafe situation then they can break the normal rules of politeness and obedience in order to keep themselves safe. They are also taught a way of screaming out if attacked.

Protection programmes will not be effective if they are not backed up by positive attitudes to children. They have to be respected. The phrase 'Children should be seen and not heard' is manna to perpetrators. If we are to keep our children safe then they must be heard, be listened to and be believed. Parents should let their children feel that they can tell them anything without constant fear of punishment.

This advice may be anathema to some parents. If children admit to having done something very wrong then surely they must be punished? Must they? Think of the example of a youngster who admits to having truanted from school. It is far better to discuss the reason for the truanting and how any difficulties can be resolved than to give the child a good hiding and ignore the problems which caused the child to truant. If small children are caught shoplifting then they have to be helped to realise the upset that theft can cause and find a way of paying back the value of what has been stolen. Children who have done something wrong can be encouraged to make amends in a way that they can acknowledge is fair.

Those who are controlled by fear and brought up in a punitive atmosphere are far more vulnerable to exploitation than those who learn to expect a considerate and gentle, if firm, response from adults. Children must be able to believe that, however wrong they feel their behaviour to have been, they need not keep it a secret from adults. It is worth stating again that child sexual abuse thrives on secrecy, but a secret shared is a danger halved.

Parents and teachers are not the only ones to have a responsibility for protecting children. There are many other people in society who should be taking their share of the responsibility:

*The judiciary*: must do something to ensure that when children identify an abuser they are treated fairly in court when they give evidence. Judges must be aware of the compulsive nature of child molestation and must not accept the excuses that perpetrators give to justify the unjustifiable.

*Manufacturers and retailers:* many manufacturers are producing clothes and cosmetics which are targeted at children to make them look like small sexy adults. Frilly underwear, suspenders, lipstick, nail polish, bras and bikinis for 5-year-old girls are unnecessary. Of course children want to be grown up and their parents find it hard to resist children's demands. If manufacturers do not produce sexy goods for small children then the children will not press their parents for them. Similarly, responsible retailers can refuse to sell inappropriate articles. Unfortunately a sexily dressed 5-year-old will unwittingly be giving the message 'I want sex' to the paedophile who if given an inch will find justification for taking a mile.

*Advertisers:* many advertisements use the sexual attraction of children to sell their products. This makes the use of children as sexual objects seem normal and acceptable. One recent advertisement for oranges shows children in rather enticing poses and has the slogan 'Small ones are juiciest'! In many entertainments seductive adult women are referred to as 'girls' or 'babes'.

In one newspaper I picked up from the lower shelves of newsagents, I found adverts for phone lines such as 'Adult *Toys*', '*Naughty girls* tell each other how they like to be pleased'. '*Play* with me'. The use of child related terms and concepts in advertising sexual services again feeds into paedophiles' belief that children are acceptable sex objects and they are not doing anything so very abnormal by having sex or playing sexy 'games' with children.

*The news media:* however knowledgable professional workers become and however many erudite books and articles circulate amongst them the problem will not be tackled until the general population has a good grasp and understanding of the issues. Wider society can really only become aware through the popular media especially television, radio and the press. Certain sections of the media have undoubtedly caused problems by using stories of child sexual abuse to titillate readers, making ill-informed and biased sweeping statements and by gross and unnecessary intrusion into privacy. The popular media, like most of society's institutions, are bastions of male domination and power; therefore there will inevitably be instances where it will accept the male perpetrator's denial and excuses.

On the other hand it has also been the news and entertainment media that has played a major part in exposing the extent of the problem. It has also enabled more victims and survivors to come forward. Time and again a referral comes about because children see a television programme and are able to say to their parents or friends 'You know what we saw on telly, well it happened to me too.' Survivors similarly have been able to speak out through radio, television and the press. It is now no longer a taboo subject.

There are presenters like Esther Ranzen and the 'That's Life' team who have exposed abuse and abusers and were the driving force behind the setting up of ChildLine. Amongst the press there are large numbers of responsible and caring journalists. In the national press there are pieces, like the moving account written by David Williams (1987), of how very young were tricked by men dressed as clowns and used for child pornography in Holland. The local press also plays its part. An example is provided by the courageous, well researched and thoughtful article by Julia Stuart (1993) who examined the controversial issue of female perpetrators.

However, programme producers and journalists will not be able to report matters accurately unless people with the relevant knowledge are prepared to share it with them. The confidentiality of children and other vulnerable people must be protected but, given safeguards, it is essential that professionals and others with significant information, communicate and cooperate with the media. Many agencies fight shy of the press and prevent their field staff – the people directly involved with the issue – from passing on their knowledge. This is misguided as organisations should see it as part of their responsibility to ensure that their staff, while being trained to ensure client confidentiality, are nevertheless encouraged to engage in a dialogue with the responsible sections of the media.

*All of us*: need to change our attitudes to masculinity and male sexuality. We need to accept that men do not have to be dominant and all powerful in society. A man can be a 'real man' even when he is weak and vulnerable. A boy who is a victim should not be made to feel diminished or less of a man if he acknowledges his victimisation.

Additionally we have to move away from the belief that once stimulated, men have a rampant need to express their sexuality, have a right to gain relief and are unable to control their sexual urges. Most societies put the onus of controlling men's sexual behaviour on women. Some societies do so explicitly and make women cover themselves from head to foot in order not to arouse any sort of sexual passion in men. Western societies may not demand this but there are more subtle pressures on females. They are allowed to dress in tight clothes, short skirts and low-cut blouses but if a man then molests a woman or girl wearing such immodest attire blame is cast on the victim for having been 'provocatively' dressed.

We must also change our attitudes to children. They are not objects nor their parents' property. They are people and like all people they have feelings, fears and wishes. They are human beings and as such have a dignity and worth. They are citizens and have rights, particularly the right to protection and security. The habit of calling a child 'it' has to be challenged. Just as we have challenged derogatory ways of referring to people of a different creed, culture, colour or those with disabilities, we must likewise challenge the references to children as 'monsters' or 'little animals'.

## In conclusion

The people with the ultimate responsibility for child sexual abuse are the perpetrators. If they use other people as sexual objects, they are the only ones to blame for any damage or distress caused. This must be a message clearly conveyed by society, enshrined in our laws and upheld by our judicial systems. But at the same time society itself and all its institutions and its individuals, that is you and me, must examine how far we reinforce abusing behaviour and how much more we could contribute to solving the problems.

# Final thoughts

# Looking after ourselves

Confronting the issue of child sexual abuse is difficult for everyone involved. There are pressures that we are all likely to experience. Advice is given about how these can be managed. Some of us encounter added dimensions to the general problems. Particular attention is paid to four groups, parents of abused children, adult survivors, professionals having to deal with child abuse cases and finally, potential or actual adult abusers. Each group is provided with some supplementary strategies for looking after themselves.

### GENERAL ISSUES

First of all there are the pressures and problems that everyone has to recognise and cope with.

### *Denial and acceptance*

Some adults find it such a difficult topic that they completely deny it happens at all or they deny that it could happen to children in their own social group, country or culture. They can comfort themselves by believing it only occurs in remote rural areas or poor Third World countries but not close to home in their neighbourhood or their own family.

The fact that you have read almost to the end is a good indicator that you do not deny that sexual abuse exists and could touch even those children close to you. However, because you accept that there is a problem you are unable to use total denial to protect yourself from the pain inherent in the subject. You might be suffering from another variation of denial. You may refuse to accept that it has any adverse effects on you whatsoever. But the likelihood is that those around you are feeling the effects. They have become aware that you are more anxious, tense, restless and easily upset than usual.

It could be that you have been able to accept that a child or adult you are in contact with has been sexually exploited and you realise that it is causing you to worry and feel under a lot of pressure. It is important to bear in mind that you are not alone in feeling like this.

### Effects on sexuality

Child sexual abuse is a difficult topic for a number of reasons, many of which we have already acknowledged. For all of us there is a tension about sexual issues. This comes from the conflict between strong sexual drives that human beings have to have in order to procreate and the controls on these that have to be imposed if the human need to live in a social, organised society is to be met.

Adults, like the fully grown members of most mammalian groups, are designed to feel protective towards their young in order to ensure the survival of the species. The majority of human beings are therefore naturally distressed at the thought of threats and danger to children. As we have already seen, most cultures have a range of stories about physical and emotional harm and neglect to children which mean that, by the time we reach adulthood, we may feel protective towards children but we have been prepared for the fact that children are physically mistreated. However we are rarely prepared for the fact that children are sexually abused; it is something that happens in secret and most societies keep it a secret. It is therefore a shock when we have to face its existence.

Many people find that in one way or another their own sexuality is affected for a while. Some people find that the whole topic is so distressing that they are unable to maintain any enthusiasm about sex even with much loved partners. Others find themselves sexually stimulated by the topic then feel guilty about the feelings that are awakened. Some men in particular have suppressed their sexual response to the extent that they have become impotent. Because most cases that come to light are of men abusing girls some women find that they become angry and disgusted with men in general for a while.

On the other hand the realisation that some women also sexually abuse leaves us in even greater turmoil. We are no longer able to view women as 'safe'. The solution to the problem of sexual abuse of children cannot lie solely in a change in attitude on the part of men and the adoption of new ways of socialising boys. For women there is a profound sense that their gender, which should be united in opposing violence and exploitation by men, has been betrayed.

## GENERAL PROTECTIVE STRATEGIES

There are a number of ways of helping yourself to cope with the pressures of involvement in a case of child sexual abuse.

### *Increased knowledge and familiarity*

One strategy that may help some people cope with child sexual abuse is to learn as much about the subject as possible. Once something becomes familiar and can be understood it becomes less overwhelming and frightening. People with a particularly distressing illness or other medical condition will sometimes find that they can cope by discovering as much as possible about the condition. What they find out might be quite painful and distressing and yet they can cope all the better for having the knowledge.

A tried and tested way of dealing with a fear or with something which you find abhorrent is to come into contact with it as much as possible. Many people find it better to face a fear and learn to master it rather than to keep running away. So facing child sexual abuse, reading all about it, watching television programmes dealing with the issue, attending training courses and discussing it with other like-minded people can, although difficult at the time, be a strengthening process in the long run.

### *Mourning and loss*

Another strategy is to recognise that your reaction may be a combination of loss and stress. When you have to face child sexual abuse there is a sense of loss of the belief in the innocence of childhood, a loss of faith and trust in fellow human beings, a loss of security, especially if you are a parent. At the same time you will feel pressurised and distressed by the burden of knowledge that you have acquired.

Recognise your grief and the fact that you will have to work through your grief. You will feel shock and then anger. Work out why you are angry, who you are angry with and what you can you do with your anger. You may be able to use it constructively to campaign on behalf of the victims or to raise money for child protective charities such as ChildLine, the NSPCC and RSSPCC.

Accept that for a while you will experience depression and despair. Again allow yourself to rest and relax. Give yourself a period of not fighting against your emotions of distress. Allow yourself to cry. Allow yourself to be grumpy or just sit staring at the wall paper feeling awful. Do not worry if you overeat or lose your appetite, feel ill and cannot sleep.

However do not allow this state to continue indefinitely. After a time start to become active again. Start to eat sensible food even if you have no appetite or only want to eat boxes of chocolates. Try to relax but at the same time attempt to shake off feelings of lethargy. If you still do not feel any better then you may need medical assistance.

### Stress relief

Make use of the various tried and tested strategies for relieving stress. Choose the ones that suit you. This will include the inevitable advice about exercise, nutrition and sleep. It may be useful to 'escape' through reading, gardening, hobbies or sport. Some people find that herbal or homeopathic remedies are useful.

Others use meditation. The more hedonistic of us might prefer to switch off through shopping trips for luxuries, parties or a spell at a beauty salon or health farm.

You may find that treating and enjoying yourself seems wrong at a time when you know that other people, maybe ones close to you are suffering. However, feeling guilty yourself will not help any victims. When young and idealistic, I went to help some friends working on a project in India where the families were very poor. There had been a long drought and food was scarce. I felt I should not be feeding myself when the people around me had so little. The result was I became malnourished, ill and my energy was completely depleted. Far from being useful I became a burden. I came back a little older, a lot thinner and very much wiser. I had learnt that if you want to be able to help others then you need to have just enough nourishment, whether physical or emotional, to give yourself sufficient energy and resilience for the task in hand.

### Talking and sharing

It is essential that you find someone you can talk to, especially a friend or colleague who has some knowledge and experience of child sexual abuse. This can serve several different functions.

Firstly, you can talk through and test out ideas and concepts. Sharing views with another equally interested person can open up fresh vistas and lead to new understanding and knowledge.

Secondly, discussing concerns can be reassuring, while other people can provide useful advice and guidance. Lastly, it is always helpful to share pressures and worries. Talking about how you feel to another person who can understand and empathise can prevent problems from getting out of proportion and can make anxieties seem more manageable.

ISSUES FOR PARENTS

### Coping with disclosure

Non-abusing parents whose child has been a victim are likely to be in a extreme state of turmoil. The first problem is that of being able to believe that your child has been molested. It is easier if there have been signs, if maybe you have been puzzled and worried about your child's changed behaviour. When you are put in the picture about the abuse everything suddenly makes sense. It is also easier to believe if the perpetrator is a stranger, distant acquaintance or someone you already felt uneasy about. It is much harder if you never suspected anything was wrong and if the accused abuser is someone you like and trust, especially your partner.

Here it is important to remember that the closer the relationship of the perpetrator to the victim the less likely the child is to be lying.

There will be added distress if your child disclosed to someone other than yourself. But remember this is not necessarily a sign of a poor relationship but rather the opposite. These children love their parents deeply and do not want to upset them, so find it easier to tell someone they care less about.

On the other hand if your child managed to tell you first then you may be worried about how you reacted. It is important to remain caring, reassuring and calm but not all of us manage to cope well in a crisis that touches us so deeply. If you feel that you reacted badly then there is time to retrieve the situation. Only if you were totally rejecting and condemning for a very long period, as Jay's parent were, will you have lost almost too much ground to catch up. As long as you showed some love and compassion you have something to build on. It is important to talk to your son or daughter and explain why you reacted badly but also give your child a chance to talk about and explain his or her feelings. Most of the conversations should focus on your child rather than on yourself.

You may have had great difficulty deciding whether to report the matter to the police or social services. This is understandable. Many of us cannot face the traumas of an investigation. On questioning several of my colleagues who work in the child protection field they admitted that if their own children were molested they would only report the matter with extreme reluctance. On the other hand if you are able to report the matter then it is easier to seek help openly for both yourself and your children.

### Coping with feelings

Hopefully by now you will have been convinced that the only person to blame for abuse are the abusers although that does not help if the perpetrator in your family's case was another of your children. Whatever positive messages your head is giving you your emotions, might well feel very negative.

Anger might seem ready to explode especially if you have had a difficult time during the investigation or any subsequent legal proceedings, and suspect that matters have been mishandled. Justice is often not seen to be done in instances of child sexual abuse; it is so often the word of a child against an that of adult with little corroborating evidence. In such cases the adversarial games played out in court are not effective at eliciting the truth – but at present we do not have a better system.

It is useful to try to see the process through the eyes of the investigators and law enforcement agencies. They are usually very busy and working with inadequate resources. They are constrained by agency policies, procedures and legal requirements. Some professionals are inadequately trained and inexperienced while the potentially good workers tend to be over-worked and under considerable stress. On the other hand it is worth identifying whether or not you have a justifiable complaint and then using agency complaints procedures. Only by people making justified protests will a deficient service or system change.

Even when the system worked well the emotional impact on you is likely to be considerable, particularly if the suspected perpetrator is your partner. In this case you may have to face very many additional worries. Firstly you may be forced to chose between your children and your partner. If your partner moves out then there may be considerable financial worries with two residences to be paid for. Your children may react badly to the departure of one parent. You could experience resentment from your in-laws, or even your own family if they take your partner's side. You might also suffer from unforgiving neighbours or, nowadays rare, media intrusion.

You are likely to be plagued by doubts about yourself 'What sort of person am I to fall in love with a person that could do that to children'. The answer to that is probably 'an average sort of person'. Remember the section on perpetrators; we know that a substantial proportion are charming, plausible, attractive and seem to be very good with children. There are many, many caring, trusting husbands, wives, partners and friends who never suspected that the person they loved was a child molester. You are not alone.

### Being kind to yourself

Whatever the damage you feel has been done by the abuser or by the system the most important people in the lives of abused children are the parents. All the research points to the fact that if one parent can give positive support, caring and love to the victims then they are much more likely to recover and be able to live without carrying too great a burden. But in order to help your child effectively you must first help yourself.

First of all, be gentle with yourself. It is worth recalling what some other parents have felt:

> *I would look at my daughter and sob. She was so beautiful and innocent . I just knew that I had done everything wrong in my parenting for this to have happened.*

and

> *I couldn't eat or sleep for days. I would think about what that man did to my child and feel so bad inside that I couldn't function. I lost several days of work because I couldn't concentrate, and I really wasn't in any shape to be of much help to Barbara when she needed me most (Hagans and Case 1990 p.71).*

Allow yourself to cry although try to do so as much as possible out of sight of your children. Scream and shout if you like but again not in front of the children. Write vitriolic letters to the abuser or to the authorities then tear them up. Over-eat or spend a bit of money on yourself for a while if that helps and if you can afford to. Take some time off work if possible, you may have sympathetic boss or you could quite truthfully say that you feel sick – even if you are not feeling physically nauseous you may be sick at heart, a sort of homesickness or yearning for the happier past, before you had to face this problem.

The only thing not to indulge are your feelings of self-recrimination and guilt. If you think that you have been an awful parent then you are likely to fulfil your own prophecy and end up becoming a less than adequate one as you wallow in self-pity and forget the needs of your child. As long as you did not knowingly take part in the abuse for your own sexual gratification and were caring and loving then your parenting was 'good enough'. If you accept that then you will be free to give more of your emotional resources to your child. If you are kind to yourself you will probably be kind to your child as well.

### Sharing problems

Your best way of helping your child is by giving him or her a sympathetic ear, though you will also need one for yourself. It is essential that you find someone who can remain fairly calm and objective and who is willing to listen patiently. You may be lucky and have a good friend otherwise your may need to turn to counselling services. If you are very distressed then the Samaritans will always be there to listen but there are usually other counsellors available locally who can give you regular planned appointments. Many of these are part of voluntary agencies such as the Family Welfare Association. If you belong to a religious group you may find that your particular church has a counselling service.

A word of warning, the dynamics of child sexual abuse are complicated and only in the last decade of the twentieth century have they been appreciated even by child protection specialists. This means that there are some counsellors who may be effective in other areas but, because they do not understand the issues, may respond inappropriately when having to deal with sexual abuse. Sheila, a survivor, found her first counsellor showed impatience and gave her the impression that she had caused all the problems herself. Encouraged by a friend, Sheila changed to a Relate trained counsellor who proved sensitive, enabling and a real life-line.

You may find it helpful to join a group of parents whose children have been abused. It is worth asking if there is an appropriate group in your area. If no group is available it may still be possible to link you to a parent in a similar position or one who has been through the same type of experience. By being part of either a group or a pair you will find you have the freedom to talk about your experiences with people who understand at first hand and you will also feel less isolated and 'different'. You may also gain some satisfaction from helping other people in the group once you begin to feel a little stronger yourself.

### ISSUES FOR ADULT SURVIVORS

#### *Parent survivors*
There are additional problems for parents of abused children who are themselves survivors. For many there is an acute sense of failure. They feel that they should be in a better position to protect their children than most other parents because they have increased awareness of the problem due to their own experiences. They may also feel that there must be something wrong with them – they appear to attract sexual abusers like a magnet.

If this describes you it is important to hang on to the statistics. We can be fairly confident that one in ten children or more are sexually abused at sometime during their childhood or early adolescence. This means that statistically a substantial proportion of children of survivors will be sexually abused. Parents can take reasonable measures to protect their children but they have to allow them independence and risks have to be taken.

You need to remember how cunning and persistent sex offenders can be. They are also good at putting the blame on to other people:

> As well as blaming the child, the offender frequently shifted responsibility for the act on to an adult female: his wife or partner, or the child's mother. The woman was blamed for allowing the man to do it by denying him sex, for not looking after the child properly or generally for neglecting the man (Mezey et al 1991 p.17).

There is a double burden of pain experienced by all survivors who are now coping with a child who has been abused; their own and that of the victim. But because most parents feel their children's pain more deeply and acutely than a less closely related person the double pain for a parent will be all the more poignant.

### *Coping with memories and flashbacks*

It is difficult for anyone, parent, friend, volunteer or professional worker, who was sexually abused as a child to face the fact that a child they know has been molested. The pain of the victim will reawaken memories of your own hurt. This could lead to the experience of 'flashbacks'; vivid recall of abusive incidents often involving several of the senses – smell, taste and touch as well as sight and hearing.

If you experience a flashback then it is important to remember they are a common experience for survivors of all manner of traumas. After the 1914-18 war even the most resilient of soldiers could suffer flashbacks many years later, reliving the horror, the fear and the stench of the trenches. You are not mad or weak. When you have one, hang on as best you can during the experience then afterwards pamper yourself. Some survivors find having a warm bath and a rest helpful. Others indulge in sweets or play with dolls; a little bit of what you fancy does you good.

Again it is useful to talk about the flashbacks and share your feelings with someone who understands. It is worth trying to find a sympathetic counsellor or a survivors' group.

### Depression and suicide

You may suddenly feel despairing and depressed. The world seems a terrible place. No one can be trusted. No child is safe. You look back at the past with pain, the present is filled with hurt and the future seems bleak. You feel suicidal.

Allow yourself some self-pity, you deserve it. Let the sense of desolation wash over you for a while. But then try to catch a glimpse of some of the good bits. Has anyone ever paid you a compliment or given you the impression that you have something to offer? Is there anything that you enjoy doing? Look after yourself physically but for a short while by forgetting yourself. Live emotionally through someone else such as your favourite character in a television soap or book. Just allow yourself to escape some of the feelings of pain and desolation for a week or two until you begin to feel a glimmer of hope.

Remember, even as the hope and happiness emerge and increase a little, you will still be volatile as your mood swings. This is normal; we all make progress unevenly with the proverbial 'two steps forward and one step back'.

It may be that the maelstrom of emotions have taken their toll, exhausted, you have developed a depressive illness. If this is the case then you will find that you cannot pull yourself together or look on the bright side. Your physical and mental functions will have slowed down. You are likely to have considerable appetite and sleep disturbances and feel tired. The remedy for this might be medication and it is certainly worth a visit to your doctor.

### When to opt out

If you are having real difficulties it may be that you have to distance yourself from child sexual abuse. This is almost impossible for parents of victims but it is an option for those less closely related. Even so, it might worry you because it appears to mean abandoning a needy child. However, if you are so emotionally distressed that you are barely able to function then you are unlikely to be of much use and it is better to try to find someone else who can help. Explain to the child you want him or her to have the best help available and this new person is really good at helping children. You should give reassurance that you will be thinking of the child and hope to keep in touch.

Another reason for distancing yourself from the case is if you find that you are inflicting pain, whether emotional or physical, on the victim. It may be that you feel that you deserve punishment because you still believe you were to blame for your own victimisation. You might find a degree of satisfaction and relief when you use abused children or young people as a substitute for yourself, hurting and punishing them. It is essential to recognise that unless you have feelings of love and concern for the abused child who once was yourself – your childself – then you are not in a position to help. This is particularly true if you are a teacher, foster carer or residential worker or in some other position of authority over young people.

### When to make use of your experiences

You might find that your problems are not over-whelming and realise that because you have survived you can use your experiences to the benefit of other victims. You are likely to have a depth of sensitivity and understanding that will convey itself.

There is, nevertheless, the problem of what to do if the victim directly asks 'Were you ever abused?'. To answer in the affirmative may mean that victims begin to worry about distressing you or feel that you must be as weak and damaged as they feel themselves. To answer in the negative means, in effect, that you are lying to the victim: this echoes what the perpetrator probably did, and you are keeping a 'guilty' secret. You have also denied yourself the opportunity to share your experience with the victim should it later become appropriate to do so.

What you say will depend on your relationship with the child and the nature of your own abuse but often a general statement is helpful. 'Yes, I did experience something similar, there are quite a few people who are like us. You are not the only child to have this happen to... now what about you'. In this way you are being open and truthful but also turning the focus away from yourself and back to the child. If the child persists in asking you about your experiences again a generally truthful reply is advised although it is essential not to overwhelm them with your experiences and emotions and to redirect the focus onto them as soon as their curiosity seems satisfied. It is important to avoid the games of 'Ain't it awful' and 'Betcha my suffering was much worse that yours'. The first is to adopt a totally negative view of the situation resulting in a pervading feeling of hopelessness. The second is a form of competitiveness which leaves the victims thinking their distress has been belittled and dismissed.

### ISSUES FOR HELPING PROFESSIONALS

There are problems for professional workers employed by helping organisations whether or not they have been abused themselves, although there are likely to be a greater number of impact issues for professionals who are also survivors.

### *Fears and threats*

All people involved in child sexual abuse could find themselves under threat. But in recent years the plight of the professional has been highlighted.

Firstly, there is the threat from client or patient violence. One colleague was instrumental in the removal of children from an abusing father. He promptly told her that because she had taken his children from him, he would pay her back by killing hers. He was a man with a very volatile personality with a history of violence and he was known to be capable of harming children. The employers and police could offer very little protection.

Other professionals have been personally threatened by perpetrators or by relatives who are furious with the 'system'. I have on file a note taken by a colleague about one abuser with whom I was working. On a home visit he told my colleague he would go out and shoot the first social worker he saw. Another father imprisoned for abusing his baby daughter threatened that on his release he would 'knife' everyone he considered had sided with his wife; I was in the cheery position of having assessed the wife as protective and capable of continuing to care for the baby.

The other threat is less direct but as pernicious. It comes from society and its base is public opinion as expressed through the media. Professionals work in constant fear that if they put a foot wrong in a child protection case then they will be subject to a public inquiry and appear on the front pages of the tabloid press under headlines such as 'Sack 'em', 'Worker lets child die' or 'Failed again'. Most professionals reading the accounts of public inquiries realise that – although, with hindsight, mistakes can be identified – given the pressures at the time they could easily have done the same.

## Organisational climates

Colleagues have often remarked on the paradox that the very organisations designed to help people are the worst at looking after their own staff. There are several reasons for this. The main one is the tendency for such organisations to divide the population into two groups. The first group are the resilient and strong who do not need help. The second are the clients or patients who are vulnerable, weak people who need help. The employees of the organisation are the help-givers therefore they must be in the resilient, strong group. Helping organisations cannot cope well with the concept that help-givers can become help-needers because that would mean that their employees become their clients.

This means that if a professional staff member begins to suffer stress because of the nature or extent of the workload the organisation simply does not want to know. It expects its employees to be resilient and strong and not in need of assistance. The helping professional who finds working with child sexual abuse very distressing is unlikely to meet much sympathy from managers.

Another reason for the lack of compassion on the part of managers is partly because they are often over-loaded themselves and yet it is essential that they stay on the resilient-strong side so they do not want any added problems. Other managers have succeeded in the present system so have a vested interest in maintaining it. If potential rivals fall by the wayside then there is less competition.

Interestingly, these organisations also cannot cope with the concept of a former help-needer crossing the great divide to become a help-giver. Members of staff who admit to having been a victim or indeed of having had any significant background problems are rather too often viewed with suspicion.

Helping organisations and their senior managers need to realise that, as illustrated in Figure 7, all human beings move

**Figure 5:**

## 1. Helping Organisations View of Human Functioning

Dividing LIne

Client/Patients        Employees

Vulnerable                          Resilient
Dependent   $\longleftrightarrow$   Independent
Needing Help                    Giving Help

## 2. Reality of Human Functioning

In Difficulty    < Employees >    When OK

In Difficulty    < Clients/Patients >    When OK

Vulnerable                          Resilient
Dependent   $\longleftrightarrow$   Independent
Needing Help                    Giving Help

up and down the emotional resilience continuum throughout their lives. Clients or patients become stronger and no longer need help whereas employees can at times become vulnerable and require assistance for themselves. After all, we have no problem accepting that shop keepers have to do their own shopping and become customers from time to time.

## Additional concerns for survivors
### Unhelpful colleagues
Survivors are likely to have to face problems from colleagues who regard them as in some way 'damaged'. They may find that in a disagreement over case management they are being accused of over-identifying with the victim or not being able to view the issues objectively.

### Limited sources of help
Another problem is that sources of help are restricted. The only people offering counselling may be colleagues or even subordinates and this can lead to embarrassment, role-conflict and fears of loss of confidentiality. At the same time the only groups for survivors in the area may be comprised of clients or patients. This again can lead to fears of loss of confidentiality on the part of the clients, role-conflict and confusion.

### Safety in numbers
One strategy adopted in some areas is for professional workers to join together and demand some time for themselves in order to give mutual support and share concerns. Sometimes the schemes are for professionals who are themselves survivors. At other times it is for any professional, survivor or not.

It makes a lot of sense for groups to be open to all workers. In some ways we are all survivors of childhood unhappiness. There must be very few people who did not experience some form of abuse even if not sexual. Children are so vulnerable and adult behaviour so often arbitrary and self-motivated that we all inevitably suffer at the hands of somebody more powerful than ourselves in childhood. Even those surrounded by adoring adults might have found themselves bullied by other children. Sexual abuse can awaken memories of those feelings of powerlessness, fear and injustice present in the vast majority of people. Helping professionals are perhaps more likely than other occupational groups to have suffered from feelings of vulnerability in childhood. It is often a recognition of those feelings which prompts them to want to help others.

If there is no group in your area again it is worth trying to find at least one or two colleagues with whom to share views. In some districts there are informal multidisciplinary lunch clubs for a range of professionals in the locality. These can be useful although it is sometimes a problem to find time to attend them.

Another strategy, if you are having to deal with a case of sexual abuse is to ask if you can have the services of a consultant particularly if your own supervisor has little knowledge of the topic. For example workers in a Barnardos project in Liverpool found the intensity of their child protection work so great that they acquired for themselves an outside consultant (Francis 1993). In some areas there is a local authority child protection consultant available for any professional to approach. In other areas a voluntary agency such as the NSPCC might offer a free consultancy service. Alternatively you may be able to acquire an informal consultant through your local networks. The general rule is 'seek and eventually, after a lot of telephone calls, persistence and patience, you shall find'.

### ISSUES FOR PERPETRATORS

This section may be helpful for those of you who know someone who has admitted to abusing a child. But it may also be helpful to you if you realise that you either have or might sexually exploit children and young people.

It is possible that you can recall having interfered with a child in your early teens and you are sure your motivation was curiosity. Since then you have had no fantasies about sex with children. Your sexual desires seem to focus entirely on fellow adults. You are not attracted to child pornography nor the portrayal of adults as children. You feel no sexual arousal when you see children or pictures of them in bathing costumes or underwear. If this describes you then it is unlikely that you are a sex abuser now and your early behaviour was indeed prompted by curiosity.

On the other hand you may have realised that you continue to be drawn to images of children having sex. You may not have engaged in sexual activity in your teens but find that from time to time you are aroused by images of children. You may feel a thrill of excitement at the idea of smacking their bottoms or catching sight of their underwear. You may enjoy their submissiveness or find yourself thinking that some children would like to have sex with you. More seriously you may have already had some sessions with what you believe are willing child participants. All this would indicate that you are a child abuser.

If you are involved as a relative, helper or professional with child sexual abuse cases then you might have discovered that you are aroused by the children's statements and catch yourself fantasising about the scenes the children described. You may find that the sexual provocativeness of some victims rather confirms your view that children really like sex and it does not do too much harm.

On the other hand you could be experiencing guilt. You have a sense of harbouring a dangerous secret. If you were also a victim then you might well be in conflict with yourself. Part of you is angry and rejecting of people who molest children but the other part of you knows that you are or could be a molester yourself. This makes you feel worthless and you despise yourself, for being both a victim and a victimiser.

You are putting yourself under intolerable pressure because you are facing considerable temptation. It is probably essential for you to withdraw from this type of work and indeed from any work from children. And yet you may not be ready for this. You may also not be ready to face up to the truth and either admit what you have done or seek help.

The problem is that if the situation continues you could well find that you are caught committing a serious offence. Rather like a compulsive gambler or someone addicted to alcohol you could find eventually that you lose everything that you value in life. The best way to help yourself is to recognise and control your behaviour.

We know that many people can only control their sexually abusive activities with concentrated external help, preferably in a residential setting. What we know less about are the numbers of perpetrators who are never caught and after committing one or two offences decide that enough is enough and stop, in much the same way that some alcoholics decide once and for all to give up drink or smokers renounce cigarettes or compulsive shop-lifters bring an abrupt end to their kleptomania. But as with all compulsive behaviours, to control the desire takes enormous will-power and determination.

There are some changes in attitude that are needed before there can be any alteration in behaviour. This requires ceasing to adopt certain defences and taking on board some new ideas and perceptions.

### *Stopping and starting*

*Denial*

The first thing is to stop denying that you are an abuser or a potential abuser. Also stop denying what you have done or could do and the seriousness of the consequences. You are likely to be minimising the extent of your desires and activities and the adverse effect they have on your victims. You could well be comforting yourself with thoughts such as 'I only touched him once'. That is once too often and once is likely eventually to lead to twice unless you take firm steps to control your activities. Your are also likely to be denying or minimising the seriousness of the consequences for yourself. You may believe that you will not be caught or that you will not be tempted by the presence of children. But you are conning yourself; you are a continuing risk to children.

Some abusers believe that because they have been to prison, through a course of therapy, married or had a religious conversion they no longer pose a risk to children. However, it is worth restating that molesting children is a compulsive behaviour which like alcohol addiction or compulsive gambling cannot be cured, it can only be controlled. The key to control is to avoid temptation as far as possible.

It is essential to start *accepting* the extent and nature of your fantasies, desires and activities and the consequences for your victims and yourself.

### *Blaming others*

It is essential to stop blaming other people for the abuse. You are the only person who can control your behaviour. It does not matter how sexy children's clothes are, how unsympathetic or sexually unexciting your partner is or how negligent the child's parent seem. Sexy clothes, unexciting partners and negligent parents do not exploit and sexually abuse children. Without you and others who behave like you there would be no sexual assaults on children. You and only you are responsible for what you have done or could do and you must start *taking responsibility* for your exploitation of those weaker, smaller, younger and less mature than yourself.

## Victimisation

You need to stop seeing yourself as the victim. It may be that you were a victim of sexual abuse as a child and you believe you were predestined to become an abuser yourself. Or you feel that you cannot really be in control of your own activities because of your helplessness as a child. You may also have acquired the habit of shifting responsibility from yourself to other people. But remember there are many millions of adults who were sexually exploited as children yet never become abusers themselves. You are now an adult and have a responsibility towards children.

You may have been victimised in other ways, being bullied or physically or emotionally abused. Again this is no excuse for your behaviour now as an adult.

You may instead feel that you are victimised by society. You might sincerely believe that children enjoy sex and agree with the slogan 'sex before eight or else its too late'. You can argue that once, under a false sense of morality homosexual relations were illegal but now they are legal and widely accepted. However the argument in relation to children is rather different. There are many activities that are not restricted in the case of adults, such as alcohol or cigarette consumption or some dangerous occupations but they are nevertheless prohibited in relation to children because they could do damage, their bodies are not fully mature, and children cannot be completely aware of all the potential advantages and disadvantages and therefore cannot give informed consent. The objections to sexual activity between children and adults is not so much about sexual morality but about the basic human right to exercise *informed consent* before being engaged in certain deeply personal activities.

You can point out that the ancient Greeks engaged legally and happily in sex with young boys and that families in many cultures sleep and have sex together. Whatever traditions may abound in other times and places the fact is that children in most present day cultures and certainly all the ones we are likely to meet in Britain do not have a relaxed attitude to sex with children. A reading of the accounts of all too many survivors indicate how profoundly distressing sexual activities with an adult are to many children even when the abuse did not cause undue physical pain. The breach of trust and feelings of helplessness cause long lasting upset.

You must start *taking control* of your behaviour and realise that you are not a helpless victim in an unfair world.

*Excuses*

You need to stop making excuses for your behaviour. Those of us working with abusers have heard so many:

- I was drunk, I didn't know what I was doing.
- I was depressed.
- I was ill.
- My partner wouldn't have sex with me.
- I was unemployed.
- I was suffering so much stress at work.
- I had money worries.
- I felt it was my duty to teach her the facts of life.
- My penis just slipped into his bottom when he came into my bed.
- I thought I was dreaming.
- I thought I was in bed with my wife.

The fact is that you find sex with children arousing and if you have already had sex with them, then you are not so much ill or depressed but an opportunist. You need also to be aware that courts and people working with perpetrators are becoming wise to the excuses given. For example, once it was thought that a man might abuse a child 'out-of-character' because he was drunk. Now we know that drink acts as a disinhibitor so that only people who are potential molesters and who want to have sex with children will do so under the influence of drink. Alcohol does not make people abuse children, they make themselves, the alcohol merely gives them the 'Dutch courage' and excuse to do so.

You have to start to *identify your vulnerabilities* and begin to realise what might act as a trigger or prompt for your activities. If you are able to recognise your own cycle of abusive

**Figure 6**

| STOP ✗ | START ✔ |
|---|---|
| Denying what you have done | Accepting what you have done |
| Blaming other people— the victim, your partner. | Taking responsibility— *you* are the adult abusing your power |
| Seeing yourself as a victim | Taking control of your own behaviour |
| Making excuses | Identifying your vulnerabilities |
| Objectifying the victim | Seeing children as people with feelings and wishes |
| Deluding yourself | Facing reality |

behaviour then you may find that you can begin to intervene before you commit any offences.

### Seeing the child as an object

It is essential that you stop seeing children as your property or as objects there for your convenience. It is only by seeing children as 'things' without feelings and wishes of their own that you will be able to abuse them. It is essential that you start to *see children as personalities* who are not there for your convenience and have their own rights, emotions and preferences which must be respected.

### Deluding yourself

This relates to several of the points already made. You need to stop deluding yourself about the extent and serious consequences of what you are doing. But most of all you need to stop deluding yourself about you own nature.

You may feel that you are some form of monster, a Jekyll and Hyde that is suddenly swept by uncontrollable urges. However there are many people who have managed to control their sexual proclivities. Few people are totally at the mercy of some internal devil or their own inexorable appetites and drives.

You may on the other hand see yourself as a really great person who has a minor Achilles heel. Whichever delusion you hold, the reality is that you are a human being with your share of good points and bad points. We all have both. What you need to do is to start to *face reality*. Try to identify your strengths and build on them and recognise your weaknesses and try to control them or reduce their effect on your behaviour.

### CONCLUDING COMMENTS

Helping sexually abused children is not just the prerogative of highly trained and qualified specialist social, legal and health workers. Everyone who comes into contact with an abused child or adult survivor, directly or indirectly, can assist by responding effectively. To act appropriately requires an understanding of the issues, sympathy with and sensitivity to the plight of the victim and a wish to act in the best interests of the child.

Hopefully, whether you are lay or professional, you now have a little more understanding of the problem and can move forward with greater confidence. Suggestions for further reading are given in the next section. It is necessary to continue to enhance your knowledge and understanding but even now you are probably in a position to give some effective assistance to the Jays of this world – the young victims of sexual exploitation.

# Glossary

**Abuse** — *see* **child abuse, sexual abuse.**

**Abuser** — the person who directly sexually assaults or exploits a child victim, other terms include **molester, offender** and **perpetrator.**

**Anatomical dolls** — soft, rag dolls with representations of the genitals, fingers, mouths which can open and tongues. They are used to enable children to demonstrate what happened to them. They can also be used to help children express how they feel about their abusive experiences. Sometimes they are called 'show and tell' or 'anatomically correct' dolls.

**Black children, people** — here a positive term used as a cultural construction implying solidarity among minorities against racism.

**Case conference** — any meeting of professionals to discuss a particular individual or 'case'. However it often specifically means the gathering of investigating and helping professionals, sometimes with the family present, to collect information and plan for the future protection of a child who has been abused by other close family members.

**Child abuse** — physical injury, physical or emotional neglect, sexual exploitation and/or emotional suffering inflicted or permitted by any person who has custody or care of the child or who is in a position of trust, power or authority over or in relation to the child.

**Child Protection Register** — files of children in a particular local authority area who are deemed to be at risk of abuse and require special protection. Information from the register is highly confidential and only available to certain designated professionals.

**Core group** — a group of professional workers and family members who meet and act in partnership to plan the most appropriate resources and plan of action to protect and help a child who has been abused. Usually the name of the child will be on the local Child Protection Register.

**Co-victim** — a person who is not directly assaulted but who is subjected to a similar process of targeting, grooming, exploitation and manipulation as the primary victim.

**Disability** — this is used as a term to denote a physical or mental limitation on the full range of human activities however it is probably more accurate to acknowledge that people with apparent disabilities are in fact 'differently able'.

**Disclosure** — a person's first statements about what has happened in relation to abusive experiences. This usually refers to a child victim who tells someone about the abuse they have experienced.

**Evidence-in-chief** — the main body of witnesses' statements which can then be subjected to cross-examination.

**Expert witness** — a witness who is a recognised expert and specialist in a particular area. He or she can give opinions as well as factual evidence.

**Extended family** — the whole family, not just parents and children but grandparents, uncles, aunts and cousins who may, or may not be resident in the household.

**External inhibitors** — a range of factors external to sex abusers which can prevent them from committing an offence. This can be an abstract idea such as the threat of imprisonment or something more tangible such as a protective parent.

**Familial** — relating to the family, hence intra-familial, something which involves or occurs within the family circle. Extra-familial is something occurring outside the family.

**Flashbacks** — sudden memories of earlier trauma, often incidents of sexual abuse. The memories are very vivid and can involve all the senses. The person is transported back and re-lives the experience. Flashbacks appear without warning and are difficult to control.

**Forensic** — concerning the law and legal matters. Therefore forensic evidence usually refers to medical or scientific findings which might be useful in court proceedings.

**Grooming** — the process by which perpetrators make their victim submit to their will. This can range from a subtle gentle bribery, a type of seduction or a series of threats and intimidation.

**Guardian ad Litem** — an independent person, often a social worker, who is appointed by the court to represent the interests of the child

**Gynaecologist** — a doctor who specialises in gynaecology. Gynecologist is the American spelling.

**Gynaecology** — a branch of medicine which is specifically devoted to the care, treatment and prevention of genital tract disorders in women. It is not concerned with pregnancy which is the area of specialism of obstetricians. Gynecology is the American spelling.

**Incest** — in legal terms, sexual intercourse between two people who are specified blood relatives. It is often more generally used to describe any form of sexual abuse within the family.

**Investigation** — when a possible case of child abuse is referred to the police, social services or NSPCC the matter will be closely examined by workers from these child protective organisations. The investigation will involve collecting information from all relevant sources including the victim and the alleged perpetrator. Investigations in relation to child abuse are often undertaken jointly between the police and a social worker.

**Internal inhibitors** — a potential perpetrator's conscience which holds him or her back from committing an offence.

**Key worker** — also commonly called a **primary worker**. When a child is placed on the Child Protection Register an individual social worker is appointed to coordinate the communications with all the main professionals involved. They will be actively involved in the child protection plan. In some areas 'key worker' is also the term applied to the member of staff in a residential setting who is allocated to a resident to have responsibility for and take a special interest in that resident.

**Masturbation** — strictly sexual activity, especially rubbing the genitals, on oneself. However the term especially when referred to as mutual masturbation is often used to denote the rubbing or fondling of the genitals of another person.

**Molest** — as a verb it means to sexually assault. In America it is often used as a noun. It can refer to any activity from non-contact voyeurism to sexual intercourse although it tends not to be synonymous with rape.

**Molester** — interchangeable with the words perpetrator, offender or abuser to denote someone who sexually assaults or exploits another person.

**Nonabusing parent** — in American literature also termed nonoffending parent. This is the mother or father of a victim who did not knowingly or directly become involved in the abuse of his or her child.

**Nuclear family** — a term applied to the most immediate family constellation, usually just parents and their offspring.

**Offender** — any one who breaks the law but is used interchangeably with **abuser, molester** and **perpetrator** to denote someone who sexually assaults or exploits a child.

**Paediatrician** — a doctor who specialised in the physical and mental development of children and disorders relating to their physical condition. Pediatrician is the American spelling.

**Paedophile** — strictly speaking an adult with an exclusive sexual preference for pre-pubertal children. However, often used more generally to indicate any one with a sexual orientation towards children and early adolescents. Pedophile is the American spelling.

**Perpetrator** — this can refer to anyone committing a crime but is usually used to refer to the person sexually abusing a child. Interchangeable with **abuser, offender** and **molester.**

**Police surgeon** — a general practitioner who gains a special expertise in working in conjunction with the police to obtain forensic medical evidence. In many cases they are the most likely doctors to give a medical examination to the victims of a crime.

**Primary worker** — see 'key worker'.

**Psychiatrist** — a qualified doctor who will diagnose and treat mental illnesses and emotional or behavioural disorders.

**Psychologist** — a person professionally trained and qualified in the study of human behaviour and mental processes. A clinical psychologist will primarily be involved in assessing and treating behaviour disorders or problems in living which cause psychological distress.

**Registration** — placing a child who is thought to have been abused on a **Child Protection Register**. This usually only occurs after a case conference is satisfied that the child is likely to have been, or to be, abused. Parents and children should be informed of the decision.

**Secondary victim** — a person close to the primary victim who has not been groomed, exploited or manipulated by the perpetrator but who nevertheless is adversely affected by the abuse of another, particularly a child.

**Sexual abuse** — the involvement of dependent, developmentally immature children and adolescents in sexual activities they do not truly comprehend, to which they are unable to give informed consent, or that violate the social taboos of family roles.

**Sibling** — a brother or sister.

**Sub**poena — a direction to appear in court as a witness under pain of a penalty for non-compliance with the order. Documents and other pieces of evidence can also be required to be presented in court under subpoena.

**Survivor** — people who have lived after suffering a major deprivation or trauma. Specifically relates to adolescents and adults who were sexually abused in childhood and have overcome many of the problems associated with sexual exploitation. This should be used as a positive term.

**Target** — a particular child selected by a perpetrator to be the victim of sexual exploitation. Any type, personality, appearance, age or gender of child can become a target. Perpetrators often have a target age or gender of child. They may also target vulnerable families, parents or institutions in order to obtain a position of power and trust thereby gaining access to children.

**Therapy** — systematic treatment often applied to psychological treatment similar to counselling.

**Trauma** — medically this can be any injury to a person resulting from outside force, however it is used specifically to refer to a psychological shock and emotional disruption often caused by abuse.

**Traumatic** — something that causes trauma (plural traumata). Often associated with a shocking or emotionally disruptive experience.

**Victim** — although it can be anyone who is subjected to mistreatment or misfortune, here it is applied specifically to a girl or boy who is sexually abused by another person.

**Witness as to fact** — witnesses in court who can give factual evidence of matters which they experienced or observed. Unlike an expert witness, they are not expected to proffer an opinion.

**Work through** — the acknowledgement of the existence and extent of a problem or set of problems and then to find a way of solving them, eventually to arrive at a stage where either they are resolved or no longer cause significant distress and worry.

# Further reading

There are so many books on child sexual abuse on the market that only a very few can be selected for comment and recommendation. Just because a book does not appear on this list does not mean that it will not be helpful. However, it is hoped that this section will provide you with a guide to additional reading. Several of the books mentioned have their own sections on suggestions of useful material to read which can be added to the list given here.

The authors, date of publication and, where appropriate, the title of the books are given in this section but there is a full reference provided in the bibliography, for those of you wishing to buy or to borrow any of them from your local library.

## CHILD ABUSE - GENERAL
It may be that children you know are not only sexually abused but physically and emotionally mistreated as well. There are a number of books which encompass all forms of abuse.

David N. Jones and colleagues (1987) *Understanding Child Abuse*. This is the most comprehensive general book on child protection. It is well informed and is sufficiently detailed to appeal to the professional reader but is clear, easy to understand and accessible to everyone who might be interested in the subject.

R. S. Kempe and C. H. Kempe (1978) *Child Abuse*. Ruth and Henry Kempe were the pioneers of child protection work. This is a classic text and although dated is still a valuable introduction.

Jean Moore (1985) *The ABC of Child Abuse Work*. Although written for a professional readership this is an accessible introduction for lay people interested in the subject. The author has followed this first book with *The ABC of Child Protection Work* (1993).

Celia Doyle. (1990) *Working with Abused Children*. This looks at abuse from the child's perspective. It examines in detail the paradox of mistreated children and young people who hide signs of abuse, defend the perpetrators and resist attempts of others to assist them. There are also practical suggestions on how abused children can be helped.

**For health professionals:**
Roy Meadow (1989) *ABC of Child Abuse*
This is a collection of papers first published in the British Medical Journal. It is informative and vividly illustrated.

Chris Hobbs and Jane Wynne (1993) *Child Abuse.*
A useful book examining some controversial issues edited by two eminent medical consultants.

**For teachers and education professionals:**
Peter Maher (ed) (1987) *Child Abuse: The Education Perspective.*
This addresses a broad range of issues relating to child abuse and although targeted at the education professional market it has much of value for the general reader.

## CHILD SEXUAL ABUSE - GENERAL

David Finkelhor (1984) *Child Sexual Abuse: New Theory and Practice.*
Although now dated much of what was written is still relevant. In particular, in this work Finkelhor introduces the idea of four preconditions having to be present before a sexual assault against a child can be perpetrated.

Diana Riley (1991) *Sexual Abuse of Children: Understanding Intervention and Prevention.*
A slim volume and easy to read, it is an excellent and by no means superficial introduction to the subject.

Kathleen Murray and David Gough (1991) *Intervening in Child Sexual Abuse.*
This is a series of chapters covering most aspects of intervention. There are sections on legal issues. Aspects of assessment and therapy are also discussed. It is particularly useful for professionals on the periphery of abuse cases.

J. La Fontaine (1990) *Child Sexual Abuse.*
Professor La Fontaine has produced a comprehensive study of the problem incorporating research findings. A brief guide with the same title is provided by the Children's Legal Centre (1992c).

Family Service Unit (1993) *Confronting the Pain.*
This contains six chapters and uses case histories and accounts by workers of how involvement with sexual abuse has influenced their own lives. It provides practical guidance on how to cope with the demands of this type of work.

**For health professionals:**
Celia Doyle (1994) *Child Sex Abuse: A Guide for Health Professionals.*
This is a comprehensive guide for nurses, doctors, occupational

therapists and physiotherapists and other health workers. Also of interest to community and family doctors is G.M. Wakely (1991) *Sexual Abuse and the Primary Care Doctor.*

**For teachers:**
Judith Milner and Eric Blyth (1988) *Coping with Child Sexual Abuse: A Guide for Teachers.*
This is an excellent guide for all teaching staff in schools. It gives useful background information, clear guidance on how to respond and exercises to help teachers develop and evaluate their understanding and abilities in relation to sexual abuse. The authors address sensitive issues such as special education needs. It is accurate and well written. It is essential reading for teachers.

## CHILD SEXUAL ABUSE - SPECIFIC ISSUES.
**Victim perspectives:**
The now classic article by Roland Summit (1983) describes the way that victims of sexual abuse 'accommodate' to their situation. His model of the accommodation syndrome helped to explain abused children's apparently paradoxical behaviour and responses at the time of disclosure. Similarly, in the opening chapters of *Working with Abused Children* by Celia Doyle (1990) the emotional forces which keep children trapped in an abusive situation are examined.

**People with disabilities:**
Hilary Brown and Ann Craft (1989) *Thinking the Unthinkable.*
This is a slim volume which covers issues relating to both adults and children with learning difficulties. It deals with sex education and preventative programmes as well as with discovering and responding to cases of abuse.

Margaret Kennedy (1989) and (1990) has highlighted the issues for children who are hearing impaired. This is further discussed in an article by S.M. Ridgeway (1993).

**Perpetrators:**
Tony Parker (1970) *The Twisting Lane.*
A now dated but still absorbing series of personal histories given by sex offenders themselves.

C.K. Li and colleagues (1990) *Children's Sexual Encounters with Children.*
This is the product of two research projects. They both contain revealing first hand accounts. In the second part of the book statements from perpetrators are both informative and disturbing.

A. Kirkwood (1993) *The Leicestershire Inquiry 1992.*
Although it might seem a daunting task to read through a lengthy official report this is well worth the effort. It reveals how one man

could manipulate both people and systems in a way that enabled him to molest children in his care for many years when he worked as a much respected head of children's residential homes.

Anna Salter (1988) *Treating Child Sex Offenders and Victims: a Practical Guide*
A.L. Horton and colleagues (1990) *The Incest Perpetrator: the Family Member No One Wants to Treat.*
These are two informative American works focusing primarily on child sex abusers.

M. Elliot (1993) *Female Sexual Abuse of Children: The Ultimate Taboo.*
To date the most comprehensive work on female perpetrators.

A demonstration of the way that the news media can bring a sensitive issue such as female abusers to the notice of the general public is given by Julia Stuart (1993) in her article for the *Northampton Chronicle and Echo* 'When mum is to blame'.

There are increasing numbers of works on adolescent offenders including, E.M. Otey and G.D. Ryan (1985) *Adolescent Sex Offenders. Issues in Research and Treatment;* Fay Honey Knopp (1985) *The Youthful Sex Offender;* Gail Ryan and Sandy Lane (1991) *Juvenile Sexual offending: Causes, Consequences and Correction;* and an article by Gail Ryan (1989) 'Victim to victimiser'.

V.R. Wiehe (1990) *Sibling Abuse: Hidden Physical, Emotional and Sexual Trauma.*
This, as the title suggests, is a comprehensive work on the abuse of children by their brothers or sisters.

**Pornography and Organised Abuse:**
Judith Ennew (1986) *The Sexual Exploitation of Children.*
The author draws on material world-wide to demonstrate how children are sexually abused and exploited. Included for scrutiny are the topics of child pornography and prostitution. Not a book for the faint-hearted.

Tim Tate (1990) *Child Pornography - an Investigation.*
Again not for the faint hearted, the author investigated child pornography working undercover in the paedophile subcultures for three years. He clearly demonstrates the cynical exploitation of children.

There are a growing number of studies of ritual abuse including a book by Pamela Hudson (1991) *Ritual Abuse, Discovery, Diagnosis and Treatment;* and articles by Snow and Sorensen (1990) and McFadyen and colleagues (1993). Sex rings are discussed by Wild and Wynne (1986).

D. Finkelhor and colleagues (1988) *Nursery Crimes: Sexual Abuse in Day Care.*
A worrying book for working parents who have to rely on childminders and nurseries. Some preschool children in the study were abused by casual staff members or relatives. Others were part of systematic organised, often ritualistic, abuse by the entire staff group when the whole centre, children and staff alike, were involved.

## Cleveland crisis:
E. Butler-Sloss (1988) *Report of the Inquiry into Child Abuse in Cleveland 1987.*
Another apparently daunting official report but in fact a very readable document. It gives a clear and balanced picture of the events during 1986 and 1987 in Cleveland which invited such intense public and media attention. It also provides basic factual information about child sexual abuse.

Beatrix Campbell (1988) *Unofficial Secrets.*
This is a contemporary analysis of the crisis in Cleveland. It is by no means a difficult read and gives interesting insights into the dynamics and leading players in the drama.

Sue Richardson and Heather Bacon (1991) *Child Sexual Abuse: Whose Problem? - Reflections from Cleveland.*
This is a series of chapters written, with hindsight, by some of the main protagonists in the Cleveland crisis. Not only does it add to an understanding of events during 1986 and 1987 but it also contains the collected wisdom of some of the most experienced child protection practitioners in Britain.

## Coping in court:
David Carson (1990) *Professionals and the Courts.*
Although this is written for 'expert witnesses' it is of use to anyone who might have to give evidence in court. It gives constructive advice about how to cope with cross-examination. A smaller but still valuable guide has been produced by B. Livesy (1988) *Giving Evidence in Court.*

Helena Kennedy (1992) *Eve Was Framed.*
This is a brilliant expose of the British judicial system and discrimination in the system against women and various disadvantaged or minority groups.

Madge Braye (1989) *Susie and the Wise Hedgehog go to Court.*
This is designed to help children who are giving evidence in court. A leaflet by Anne Peake (1991) called *Going to Court* is particularly helpful for children aged from about eight to sixteen years. Similarly several leaflets for children or for adults supporting child witnesses have been prepared by the Children's Legal Centre (1992a, 1992b).

There are a number of works examining the plight of child witnesses including those by J. Morton and J. Plotnikoff (1990); N.W. Perry and L.S. Wrightsman (1991); J.R. Spencer (1990) and R. Flin (1991)

## MEDIA RELATIONS

A. Fry (1987) *Media Matters.*
This is a useful guide on how to communicate with the news and popular media. Although written primarily for social services personnel it has many useful hints for any one interested in making links with the press, radio and television. Two good examples of responsible reporting on the issue of child sexual abuse are provided by journalists David Williams (1987) and Julia Stuart (1993).

## FOR PARENTS

Kathryn Hagans and Joyce Case (1990) *When Your Child Has Been Molested.*
This book was drawn to my attention by the mother of Lisa, who found it tremendously helpful, when the family was having to cope with their feelings in the wake of Lisa's disclosure. It is very clearly set out and deals with aftermath of abuse, helping parents to understand their own reactions, those of their children and the response of the system. Its only slight drawback for some readers is that it is American so that some of the procedures are slightly different in Britain, Europe and elsewhere.

Clodagh Corcoran (1987) *Take Care!*
Set in the context of Irish procedures this book is nevertheless universally useful. It covers all aspects of sexual abuse which parents may have to address from ways of protecting children from abuse to coping with a disclosure and with the future after an investigation.

Caren Adams and Jennifer Fay (1992) *Helping Your Child to Recover from Sexual Abuse.*
This provides guidance for parents to empower them to deal more effectively with every situation from disclosure to the future, when as the children grow 'We'll need to talk again' and eventually 'Its better now'. It has information for parents on the left-hand side of the page and responses and activities for families on the opposite page.

W. Ovaris (1991) *After the Nightmare: The Treatment of Non-Offending Mothers of Sexually Abused Children.*
A supportive mother who believes her child is one of the major factors in the healing process for any young victim. This book acknowledges the emotional impact on the mother especially in cases of father-child and sibling abuse. As one reviewer observed it is to be hoped that the author tackles a text for non-offending fathers in the near future.

There are many situations where fathers are not the abusers and are coping with considerable distress such as where the parents are separated and the step-father is the offender, and in instances of sibling or non-family abuse.

## HELPING CHILDREN AND YOUNG PEOPLE
**Sex education:**
Peter Mayle (1978a) *Where Did I Come From?*
Recently reprinted this is a delightfully illustrated series of cartoons with explanations of the facts of life suitable for all ages of children from the inquisitive toddler to the less knowledgeable teenager. For older children and adolescents there is the companion book *What's Happening to Me?* This makes becoming a teenager seem like good fun! A popular general book *The Body Book* has been written by Clare Rayner (1989). *The Playbook for Kids Abuse Sex* by Blank (1980) is a lively American sex education workbook for children.

**Protecting children:**
David Pithers and Sarah Green (1990) *We Can Say NO!*
This is a series of four short stories about two children, Joanne and Tom who avoid being tricked into potentially dangerous situations. One of its advantages is that it emphasises that dangerous strangers can look very ordinary. It is also useful because in one scenario one of the threatening adults is a women and in another the children know the adult, so he is not a complete stranger. The problems are that this book does not deal with abuse from family members, the children represented are stereotypically white and the dominant of the two youngsters is the boy. More importantly, I am not sure how the book leaves those children who have been tricked and have found themselves unable to be 'strong, be clever, be careful'. Is the opposite message conveyed to those who have been deceived and exploited 'you are weak, stupid and careless'? I hope not.

Michelle Elliot (1986) *Keeping Safe: a Practical Guide to Talking with Children.*
The author is one of the leading figures in the field of protection programmes for children. This is a useful book for parents and teachers. Although its focus is protection from sexual exploitation it also looks at all forms of bullying. In addition, Michelle Elliot has produced a training pack for front-line carers (1992). Although expensive for an individual parent it is a useful purchase for groups of carers such as childminders, nursery staff, education welfare officers and community nurses.

Jan Hindman (1985) *A Very Touching Book.*
When first produced in 1983 it was one of the few amusing yet sensitive books designed to help children protect themselves from

abuse. It has recently been reprinted. It is most suitable for children from about seven to teens although a younger child would enjoy the brilliant, mostly fun-filled illustrations. The author, while exhorting children to say No and tell, recognises in a simple, very sad little drawing that sometimes the abuser is 'so... so... so... big and important that you feel too... too... too... little to tell.' A child unable to say No and tell is not left feeling guilty or foolish.

Kadj Rouf (1989c) *My Body, My Book.*
This is a drawing book for children. One of its strengths is that the illustrations reflect children with disabilities and those with distinct racial features or wearing traditional ethnic dress. Kadj Rouf has also written *Mousie* (1989a) a story book for younger children and *Secrets* (1989b) which is for teenagers. This comes in two versions one featuring a black family and the other a white one. These have all proved very useful in my work with abused children.

**For Black children:**
Kadj Rouf (1990) *Black Girls Speak Out*
This is written by Kadj who has a dual heritage and Charmaine whose parents were born in the Caribbean. Their hand-written experiences have a special poignancy. Of particular interest is the way they describe their experiences of joining a therapy group.

**For child and adolescent victims:**
The books by Kadj Rouf and Jan Hindman mentioned in the previous section are also useful in helping children who have already been abused.

Ouaine Bain and Maureen Sanders (1990) *Out in the Open.*
This is probably one of the best books for teenagers and young adults who have been abused. It is also helpful reading for older survivors and parents. It acknowledges that some youngsters may be feeling suicidal. One of the most interesting sections is on forgiving. They recognise that some victims can feel forgiveness and compassion and make peace with their past. Others cannot and their wise comment is 'Why should you forgive? Your abuser has stolen from you - he has no right to expect forgiveness too. You have given enough'. (p.90). Another American published book for teenage victims is by B. Bean and S. Bennet (1993) *The Me Nobody Knows: A Recovery Guide for Teenagers.*

## FOR SURVIVORS

**General:**
Eliana Gil (1983) *Outgrowing the Pain.*
This is a wonderful book for all survivors of childhood abuse of whatever form. It reads as if the author is talking to you with

kindness and compassion but without sentimentality. The text is punctuated by simple cartoons which also speak volumes. *Treatment of Adult Survivors.* (1988) is more detailed but by the same author and reflecting her concern and understanding of abuse victims.

Moira Walker (1992) *Surviving Secrets.*
In this the author demonstrates the effects and implications for adult survivors and the way in which they can be helped. There are detailed accounts by former victims which illustrate the issues under discussion. *Out of the Shadows* (1993) is by the same author.

**For female survivors:**
Ellen Bass and Laura Davis (1990) *The Courage to Heal.*
This is probably one of the largest and most comprehensive volumes written for survivors of sexual abuse. It is full of advice.

Liz Hall and Siobhan Lloyd (1989) *Surviving Child Sexual Abuse.*
This is a large book and its small print makes it quite a daunting read. However any survivor who makes the effort will find this a treasure chest of understanding, good sense and hope. It covers every aspect of being a victim and survivor. It is the book to take as route map, companion and sustenance for a long hard journey. Take it steadily and when you are exhausted rest and pause along the way. For anyone helping survivors it is equally useful and there is a section specifically for helpers.

**For male survivors:**
Frank Bolton and colleagues (1989) *Males at Risk: The Other Side of Child Sexual Abuse.*
For many years the focus of work was on father-daughter incest. It has only slowly been recognised that boys can be victims too. This is one of the first books to thoroughly examine the issues for boy victims. Understanding is also provided in the book by Eugene Porter (1986) *Treating the Young Male Victim of Sexual Assault.*

Jim Christopherson and colleagues (1989) *Working with Sexually Abused Boys.*
A broad range of topics relating to the abuse of boys are addressed including sex rings, residential care and issues of race.

Mike Lew (1988) *Victims No Longer: Men Recovering from Incest.*
This is one of the few books written specifically for male victims and is written in an accessible form.

There are several biographical works describing abuse, including sexual abuse, to boys. No young man need feel isolated and set apart from his peers. Details of the accounts of boy victims are given in the next section.

## BIOGRAPHIES

### Boys' accounts:

Ben (1991) *Things in My Head.*

This was written partly as a therapeutic exercise by a young man coping with a childhood during which he was savagely physically and emotionally abused by his adoptive mother. He escaped from home to the care of his uncle only to find himself sexually abused and exploited by his uncle. What comes over firstly is the intense pain and suffering of Ben's childhood. But by far the most important impression is the one we form of Ben himself. If ever there was a noble survivor, a person of courage, strength and integrity despite horrific experiences, Ben is one such.

J. MacVeigh (1982) *Gaskin.*

This is the biography of a young man whose mother committed suicide and whose father could not cope, so at a tender age he started what was to be a disastrous career in care. If anyone needs an argument against corporal punishment and the institutionalisation of children, the true story of Graham Gaskin's life provides a powerful and compelling one. An innocent victim, he was abused and exploited at every turn. When in young adulthood he lost that innocence and ran foul of the law it is hard to condemn him. We are left with the feeling that as members of society, we are the guilty ones for permitting children to be treated in this way when they are meant to be in the 'care' of the state.

Peter Quinn (1988) *Cry Out!*

This is the story of a boy who was physically and emotionally abused in both foster and adoptive homes. Although not about sexual abuse it is the autobiography of a boy who was a victim and clearly demonstrates that there is nothing weak or unmanly about coping with suffering. A similar account of physical and emotional abuse and neglect is given by Tom O'Neill (1981) in *A Place Called Hope.* Not only was Tom a victim but he gives a moving account of his brother who, placed in care with another brother, Terry, was tortured, beaten, starved and finally killed by his foster father at Bank Farm in Hope Valley. The boys' ill-treatment and Dennis' death lead to the setting-up of Children's Departments in Britain.

### Girls' accounts:

Maya Angelou (1984) *I Know Why the Caged Bird Sings.*

This is the autobiography of an African American growing up with her grandmother, uncle and brother in the southern states of America and on occasions staying with her parents in St Louis and California. She vividly describes being 'groomed' then raped by her mother's boyfriend, the subsequent trial and the emotional aftermath of these traumas. The book also gives a vivid picture of poverty, discrimination and the oppression of Black people.

Sylvia Fraser (1989) *My Father's House.*
The story of a pretty, blond Canadian girl's abuse by her father and the way in which she coped by splitting her personality into two or three people so that she could live at least one life free from abuse. As sometimes happens, her father's abuse rendered her vulnerable to other exploitation and she was also sexually abused by a lodger.

Kathy Evert and Inie Bijkerk (1987) *When You're Ready.*
Kathy is Native American (North American Indian) and was physically and sexually abused by her mother. Like Sylvia, she was rendered vulnerable and was also abused by her mother's cousin. Much of the book is about the painful journey through therapy and the support Kathy received from Inie Bijkerk, her therapist.

Jacqueline Spring (1987) *Cry Hard and Swim.*
This is the account of a Scottish woman who receives therapy when she recognises that her relationship with her children is effected by the sexual abuse she suffered at the hands of her father who tyrannised and abused his large, 'happy' family of children.

**Other biographies include:**
C.A. Matthews (1986) *No Longer a Victim.*
The author recalls in later life long forgotten experiences of abuse at the hands of her father.

Sheila Sisk and Charlotte Hoffman (1987) *Inside Scars.*
This is another joint work by survivor and therapist. In this case the perpetrator was the step-father.

C.E. Wynne (1987) *That Looks Like a Nice House.*
This is account of recovery from sexual abuse also contains illustrations.

K. Brady (1979) *Father's Days.*
This was written before the majority of accounts, is a courageous first person account of a girl's sexual abuse by her father.

L. Armstrong (1978) *Kiss Daddy Goodnight.*
This is another comparatively early work. This is a collection of first hand accounts gathered by the author who found far more women had been abused than anticipated.

Toni McNaron and Yarrow Morgan (1982) *Voices in the Night.*
Another collection of first hand accounts and descriptions of feelings about having been abused, by a number of women.

## FICTION

Alice Walker (1983) *The Color Purple.*
This is a series of letters between Celie and her sister Nettie or from Celie to God. For some readers it might be difficult to start because of the letter format and the unfamiliar grammar. But it is well worth persevering because it will prove to be a memorable experience. The novel encompasses a vast vista of life for Black people, or people of colour, in the American deep south between the wars, and in Africa. It describes sexual abuse as well as poverty, oppression and the exploitation of Black people.

D. Moggach (1983) *Porky.*
Another possibly difficult book to start reading, it nevertheless gives vivid insights into the developmental problems of a girl who has been sexually abused by her father.

Michelle Morris (1982) *If I Should Die Before I Wake.*
The story of a girl abused by her father. Although fictional it reflects the suffering of children who are exploited in this way.

T. Hart (1979) *Don't Tell Your Mother.*
This is comparatively early work. It describes not only the sexual abuse of a girl by her father but the consequences of the legal action taken.

*The majority of these books can be obtained from good local bookshops but a few, especially those published in America, may be difficult for people in Britain to obtain. In this event it is often possible to obtain them from Bookstall Services, 86 Abbey Street, Derby, DE22 3SQ, UK. Tel. Derby (0332) 368039.*

# Bibliography

Adams, C. and Fay, J. (1992) *Helping Your Child to Recover from Sexual Abuse*. Seattle: University of Washington Press.

Ahmad, B. (1989) Protecting black children from abuse. Social Work Today, June 8, 24.

Allen, C.V. (1980) *Daddy's Girl*. New York: Berkeley.

Angelou, M. (1984) *I Know Why the Caged Bird Sings*. London: Virago.

Armstrong, L. (1978) *Kiss Daddy Goodnight*. New York: Pocket Books.

Bain, O. and Sanders, M. (1990) *Out in the Open: A Guide for Young People Who Have Been Sexually Abused*. London: Virago.

Baker, A.W. and Duncan, S.P. (1985) Child sexual abuse: a study of prevalence in Great Britain. *Child Abuse and Neglect*, 9 (4), 457-68.

Bamford, F. and Roberts, R. (1989) Child sexual abuse - II in Meadows, R. (ed.) *ABC of Child Abuse* . London: British Medical Journal, 31-36.

Bass, E. and Davis, L. (1990) *The Courage to Heal: A Guide for Women Survivors of Child Sexual Abuse*. London: Cedar.

Bays, J. and Chadwick, D. (1993) Medical diagnosis of sexually abused children. *Child Abuse and Neglect*, 17 (1), 91-110.

Bean, B. and Bennet, S. (1993) *The Me Nobody Knows: A Recovery Guide for Teenagers*. Massachussets: Lexington.

Ben (1991) *Things in My Head*. Dublin: Glendale Publishing.

Bennetts, C., Brown, M. and Sloan, J. (1992) *AIDS: The Hidden Agenda in Child Sexual Abuse*. Harlow, Essex: Longman.

Blank, J. (1980) *The Playbook for Kids About Sex*. Burlingame, CA: Down There Press.

Bolton, F.G. Jr., Morris, L.A. and MacEachron, A.E. (1989) *Males At Risk: The Other Side of Child Sexual Abuse*. Newbury Park: Sage.

Brady, K. (1979) *Father's Days: A True Story of Incest*. New York: Dell.

Bray, M. (1989) *Susie and the Wise Hedgehog Go to Court*. London: Hawksmere.

Brown, H. and Craft, A. (eds.) (1989) *Thinking the Unthinkable: Papers on Sexual Abuse and People with Learning Difficulties*. London: FPA Education Unit.

Butler-Sloss, E. Right Honourable Lord (1988) *Report of the Inquiry into Child Abuse in Cleveland 1987*. London: HMSO.

Campbell, B. (1988) *Unofficial Secrets: Child Sexual Abuse — The Cleveland Case*. London: Virago.

Carson, D. (1990) *Professionals and the Courts: A Handbook for Expert Witnesses*. Birmingham: Venture.

Children's Legal Centre (1992a) *The Child Witness*. London: Children's Legal Centre.

Children's Legal Centre (1992b) *Being a Witness*. London: Children's Legal Centre.

Children's Legal Centre (1992c) *Child Sexual Abuse*. London: Children's Legal Centre.

Christopherson, J., Furniss, T., O'Mahoney, B., Peake, A. with Armstrong, H. and Hollows, A. (1989) *Working with Sexually Abused Boys*. London: National Children's Bureau.

Corcoran, C. (1987) *Take Care! Preventing Child Sexual Abuse*. Dublin: Poolberg Press.

Doyle, C. (1986) Management sensitivity in CSA. *Child Abuse Review*, 1 (4), 8-9.

Doyle, C. (1987) *Profile of Child Sexual Abuse Drawn from the Northamptonshire Child Protection Register*. Unpublished.

Doyle, C. (1990) *Working with Abused Children*. London: Macmillan.

Doyle, C. (1994) *Child Sex Abuse: a Guide for Health Professionals*. London: Chapman and Hall.

Elliot, M. (1986) *Keeping Safe: A Practical Guide to Talking with Children*. London: Bedford Square Press.

Elliot, M. (1992) *Protecting Children: Training Pack for Front-Line Carers*. London: HMSO.

Elliot, M. (ed.) (1993) *Female Sexual Abuse of Children: The Ultimate Taboo*. Harlow, Essex: Longman.

Ennew, J. (1986) *The Sexual Exploitation of Children*. Cambridge: Polity Press.

Evans, K. (1994) Jailed for being raped. *Marie Claire*, June, 53-62.

Evert, K. and Bijkerk, I. (1987) *When You're Ready*. Walnut Creek: Launch Press.

Family Service Units (1993) *Confronting the Pain*. London: FSU.

Finkelhor, D. (1979) What's wrong with sex between adults and children? *American Journal of Orthopsychiatry*, 49 (4), 692-700.

Finkelhor, D. (1984) *Child Sexual Abuse: New Theory and Research*. New York: The Free Press.

Finkelhor, D. et al. (1986) *A Sourcebook on Child Sexual Abuse*. Newbury Park: Sage.

Finkelhor, D., Williams, L.M. and Burns, N. (1988) *Nursery Crimes: Sexual Abuse in Day Care*. Newbury Park: Sage.

Flin, R. (1991) Sources of stress for child witnesses in court in Murray, K. and Gough, D. (eds.) *Intervening in Child Sexual Abuse*. Edinburgh: Scottish Academic Press.

Francis, J. (1993) Honest revelations. *Community Care*, 12 Aug, 17.

Fraser, S. (1989) *My Father's House*. London: Virago.

Fromuth, M.E. (1986) The relationship of childhood sexual abuse with later psychological and sexual adjustment in a sample of college women. *Child Abuse and Neglect*, 10, 5-15.

Fry, A. (1987) *Media Matters*. Wallington Surrey: Reed Publishing.

Gil, E. (1983) *Outgrowing the Pain*. Walnut Creek: Launch Press.

Gil, E. (1988) *Treatment of Adult Survivors of Child Abuse*. Walnut Creek: Launch Press.

Glaser, D. and Collins, C. (1989) The response of young, non-sexually abused children to anatomically correct dolls. *Journal of Child Psychology and Psychiatry*, 30 (4), 547-60.

Glaser, D. and Frosh, S. (1988) *Child Sexual Abuse*. London: Macmillan.

Glaser, D. and Frosh, S. (1993) *Child Sexual Abuse*. Second Edition. London: Macmillan.

Gonzalez, L.S., Waterman, J., Kelly, R.J., McCord, J. and Oliveri, M.K. (1993) Children's patterns of disclosures and recantations of sexual and ritualistic abuse allegations in psychotherapy. *Child Abuse and Neglect*, 17 (2) 281-90.

Goodwin, J. (1994) *The Price of Honor*. London: Little Brown & Co.

Hagans, K.B. and Case, J. (1990) *When Your Child Has Been Molested: A Parent's Guide to Healing and Recovery*. Massachusetts: Lexington.

Hall, L. and Lloyd, S. (1989) *Surviving Child Sexual Abuse: A Handbook for Helping Women Challenge their Past*. Basingstoke: The Falmer Press.

Harrison, H. (1993) Female abusers — what children and young people have told ChildLine in Elliot, M. (ed.) *Female Sexual Abuse of Children: The Ultimate Taboo*. Harlow, Essex: Longman 95-8.

Hart, T. (1979) *Don't Tell Your Mother*. London: Quartet Books.

Hindman, J. (1985) *A Very Touching Book*. Second Edition. Ontario, Oregan: Alexandria Associates.

Hobbs, C.J. and Wynne, J.M. (eds.) (1993) *Child Abuse*. London: Bailliere Tindal.

Home Office (1992) *Memorandum of Good Practice: on Video Recorded Interviews with Child Witnesses for Criminal Proceedings*. London: HMSO.

Horton, A.L., Johnson, B. L., Roundy, L. M. and Williams, D. (eds.) (1990) *The Incest Perpetrator: The Family Member No-One Wants to Treat*. Newbury Park: Sage.

Hudson, P.S. (1991) *Ritual Child Abuse, Discovery, Diagnosis and Treatment*. New York: Safer Society Press.

Jewett, C.L. (1984) *Helping Children Cope with Separation and Loss*. London: Batsford.

Jones, D.N., Pickett, J., Oates, M. and Barbor, P. (1987) *Understanding Child Abuse. Second Edition*. London: Macmillan.

Jones, D.P.H. and McQuiston, M.G. (1988) *Interviewing the Sexually Abused Child*. London: Gaskell.

Kempe, R.S. and Kempe, C. H. (1978) *Child Abuse*. London: Fontana/ Open Books.

Kennedy, H. (1992) *Eve Was Framed: Women and British Justice*. London: Chatto and Windus.

Kennedy, M. (1989) The abuse of deaf children. *Child Abuse Review*, 3 (1), 3-6.

Kennedy, M. (1990) The deaf child who is sexually abused - is there a need for a dual specialist? *Child Abuse Review,* 4 (2), 3-6.

Kirkwood, A. (1993) *The Leicestershire Inquiry 1992.* Leicestershire: Leicestershire County Council.

Knopp, F.H. (1985) *The Youthful Sex Offender: The Rationale and Goals of Early Intervention & Treatment.* Orwell: Safer Society Press.

Knuston, J.N. (1980) The dynamics of the hostage taker: some major variants. *Annals of the New York Academy of Sciences,* 347, 117-27.

Kubler-Ross, E. (1970) *On Death and Dying.* London: Tavistock.

La Fontaine, J. (1990) *Child Sexual Abuse.* Cambridge: Polity Press.

Lamb, S. and Coakley, M. (1993) 'Normal' childhood sexual play and games: differentiating play from abuse. *Child Abuse and Neglect,* 17 (4), 515-26.

Lew, M. (1988) *Victims No Longer: Men Recovering from Incest.* New York: Nevraumont Publishers.

Li, C.K., West, D.J. and Woodhouse, T.P. (1990) *Children's Sexual Encounters with Adults.* London: Duckworth.

Livesy, B. (1988) *Giving Evidence in Court.* York: BASPCAN.

MacFarlane, K., Waterman, J., Conerly, Damon, L., Durfee, M. and Long, S. (1986) *Sexual Abuse of Young Children.* London: Holt, Rinehart and Winston.

MacFarlane, K. (1990) Cindy's poem in Horton, A.L., Johnson, B. L., Roundy, L. M. and Williams, D. (eds.) *The Incest Perpetrator: The Family Member No-One Wants to Treat.* Newbury Park: Sage.

MacVeigh, J. (1982) *Gaskin.* London: Jonathan Cape.

Maher, P (ed.) (1987) *Child Abuse: The Education Perspective.* Oxford: Basil Blackwell.

Matthews, C.A. (1986) *No Longer a Victim.* Canberra: Acorn Press.

Mayle, P. (1978a) *Where Did I Come From?* London: Macmillan.

Mayle, P. (1978b) *What's Happening to Me?* London: Macmillan.

McCann, J., Voris, J., Simon, M. and Wells, R. (1989) Perianal findings in prepubertal children selected for nonabuse: a descriptive study. *Child Abuse and Neglect,* 13, 179-93.

McElroy, L.P. (1992) Early indicators of pathological dissociation in sexually abused children. *Child Abuse and Neglect,* 16 (6), 833-46.

McFadyen, A. Hanks, H. and James, C. (1993) Ritual abuse: a definition. *Child Abuse Review,* 2 (1), 35-41.

McNaron, T. and Morgan, Y. (eds.) (1982) *Voices in the Night: Women Speaking About Incest.* Minneapolis: Cleis Press.

Meadow, R. (ed.) (1989) *ABC of Child Abuse.* London: British Medical Journal.

Mezey, G., Vizard, E., Hawkes, C. and Austin, R. (1991) A community treatment programme for convicted child sex offenders: a preliminary report. *Journal of Forensic Psychiatry,* 2 (1), 11-26.

Milner, J. and Blyth, E. (1988) *Coping with Child Sexual Abuse: A Guide for Teachers.* London: Longman.

Moggach, D. (1983) *Porky.* Harmondsworth: Penguin.

Moore, J. (1985) *The ABC of Child Abuse Work.* Aldershot: Gower.

Moore, J. (1993) *The ABC of Child Protection.* Basingstoke: Ashgate.

Morris, M. (1982) *If I Should Die Before I Wake.* London: Black Swan

Books.

Morton, J. and Plotnikoff, J. (1990) Children as victims of crime in Spencer, J., Nicholson, G., Flin, R. and Bull, R. (eds.) *Children's Evidence in Legal Proceedings.* London: Hawksmere.

Mrazek, P.B. and Kempe, C.H. (eds.) (1981) *Sexually Abused Children and their Families.* Oxford: Pergamon.

Murray, K. and Gough, D. A. (eds.) (1991) *Intervening in Child Sexual Abuse.* Edinburgh: Scottish Academic Press.

O'Neill, T. (1981) *A Place Called Hope.* Oxford: Basil Blackwell.

Otey, E.M. and Ryan, G.D. (1985) *Adolescent Sex Offenders. Issues in Research and Treatment.* Rockville, Maryland: National Institute of Mental Health.

Ovaris, W. (1991) *After the Nightmare: The Treatment of Non-Offending Mothers of Sexually Abused Children.* Holmes Beach: Learning Publications.

Palmer, R.L., Oppenheimer, R., Chaloner, D.A. and Howells, K. (1990) Childhood sexual experiences with adults reported by women with eating disorders: an extended series. *British Journal of Psychiatry,* 156, 699-703.

Parker, T. (1970) *The Twisting Lane: Some Sex Offenders.* London: Panther.

Peake, A (1991) *Going To Court.* London: The Children's Society.

Perry, N.W. and Wrightsman, L.S. (1991) *The Child Witness: Legal Issues and Dilemmas.* London: Sage.

Pithers, D. and Greene, S. (1990) *We Can Say NO!* London: Red Fox.

Porter, E. (1986) *Treating the Young Male Victim of Sexual Assault: Issues and Intervention Strategies.* Orwell: The Safer Society Press.

Quinn, P. (1988) *Cry Out!* Eastbourne: Kingsway.

Rayner, C. (1989) *The Body Book.* London: Piccolo.

Redding, D. (1989) Smashing a subculture. *Community Care,* 1 June, 14-15.

Richardson, S. and Bacon, H., Dunn, M., Wyatt, G., Higgs, M., Cashman, H. and Lamballe-Armstrong, A. (eds.) (1991) *Child Sexual Abuse: Whose Problem? - Reflections from Cleveland.* Birmingham: Venture Press.

Ridgeway, S.M. (1993) Abuse and deaf children: some factors to consider. *Child Abuse Review,* 2 (3), 166-73.

Riley, D. (ed.) (1991) *Sexual Abuse of Children: Understanding, Intervention and Prevention.* Oxford: Radcliffe Medical Press.

Rouf, K. (1989a) *Mousie.* London: The Children's Society

Rouf, K. (1989b) *Secrets.* London: The Children's Society

Rouf, K. (1989c) *My Body, My Book.* London: The Children's Society

Rouf, K. (1991a) *Black Girls Speak Out.* London: The Children's Society.

Rouf, K. (1991b) *Into Pandora's Box.* London: The Children's Society.

Ryan, G. (1989) Victim to victimizer: rethinking victim treatment. *Journal of Interpersonal Violence,* 4 (3) 325-41.

Ryan, G.D. and Lane, S.L. (1991) *Juvenile Sexual Offending: Causes, Consequences and Correction.* Lexington, M.A.: Lexington Books.

Salter, A. (1988) *Treating Child Sex Offenders and Victims: A Practical Guide.* Newbury Park: Sage.

Schechter, M.D. and Roberge, L. (1976) Child sexual abuse in Helfer, R. and Kempe, C.H. (eds.) *Child Abuse and Neglect: The Family and the Community*. Cambridge, Massachussets: Ballinger.

Seven, P. (1991) Treating sex offenders in prison. *Journal of Forensic Psychiatry*, 2 (1), 8-9.

Sisk, S.L. and Hoffman, C.F. (1987) *Inside Scars: Incest Recovery as Told by a Survivor and Her Therapist*. Gainesville, Florida: Pandora Press.

Sivan, A.B., Schor, D.P., Koeppl, G.K. and Noble, L.D. (1988) Interaction of normal children with anatomical dolls. *Child Abuse and Neglect*, 12, 295-304.

Snow, B. and Sorensen, T. (1990) Ritualistic child abuse in a neighbourhood setting. *Journal of Interpersonal Violence*, Dec, 474-87.

Spencer, J.R. (1990) Persuading the courts to listen to children in Bannister, A., Barrett, K. and Shearer, E. (eds.) *Listening to Children: The Professional Response to Hearing the Abused Child*. Harlow, Essex: Longman.

Spring, J. (1987) *Cry Hard and Swim: The Story of an Incest Survivor*. London: Virago.

Strenz, T. (1980) The Stockholm syndrome: law enforcement policy and the ego defenses of the hostage. *Annals of the New York Academy of Sciences*, 347, 137-50.

Stuart, J. (1993) When mum is to blame. *Northampton Chronicle and Echo*, March 24, 10.

Summit, R.C. (1983) The child sexual abuse accommodation syndrome. *Child Abuse and Neglect*, 7, 177-93.

Tate, T. (1990) *Child Pornography - An Investigation*. London: Methuen.

Wakley, G. (1991) *Psychosexual Medicine Series 3: Sexual Abuse and the Primary Care Doctor* .London: Chapman and Hall.

Walker, A. (1983) *The Color Purple*. London: The Women's Press.

Walker, M. (1992) *Surviving Secrets*. Buckingham: Open University Press.

Walker, M. (1993) *Out of the Shadows*. Buckingham: Open University.

Wiehe, V.R. (1990) *Sibling Abuse: Hidden Physical, Emotional, and Sexual Trauma*. Lexington: Lexington Books.

Wild, N.J. and Wynne, J.M. (1986) Child sex rings. *British Medical Journal*, 293, 183-5.

Williams, D. (1987) Suffer little children. *Daily Mail*, Friday 12 June, 8.

Wynne, C.E. (1987) *That Looks Like a Nice House*. Walnut Creek: Launch Press.

# Index

Abuse 195, 200-202
  by children 13, 16, 18, 76-78, 90-91, 203
  child sexual abuse, definition 16, 26
  ritual and organised 16, 22-24
Abusers 195
  adolescent 16, 76-78
  female 16, 30, 47, 73-76, 173, 203
  who kill 25, 72, 85, 99, 183
  *also see* perpetrators
Access visits 19
Acquired immune deficiency syndrome, see AIDS
Addiction 165, 189
  *also see* alcohol, compulsive behaviour, substance abuse
Adolescents
  abusing behaviour 16, 76-78, 202-203
  as victims 5, 13, 16, 97, 98, 110, 133, 206
  treatment of offenders 203
Adults abused as children 8, 26, 27, 36, 41, 63, 99, 131, 136, 139, 179-
  183, 186, 193, 199, 207-210
AIDS 4, 10, 87-88
  *also see* venereal disease
Alcohol 46, 165, 188, 189, 190, 191
Anal assault 14, 22, 53, 72, 86-87, 90, 96, 112, 128, 133, 150
Anal dilatation 86-87, 133
Anatomical dolls 126-128, 195
Anger 5
  of child victims 48, 59, 108, 125, 133, 158, 160
  of helpers 42-45, 102, 109, 174
  of parents 102, 176
  of survivors 42-45, 137
Anorexia nervosa, see eating disorders

Babies, subject to abuse 5, 27, 31, 64, 74, 122
Baby-sitters as abusers 19-20, 47, 58, 93
Barnardos 187
Belief, in child's disclosures 9, 40, 51-54, 150
Bereavement 160-161
  *see also* loss, mourning